BLACK ON BLACK

ARNOLD ADOFF, a native New Yorker, graduated from the College of the City of New York and did graduate work at Columbia University. He is a poet and teacher who has spent many years in the public schools of Harlem and the upper west side of Manhattan. He has also been an instructor in federal projects at New York University and Connecticut College and is the editor of *I Am the Darker Brother: An Anthology of Modern Poems by Negro Americans*. Mr. Adoff is married and has two children.

BLACK

ON BLACK

Commentaries
by Negro Americans

EDITED BY ARNOLD ADOFF

Foreword by Roger Mae Johnson

THE MACMILLAN COMPANY • NEW YORK

The Macmillan Company, New York
Collier-Macmillan Canada, Ltd., Toronto, Ontario

Library of Congress catalog card number: 68-24101

PRINTED IN THE UNITED STATES OF AMERICA
First Printing

ACKNOWLEDGMENTS

Thanks are due to the following for permission to include copyrighted selections.

JAMES BALDWIN for "Unnameable Objects, Unspeakable Crimes," first published in *Ebony*.

CITADEL PRESS INC. for "To a Schoolgirl, 1905" and "Twenty-fifth Birthday, 1893" by W. E. B. DuBois (from *A Documentary History of the Negro People in the United States* by Herbert Aptheker).

COWARD-McCANN, INC. for selections from *Go Up for Glory* by Bill Russell as told to William McSweeny, Copyright © 1966 by William Felton Russell and William Francis McSweeny.

CRISIS MAGAZINE for "The Name 'Negro,'" an exchange of letters between Dr. W. E. B. DuBois and Roland Barton, first published in March, 1928.

JOAN DAVES for "Letter from Birmingham Jail" from *Why We Can't Wait* by Martin Luther King, Jr., Copyright © 1963 by Martin Luther King, Jr.

OSSIE DAVIS for "On Malcolm" ("Why I Eulogized Malcolm X").

DOUBLEDAY & COMPANY, INC. for a selection from *White Man, Listen!* by Richard Wright, Copyright © 1957 by Richard Wright.

E. P. Dutton & Co., Inc. for selections from *nigger:* An Autobiography by Dick Gregory with Robert Lipsyte, Copyright © 1964 by Dick Gregory Enterprises, Inc.

Ebony Magazine and Lerone Bennett for the article "The White Problem in America," first published in August, 1965.

Grove Press, Inc. for selections from *The Autobiography of Malcolm X,* with the assistance of Alex Haley, Copyright © 1964 by Alex Haley and Malcolm X; Copyright © 1965 by Alex Haley and Betty Shabazz.

Harcourt, Brace & World, Inc. for a selection from *Dusk of Dawn* by W. E. Burghardt DuBois, Copyright 1940 by Harcourt, Brace & World, Inc.

Harper & Row, Publishers for selections from *Dark Ghetto* by Kenneth B. Clark, Copyright © 1965 by Kenneth B. Clark; Chapter 24 from *A Choice of Weapons* by Gordon Parks, Copyright © 1965, 1966 by Gordon Parks; selections from *Black Boy* by Richard Wright, Copyright 1937, 1942, 1944, 1945 by Richard Wright.

Hawthorn Books, Inc. for a selection from *Black Drama* by Loften Mitchell, Copyright © 1967 by Hawthorn Books, Inc.

Hill & Wang, Inc. for a selection from *The Big Sea* by Langston Hughes, Copyright 1940 by Langston Hughes.

John O. Killens and The New York Times for "Explanation of the Black Psyche" by John O. Killens, © 1964 by The New York Times Company.

Conrad J. Lynn for a selection from "U.S.A.: The Potential of a Minority Revolution" by Robert F. Williams.

Marzani & Munsell, Inc. for a selection from *Negroes with Guns* by Robert F. Williams.

William Morrow and Company, Inc. for selections from *Home* by LeRoi Jones, Copyright © 1961, 1962, 1963, 1964, 1965, 1966 by LeRoi Jones.

The New American Library, Inc. for selections from *This Is My Country Too* by John A. Williams, Copyright © 1964–1965 by John A. Williams.

Harold Ober Associates Inc. for "In Love with Harlem" by Langston Hughes, Copyright © 1963 by Freedomways Magazine.

Ted Poston for "The Revolt of the Evil Fairies."

Random House, Inc. for selections from *Black Power* by Stokely Carmichael and Charles V. Hamilton, Copyright © 1967 by Stokely Carmichael and Charles V. Hamilton.

Trident Press for selections from *Black Man's Burden* by John Oliver Killens, Copyright © 1965 by John Oliver Killens.

The Viking Press, Inc. for the interview with Ralph Ellison from *Writers at Work:* The Paris Review Interviews, Second Series, Copyright © 1963 by The Paris Review, Inc.

Mrs. Walter White for a selection from "I Investigate Lynchings," by Walter White.

Thanks are due also to Quandra Prettyman Stadler for her friendship and the generous sharing of her exceptional private library; and to Shirley Dolgoff, my editor, for her concern and commitment.

For Virginia Hamilton Adoff
In Memory of Dr. Martin Luther King, Jr.

"Black is beautiful,
And it's so beautiful
To be black."
—SOUTHERN CHRISTIAN LEADERSHIP CONFERENCE

FOREWORD

All treasure is not discovered at the bottom of the sea. Treasure can be found under an upturned rock, in a trunk, in a castle, on a poor city street. In a ghetto in Cleveland there is a Treasure House Public Library designed especially for youth. As librarian there, I meet many children and young people who come to enjoy the pleasures of books and reading. Like others, they are influenced by books, and they and many more are certain to find stimulation in *Black on Black*, a selection from Negro voices relating their experiences in white America. In reading and listening, young people will seek and find their own individual voices and personal approaches.

The speeches, letters, excerpts from books, personal interviews, and exhortations that follow are representative of many areas of life in America. Some are bitter preachments with racial overtones; some are tense sarcasms and condemnations of the peculiar American society in which these men have lived. There are humor and irony, but the underlying theme is a strong-willed sense of survival. Paralleling this will to survive is the presence of interests and pleasures that all men enjoy—the arts, travel, and sports. These binding threads that give us our common culture—discussed in terms of the urgent need for the Negro to be given the right to develop his appreciation and love of man's common joys —are spoken of in the historical and sociological excerpts and in the contributions by civil rights leaders.

Black on Black offers a variety of human experiences, opinions, and facts. It is hoped that this book will lead the youthful reader to the larger works of these spokesmen. Youth must find its own voice, but until that time comes it would be well if it can hear another and inspired message.

ROGER MAE JOHNSON

Cleveland, Ohio
1968

PREFACE

Black on Black presents some of the best literature by Negro Americans written over the last hundred years. From the time of Frederick Douglass to the present, black men have moved forward, only to discover that society has had little desire to let them proceed. The commentaries in this collection underline the continual rediscovery of the barriers placed before black Americans and delineate how some of these barriers can be overcome to achieve real equality.

To be American and black, with the ability to write astutely of a separate citizenship spanning a century, is to create a unique literary heritage. Such is the contribution Negro Americans have given their country and the world. This anthology could have been a dozen volumes, so great is the quantity of serious prose writing and scholarly works from mid eighteenth century America to the present.

The authors represented here have been selected for their individuality of thought and the persuasive power of their prose. It is no accident that the word "power" is used in describing the contents of this collection. These writers have lived and written as creative men and survived as men as well as artists in the hostile environment of racist attitudes. Even where assassination or exile eliminated the force of their physical presence, the power of their thought remained to challenge each young person coming in contact with their writing.

Black on Black is a proud presentation of ideas by men whose experiences are as diverse as the classroom, newspaper office, basketball court, pulpit, or the street. For over ten years I have examined this literature with my students to explode myth and miseducation. Like my students, millions of our citizens will be hurrying to school or job, or tragic conflict in the years ahead. This anthology is a celebration of black vision for Americans of *every* vision and color.

ARNOLD ADOFF

New York City
1968

CONTENTS

CONTENTS

CONTENTS

BLACK ON BLACK

FREDERICK DOUGLASS

Those who profess to favor freedom yet deprecate agitation, are men who want crops without plowing up the ground; they want rain without thunder and lightning. They want the ocean without the awful roar of its many waters. . . . Power concedes nothing without demand. It never did and it never will. Find out just what any people will quietly submit to and you have found out the exact measure of injustice and wrong which will be imposed upon them, and these will continue till they are resisted with either words or blow, or with both. The limits of tyrants are prescribed by the endurance of those whom they oppress. [This passage is from Douglass's West India Emancipation Speech of August, 1857. —Ed. Note]

"What to the Slave Is the Fourth of July?"

The following is a speech given in Rochester, New York, on July 4, 1852.

Fellow citizens: Pardon me, and allow me to ask, why am I called upon to speak here today? What have I or those I represent to do with your national independence? Are the great principles of political freedom and of natural justice, embodied in that Declaration of Independence, extended to us? And am I,

1

therefore, called upon to bring our humble offering to the national altar, and to confess the benefits, and express devout gratitude for the blessings resulting from your independence to us?

Would to God, both for your sakes and ours, that an affirmative answer could be truthfully returned to these questions. Then would my task be light, and my burden easy and delightful. For who is there so cold that a nation's sympathy could not warm him? Who so obdurate and dead to the claims of gratitude, that would not thankfully acknowledge such priceless benefits? Who so stolid and selfish that would not give his voice to swell the halleluiahs of a nation's jubilee, when the chains of servitude had been torn from his limbs? I am not that man.

. . . I say it with a sad sense of disparity between us. I am not included within the pale of this glorious anniversary! Your high independence only reveals the immeasurable distance between us. The blessings in which you this day rejoice are not enjoyed in common. The rich inheritance of justice, liberty, prosperity, and independence bequeathed by your fathers is shared by you, not by me. The sunlight that brought life and healing to you has brought stripes and death to me. This Fourth of July is *yours,* not *mine. You* may rejoice, *I* must mourn. To drag a man in fetters into the grand illuminated temple of liberty, and call upon him to join you in joyous anthems, were inhuman mockery and sacrilegious irony. Do you mean, citizens, to mock me, by asking me to speak today? If so, there is a parallel to your conduct. And let me warn you, that it is dangerous to copy the example of a nation whose crimes, towering up to heaven, were thrown down by the breath of the Almighty, burying that nation in irrecoverable ruin. I can today take up the lament of a peeled and woe-smitten people.

"By the rivers of Babylon, there we sat down. Yes! We wept when we remembered Zion. We hanged our harps upon the willows in the midst thereof. For there they that carried us away captive, required of us a song; and they who wasted us, required of us mirth, saying, Sing us one of the songs of Zion. How can we sing the Lord's song in a strange land? If I forget thee, O

Jerusalem, let my right hand forget her cunning. If I do not remember thee, let my tongue cleave to the roof of my mouth."

Fellow citizens, above your national, tumultuous joy, I hear the mournful wail of millions, whose chains, heavy and grievous yesterday, are today rendered more intolerable by the jubilant shouts that reach them. If I do forget, if I do not remember those bleeding children of sorrow this day, "may my right hand forget her cunning, and may my tongue cleave to the roof of my mouth!" To forget them, to pass lightly over their wrongs, and to chime in with the popular theme, would be treason most scandalous and shocking, and would make me a reproach before God and the world. My subject, then, fellow citizens, is "American Slavery." I shall see this day and its popular characteristics from the slave's point of view. Standing here, identified with the American bondman, making his wrongs mine, I do not hesitate to declare, with all my soul, that the character and conduct of this nation never looked blacker to me than on this Fourth of July. Whether we turn to the declarations of the past, or to the professions of the present, the conduct of the nation seems equally hideous and revolting. America is false to the past, false to the present, and solemnly binds herself to be false to the future. Standing with God and the crushed and bleeding slave on this occasion, I will, in the name of humanity, which is outraged, in the name of liberty, which is fettered, in the name of the Constitution and the Bible, which are disregarded and trampled upon, dare to call in question and to denounce, with all the emphasis I can command, everything that serves to perpetuate slavery—the great sin and shame of America! "I will not equivocate; I will not excuse"; I will use the severest language I can command, and yet not one word shall escape me that any man, whose judgment is not blinded by prejudice, or who is not at heart a slave-holder, shall not confess to be right and just.

But I fancy I hear some of my audience say it is just in this circumstance that you and your brother Abolitionists fail to make a favorable impression on the public mind. Would you argue more and denounce less, would you persuade more and rebuke less, your cause would be much more likely to succeed. But, I submit, where all is plain there is nothing to be argued. What point in the anti-slavery creed would you have me argue? On what branch of the subject do the people of this country need light? Must I undertake to prove that the slave is a man? That point is conceded already. Nobody doubts it. The slave-holders themselves acknowledge it in the enactment of laws for their government. They acknowledge it when they punish disobedience on the part of the slave. There are seventy-two crimes in the State of Virginia, which, if committed by a black man (no matter how ignorant he be), subject him to the punishment of death; while only two of these same crimes will subject a white man to like punishment. What is this but the acknowledgment that the slave is a moral, intellectual, and responsible being? The manhood of the slave is conceded. It is admitted in the fact that Southern statute-books are covered with enactments, forbidding, under severe fines and penalties, the teaching of the slave to read and write. When you can point to any such laws in reference to the beasts of the field, then I may consent to argue the manhood of the slave. When the dogs in your streets, when the fowls of the air, when the cattle on your hills, when the fish of the sea, and the reptiles that crawl, shall be unable to distinguish the slave from a brute, then I will argue with you that the slave is a man!

For the present it is enough to affirm the equal manhood of the Negro race. Is it not astonishing that, while we are plowing, planting, and reaping, using all kinds of mechanical tools, erecting houses, constructing bridges, building ships, working in metals of brass, iron, copper, silver, and gold; that while we are reading, writing, and cyphering, acting as clerks, merchants, and secretaries, having among us lawyers, doctors, ministers, poets, authors, editors, orators, and teachers; that while we are engaged in all the enterprises common to other men—digging gold in California, capturing the whale in the Pacific, feeding sheep and cattle on the hillside, living, moving, acting, thinking, planning, living in families as husbands, wives, and children, and above all, confessing

4

and worshipping the Christian God, and looking hopefully for life and immortality beyond the grave—we are called upon to prove that we are men?

Would you have me argue that man is entitled to liberty? That he is the rightful owner of his own body? You have already declared it. Must I argue the wrongfulness of slavery? Is that a question for republicans? Is it to be settled by the rules of logic and argumentation, as a matter beset with great difficulty, involving a doubtful application of the principle of justice, hard to understand? How should I look today in the presence of Americans, dividing and subdividing a discourse, to show that men have a natural right to freedom, speaking of it relatively and positively, negatively and affirmatively? To do so would be to make myself ridiculous, and to offer an insult to your understanding. There is not a man beneath the canopy of heaven who does not know that slavery is wrong *for him.*

What! Am I to argue that it is wrong to make men brutes, to rob them of their liberty, to work them without wages, to keep them ignorant of their relations to their fellow men, to beat them with sticks, to flay their flesh with the last, to load their limbs with irons, to hunt them with dogs, to sell them at auction, to sunder their families, to knock out their teeth, to burn their flesh, to starve them into obedience and submission to their masters? Must I argue that a system thus marked with blood and stained with pollution is wrong? No; I will not. I have better employment for my time and strength than such arguments would imply.

What, then, remains to be argued? Is it that slavery is not divine; that God did not establish it; that our doctors of divinity are mistaken? There is blasphemy in the thought. That which is inhuman cannot be divine. Who can reason on such a proposition? They that can, may; I cannot. The time for such argument is past.

At a time like this, scorching irony, not convincing argument, is needed. Oh! had I the ability, and could I reach the nation's ear, I would today pour out a fiery stream of biting ridicule, blasting reproach, withering sarcasm, and stern rebuke. For it is not light that is needed, but fire; it is not the gentle shower, but

5

thunder. We need the storm, the whirlwind, and the earthquake. The feeling of the nation must be quickened; the conscience of the nation must be roused; the propriety of the nation must be startled; the hypocrisy of the nation must be exposed; and its crimes against God and man must be denounced.

What to the American slave is your Fourth of July? I answer, a day that reveals to him more than all other days of the year, the gross injustice and cruelty to which he is the constant victim. To him your celebration is a sham; your boasted liberty an unholy license; your national greatness, swelling vanity; your sounds of rejoicing are empty and heartless; your denunciation of tyrants, brass-fronted impudence; your shouts of liberty and equality, hollow mockery; your prayers and hymns, your sermons and thanksgivings, with all your religious parade and solemnity, are to him mere bombast, fraud, deception, impiety, and hypocrisy—a thin veil to cover up crimes which would disgrace a nation of savages. . . .

"What Is Slavery?"

This selection is from a speech presented at a reception for Mr. Douglass in England, in 1846.

SLAVERY

Slavery in the United States is the granting of that power by which one man exercises and enforces a right of property in the body and soul of another. The condition of a slave is simply that of the brute beast. He is a piece of property—a marketable commodity, in the language of the law, to be bought and sold at the will and caprice of the master who claims him to be his property; he is spoken of, thought of, and treated as property. His own good, his conscience, his intellect, his affections, are all set aside by the master. The will and the wishes of the master are the law of the slave. He is as much a piece of property as a horse. If he is fed, he is fed because he is property. If he is clothed, it is with a view to the increase of his value as property. Whatever of comfort is necessary to him for his body or soul that is inconsistent with his being property is carefully wrested from him, not only by public opinion, but by the law of the country. He is carefully deprived of everything that tends in the slightest degree to detract from his value as property. He is deprived of education. God has given him an intellect; the slaveholder declares it shall not be cultivated. If his moral perception leads him in a course contrary to his value as property, the slaveholder declares he shall not exercise it. The marriage institution cannot exist among slaves, and one-sixth of the population of democratic America is denied its privileges by the law of the land. What is to be thought of a nation boasting of its liberty, boasting of its humanity, boasting of its Christianity, boasting of its love of justice and purity, and yet having within its own borders three millions of persons denied by law the right of marriage?—what must be the condition of that people?

The Slave Trade

Behold the practical operation of this internal slave-trade, the American slave-trade, sustained by American politics and American religion. Here you will see men and women reared like swine for the market. You know what is a swine-drover? I will show you a man-drover. They inhabit all our Southern states. They perambulate the country, and crowd the highways of the nation, with droves of human stock. You will see one of these human flesh jobbers, armed with pistol, whip, and bowie-knife, driving a company of a hundred men, women, and children, from the Potomac to the slave market at New Orleans. These wretched people are to be sold singly, or in lots, to suit purchasers. They are food for the cotton-field and the deadly sugar-mill. Mark the sad procession, as it moves wearily along, and the inhuman wretch who drives them. Hear his savage yells and his blood-curdling oaths, as he

7

hurries on his affrighted captives! There, see the old man with locks thinned and gray. Cast one glance, if you please, upon that young mother, whose shoulders are bare to the scorching sun, her briny tears falling on the brow of the babe in her arms. See, too, that girl of thirteen, weeping, *yes!* weeping, as she thinks of the mother from whom she has been torn! The drove moves tardily. Heat and sorrow have nearly consumed their strength; suddenly you hear a quick snap, like the discharge of a rifle; the fetters clank, and the chain rattles simultaneously; your ears are saluted with a scream, that seems to have torn its way to the centre of your soul! The crack you heard was the sound of the slave-whip; the scream you heard was from the woman you saw with the babe. Her speed had faltered under the weight of her child and chains! That gash on her shoulder tells her to move on. Follow this drove to New Orleans. Attend the auction; see men examined like horses; see the forms of women rudely and brutally exposed to the shocking gaze of American slave-buyers. See this drove sold and separated forever; and never forget the deep, sad sobs that arose from that scattered multitude. Tell me, citizens, WHERE, under the sun, you can witness a spectacle more fiendish and shocking. Yet this is but a glance at the American slave-trade, as it exists, at this moment, in the ruling part of the United States.

I was born amid such sights and scenes. To me the American slave-trade is a terrible reality. When a child, my soul was often pierced with a sense of its horrors. I lived on Philpot Street, Fell's Point, Baltimore, and have watched from the wharves the slave ships in the Basin, anchored from the shore, with their cargoes of human flesh, waiting for favorable winds to waft them down the Chesapeake. There was, at that time, a grand slave mart kept at the head of Pratt Street, by Austin Woldfolk. His agents were sent into every town and county in Maryland, announcing their arrival, through the papers, and on flaming *"hand-bills,"* headed CASH FOR NEGROES. These men were generally well dressed men, and very captivating in their manners; ever ready to drink, to treat, and to gamble. The fate of many a slave has depended upon the turn of a single card; and many a child has been

snatched from the arms of its mother by bargains arranged in a
state of brutal drunkenness.

From *Life and Times of Frederick Douglass*

LIFE AS A FREEMAN

My free life began on the third of September, 1838. On the
morning of the 4th of that month, after an anxious and most
perilous but safe journey, I found myself in the big city of New
York, a *free man*, one more added to the mighty throng which,
like the confused waves of the troubled sea, surged to and fro
between the lofty walls of Broadway. Though dazzled with the
wonders which met me on every hand, my thoughts could not
be much withdrawn from my strange situation. For the moment
the dreams of my youth and the hopes of my manhood were
completely fulfilled. The bonds that had held me to "old master"
were broken. No man now had a right to call me his slave or
assert mastery over me. I was in the rough and tumble of an
outdoor world, to take my chance with the rest of its busy
number. I have often been asked how I felt when first I found
myself on free soil. My readers may share the same curiosity.
There is scarcely anything in my experience about which I could
not give a more satisfactory answer. A new world had opened
upon me. If life is more than breath, and the "quick round of
blood," I lived more in one day than in a year of my slave life.
It was a time of joyous excitement which words can but tamely
describe. In a letter written to a friend soon after reaching New
York, I said: "I felt as one might feel upon escape from a den
of hungry lions." Anguish and grief, like darkness and rain, may
be depicted, but gladness and joy, like the rainbow, defy the
skill of pen or pencil. During ten or fifteen years I had, as it
were, been dragging a heavy chain which no strength of mine

could break. I was not only a slave, but a slave for life. I might become a husband, a father, an aged man, but through all, from the cradle to the grave, I had felt myself doomed. All efforts I had previously made to secure my freedom, had not only failed, but had seemed only to rivet my fetters the more firmly and to render my escape more difficult. Baffled, entangled and discouraged, I had at times asked myself the question, May not my condition after all be God's work and ordered for a wise purpose, and if so, was not submission my duty? A contest had in fact been going on in my mind for a long time, between the clear consciousness of right and the plausible makeshifts of theology and superstition. The one held me an abject slave—a prisoner for life, punished for some transgressions in which I had no lot or part; the other counseled me to manly endeavor to secure my freedom. This contest was now ended; my chains were broken, and the victory brought me unspeakable joy. But my gladness was short-lived, for I was not yet out of the reach and power of the slaveholders.

I soon found that New York was not quite so free or so safe a refuge as I had supposed, and a sense of loneliness and insecurity again oppressed me most sadly. I chanced to meet on the street, a few hours after my landing, a fugitive slave whom I had once known well in slavery. The information received from him alarmed me. The fugitive in question was known in Baltimore as "Allender's Jake," but in New York he wore the more respectable name of "William Dixon." Jake, in law, was the property of Doctor Allender, and Tolly Allender, the son of the doctor, had once made an effort to recapture *Mr. Dixon,* but had failed for want of evidence to support his claim. Jake told me the circumstances of this attempt and how narrowly he escaped being sent back to slavery and torture. He told me that New York was then full of Southerners returning from the watering places north; that the colored people of New York were not to be trusted; that there were hired men of my own color who would betray me for a few dollars; that there were hired men ever on the lookout for fugitives; that I must trust no man with my secret; that I must not think of going either upon the wharves, or into any colored boarding house, for all such places were closely watched; that he was himself unable to help me; and, in fact, he seemed while speaking to me, to fear lest I myself might be a spy and a betrayer. Under this apprehension, as I suppose, he showed signs of wishing to be rid of me, and with whitewash brush in hand, in search of work, he soon disappeared.

This picture, given by poor Jake, of New York, was a damper to my enthusiasm. My little store of money would soon be exhausted, and since it would be unsafe for me to go on the wharves for work and I had no introductions elsewhere, the prospect for me was far from cheerful. I saw the wisdom of keeping away from the shipyards, for, if pursued, as I felt certain I would be, Mr. Auld would naturally seek me there among the calkers. Every door seemed closed against me. I was in the midst of an ocean of my fellow men, and yet a perfect stranger to every one. I was without home, without acquaintances, without money, without credit, without work, and without any definite knowledge as to what course to take or where to look for succor. In such an extremity, a man has something besides his new-born freedom of which to think. While wandering about the streets of New York, and lodging at least one night among the barrels on one of the wharves, I was indeed free—from slavery, but free from food and shelter as well.

I kept my secret to myself as long as I could, but was compelled at last to seek some one who should befriend me without taking advantage of my destitution to betray me. Such an one I found in a sailor named Stuart, a warm-hearted and generous fellow, who, from his humble home on Center Street, saw me standing on the opposite sidewalk, near "The Tombs." As he approached me I ventured a remark to him which at once enlisted his interest in me. He took me to his home to spend the night, and in the morning went with me to Mr. David Ruggles, the secretary of the New York Vigilance Committee, a coworker with Isaac T. Hopper, Lewis and Arthur Tappan, Theodore S. Wright, Samuel Cornish, Thomas Downing, Philip A. Bell, and other true men of their time. All these (save Mr. Bell, who still lives, and is editor and publisher of a paper called the *Elevator,* in San Francisco) have finished their work on earth. Once in the hands of these brave and wise men, I felt comparatively safe.

With Mr. Ruggles, on the corner of Lispenard and Church Streets, I was hidden several days, during which time my intended wife came on from Baltimore at my call, to share the burdens of life with me. She was a free woman, and came at once on getting the good news of my safety. We were married by Rev. J. W. C. Pennington, then a well-known and respected Presbyterian minister. I had no money with which to pay the marriage fee, but he seemed well pleased with our thanks.

Mr. Ruggles was the first officer on the underground railroad with whom I met after coming north, and was indeed the only one with whom I had anything to do, till I became such an officer myself. Learning that my trade was that of a calker, he promptly decided that the best place for me was in New Bedford, Mass. He told me that many ships for whaling voyages were fitted out there, and that I might there find work at my trade and make a good living. So, on the day of the marriage ceremony, we took our little luggage to the steamer *John W. Richmond,* which at that time was one of the line running between New York and Newport, R. I. Forty-three years ago colored travelers were not permitted in the cabin, nor allowed abaft the paddle wheels of a steam vessel. They were compelled, whatever the weather might be, whether cold or hot, wet or dry, to spend the night on deck. Unjust as this regulation was, it did not trouble us much. We had fared much harder before.

We arrived at Newport the next morning, and soon after an old-fashioned stagecoach with "New Bedford" in large, yellow letters on its sides, came down to the wharf. I had not money enough to pay our fare and stood hesitating to know what to do. Fortunately for us, there were two Quaker gentlemen who were about to take passage on the stage—Friends William C. Taber and Joseph Ricketson—who at once discerned our true situation, and in a peculiarly quiet way, addressing me, Mr. Taber said, "Thee get in." I never obeyed an order with more alacrity, and we were soon on our way to our new home. When we reached

Stone Bridge the passengers alighted for breakfast and paid their fares to the driver. We took no breakfast, and when asked for our fares I told the driver I would make it right with him when we reached New Bedford. I expected some objection to this on his part, but he made none. When, however, we reached New Bedford he took our baggage, including three music books—two of them collections by Dyer, and one by Shaw—and held them until I was able to redeem them by paying to him the sums due for our rides. This was soon done, for Mr. Nathan Johnson not only received me kindly and hospitably, but, on being informed about our baggage, at once loaned me the two dollars with which to square accounts with the stage-driver. Mr. and Mrs. Nathan Johnson reached a good old age and now rest from their labors. I am under many grateful obligations to them. They not only "took me in when a stranger," and "fed me when hungry," but taught me how to make an honest living.

Thus, in a fortnight after my flight from Maryland, I was safe in New Bedford—a citizen of the grand old Commonwealth of Massachusetts.

Once initiated into my new life of freedom and assured by Mr. Johnson that I need not fear recapture in that city, a comparatively unimportant question arose, as to the name by which I should be known thereafter, in my new relation as a free man. The name given me by my dear mother was no less pretentious and long than Frederick Augustus Washington Bailey. I had, however, while living in Maryland, disposed of the Augustus Washington, and retained only Frederick Bailey. Between Baltimore and New Bedford, the better to conceal myself from the slave-hunters, I had parted with Bailey and called myself Johnson, but finding that in New Bedford the Johnson family was already so numerous as to cause some confusion in distinguishing one from another, a change in this name seemed desirable. Nathan Johnson, mine host, was emphatic as to this necessity, and wished me to allow him to select a name for me. I consented, and he called me by my present name—the one by which I have been known for three and forty years—Frederick Douglass. Mr. Johnson had just been reading the *Lady of the Lake,* and so pleased was he with its great character that he wished me to bear this name. Since reading that charming poem myself, I have often thought that, considering the noble hospitality and manly character of Nathan Johnson, black man though he was, he, far more than I, illustrated the virtues of the Douglas of Scotland. Sure am I that if any slave-catcher had entered his domicile with a view to my recapture, Johnson would have been like him of the "stalwart hand."

Living in Baltimore as I had done for many years, the reader may be surprised, when I tell the honest truth of the impressions I had in some way conceived of the social and material condition of the people at the North. I had no proper idea of the wealth, refinement, enterprise, and high civilization of this section of the country. My *Columbian Orator,* almost my only book, had done nothing to enlighten me concerning northern society. I had been taught that slavery was the bottom-fact of all wealth. With this foundation idea, I came naturally to the conclusion that poverty must be the general condition of the people of the free states. A white man holding no slaves in the country from which I came, was usually an ignorant and poverty-stricken man. Men of this class were contemptuously called "poor white trash." Hence I supposed that since the non-slaveholders at the South were, as a class, ignorant, poor, and degraded, the non-slave-holders at the North must be in a similar condition. New Bedford, therefore, which at that time was in proportion to its population, really the richest city in the Union, took me greatly by surprise, in the evidences it gave of its solid wealth and grandeur. I found that even the laboring classes lived in better houses, that their houses were more elegantly furnished and were more abundantly supplied with conveniences and comforts, than the houses of many who owned slaves on the Eastern Shore of Maryland. This was true not only of the white people of that city, but it was so of my friend, Mr. Johnson. He lived in a nicer house, dined at a more ample board, was the owner of more books, the reader of more newspapers, was more conversant with the moral, social, and political condition of the country and the world, than nine-tenths of the slaveholders in all Talbot County.

I was not long in finding the cause of the difference, in these

14

respects, between the people of the North and South. It was the superiority of educated mind over mere brute force. I will not detain the reader by extended illustrations as to how my understanding was enlightened on this subject. On the wharves of New Bedford I received my first light. I saw there industry without bustle, labor without noise, toil—honest, earnest and exhaustive—without the whip. There was no loud singing or hallooing, as at the wharves of southern ports when ships were loading or unloading, no loud cursing or quarreling; everything went on as smoothly as well-oiled machinery. One of the first incidents which impressed me with the superior mental character of labor in the North over that of the South, was the manner of loading and unloading vessels. In a southern port twenty or thirty hands would be employed to do what five or six men, with the help of one ox, would do at the wharf in New Bedford. Main strength—human muscle—unassisted by intelligent skill, was slavery's method of labor. With a capital of about sixty dollars in the shape of a good-natured old ox attached to the end of a stout rope, New Bedford did the work of ten or twelve thousand dollars, represented in the bones and muscles of slaves, and did it far better. In a word, I found everything managed with a much more scrupulous regard to economy, both of men and things, time and strength, than in the country from which I had come. Instead of going a hundred yards to the spring, the maidservant had a well or pump at her elbow. The wood used for fuel was kept dry and snugly piled away for winter. Here were sinks, drains, self-shutting gates, pounding-barrels, washing-machines, wringing machines, and a hundred other contrivances for saving time and money. The ship-repairing docks showed the same thoughtful wisdom as seen elsewhere. Everybody seemed in earnest. The carpenter struck the nail on its head, and the calkers wasted no strength in idle flourishes of their mallets. Ships brought here for repairs were made stronger and better than when new. I could have landed in no part of the United States where I should have found a more striking and gratifying contrast, not only to life generally in the South, but in the condition of the colored people there, than in New Bedford. No colored man was really free while residing in a slave state. He was ever more or less subject to the condition of his slave brother. In his color was his badge of bondage. I saw in New Bedford the nearest approach to freedom and equality that I had ever seen. I was amazed when Mr. Johnson told me that there was nothing in the laws or constitution of Massachusetts that would prevent a colored man from being governor of the State, if the people should see fit to elect him. There, too, the black man's children attended the same public schools with the white man's children, and apparently without objection from any quarter. To impress me with my security from recapture and return to slavery, Mr. Johnson assured me that no slaveholder could take a slave out of New Bedford, that there were men there who would lay down their lives to save me from such a fate.

A threat was once made by a colored man to inform a southern master where his runaway slave could be found. As soon as this threat became known to the colored people they were furious. A notice was read from the pulpit of the Third Christian Church (colored) for a public meeting, when important business would be transacted (not stating what the important business was). In the meantime special measures had been taken to secure the attendance of the would-be Judas, and these had proved successful, for when the hour of meeting arrived, ignorant of the object for which it was called, the offender was promptly in attendance. All the usual formalities were gone through with, the prayer, appointments of president, secretaries, etc. Then the president, with an air of great solemnity, rose and said: "Well, friends and brethren, we have got him here, and I would recommend that you, young men, should take him outside the door and kill him." This was enough—there was a rush for the villain, who would probably have been killed but for his escape by an open window. He was never seen again in New Bedford.

Vast Changes

I delivered a lecture in National Hall, Philadelphia, and at its close a gentleman approached me and said, "Mr. Douglass, do you know that your once mistress has been listening to you tonight?" I replied that I did not, nor was I inclined to believe it. I had four or five times before had a similar statement made to me by different individuals in different states and this made me skeptical in this instance. The next morning, however, I received from a Mr. Wm. Needles a very elegantly written note, which stated that she who was Amanda Auld, daughter of Thomas and Lucretia Auld, and granddaughter to my old master, Capt. Aaron Anthony, was now married to Mr. John L. Sears, a coal merchant in West Philadelphia. The street and number of Mr. Sears's office was given, so that I might, by seeing him, assure myelf of the facts in the case, and perhaps learn something of the relatives whom I left in slavery. This note, with the intimation given me the night before, convinced me there was something in it, and I resolved to know the truth. I had now been out of slavery twenty years, and no word had come to me from my sisters, or my brother Perry, or my grandmother. My separation had been as complete as if I had been an inhabitant of another planet. A law of Maryland at that time visited with heavy fine and imprisonment any colored person who should come into the state, so I could not go to them any more than they could come to me.

Eager to know if my kinsfolk still lived, and what was their condition, I made my way to the office of Mr. Sears, found him in, and handed him the note I had received from Mr. Needles, and asked him to be so kind as to read it and to tell me if the facts were as there stated. After reading the note, he said it was true but he must decline any conversation with me, since not to do so would be a sacrifice to the feelings of his father-in-law. I deeply regretted his decision, spoke of my long separation from my relations and appealed to him to give me some information concerning them. I saw that my words were not without their effect. Presently he said, "You publish a newspaper, I believe?" "I do," I said, "but if that is your objection to speaking with me, no word of our conversation shall go into its columns." To make a long story short, we had then quite a long conversation, during which Mr. Sears said that in my *Narrative* I had done his father-in-law injustice, for he was really a kind-hearted man, and a good master. I replied that there must be two sides to the relation of master and slave, and what was deemed kind and just to the one was the opposite to the other. Mr. Sears was not disposed to be unreasonable and the longer we talked the nearer we came together. I finally asked permission to see Mrs. Sears, the little girl of seven or eight years when I left the Eastern Shore of Maryland. This request was at first a little too much for him, and he put me off by saying that she was a mere child when I last saw her and that she was now the mother of a large family of children and I would not know her. He, as well as she, could tell me everything about my people. I pressed my suit, however, insisting that I could select Miss Amanda out of a thousand other ladies, my recollection of her was so perfect, and begged him to test my memory at this point. After much parley of this nature, he at length consented to my wishes, giving me the number of his house and name of street, with permission to call at three o'clock P.M. on the next day. I left him, delighted, and prompt to the hour was ready for my visit. I dressed myself in my best, and hired the finest carriage I could get to take me, partly because of the distance, and partly to make the contrast between the slave and the free man as striking as possible. Mr. Sears had been equally thoughtful. He had invited to his house a number of friends to witness the meeting between Mrs. Sears and myself.

I was somewhat disconcerted when I was ushered into the large parlors occupied by about thirty ladies and gentlemen, to all of whom I was a perfect stranger. I saw the design to test my memory by making it difficult for me to guess who of the company was "Miss Amanda." In her girlhood she was small and slender, and hence a thin and delicately formed lady was seated in a rocking-chair near the center of the room with a little girl by her side. The device was good, but it did not succeed. Glancing around the room, I saw in an instant the lady who was a child twenty-five years before, and the wife and mother now. Satisfied of this, I said, "Mr. Sears, if you will allow me, I will select Miss Amanda from this company." I started towards her, and she, seeing that I recognized her, bounded to me with joy in every feature, and expressed her great happiness at seeing me. All thought of slavery, color, or what might seem to belong to the dignity of her position vanished, and the meeting was as the meeting of friends long separated, yet still present in each other's memory and affection.

Amanda made haste to tell me that she agreed with me about slavery, and that she had freed all her slaves as they had become of age. She brought her children to me, and I took them in my arms, with sensations which I could not if I would stop here to describe. One explanation of the feeling of this lady towards me was that her mother, who died when she was yet a tender child, had been briefly described by me in a little *Narrative of My Life,* published many years before our meeting, and when I could have had no motive but the highest for what I said of her. She had read my story and had through me learned something of the amiable qualities of her mother. She also recollected that as I had had trials as a slave she had had her trials under the care of a stepmother, and that when she was harshly spoken to by her father's second wife she could always read in my dark face the sympathy of one who had often received kind words from the lips of her beloved mother. Mrs. Sears died three years ago in Baltimore, but she did not depart without calling me to her bedside, that I might tell her as much as I could about her mother, whom she was firm in the faith that she should meet in another and better world. She especially wished me to describe to her the personal appearance of her mother, and desired to know if any of her own children then present resembled her. I told her that the young lady standing in the corner of the room was the image of her mother in form and features. She looked at her daughter and said, "Her name is Lucretia—after my mother." After telling me that her life had been a happy one, and thanking me for coming to see her on her deathbed, she said she was ready to die. We parted to meet no more in life. The interview touched me deeply, and was, I could not help thinking, a strange one—another proof that "truth is often stranger than fiction."

If any reader of this part of my life shall see in it the evidence of a want of manly resentment for wrongs inflicted by slavery upon myself and race, and by the ancestors of this lady, so it must be. No man can be stronger than nature, one touch of which, we are told, makes all the world akin. I esteem myself a good, persistent hater of injustice and oppression, but my resentment ceases when they cease, and I have no heart to visit upon children the sins of their fathers.

W. E. B. DuBOIS

I have seen a land right merry with the sun, where children sing, and rolling hills lie like passioned women wanton with harvest. And there in the King's Highway sat and sits a figure veiled and bowed, by which the traveller's footsteps hasten as they go. On the tainted air broods fear. Three centuries' thought has been the raising and unveiling of that bowed human heart, and now behold a century new for the duty and the deed. The problem of the Twentieth Century is the problem of the color-line. [*This passage is from* The Souls of Black Folk.—*Ed. Note*]

Twenty-fifth Birthday, 1893

Program for the celebration of my twenty-fifth birthday. . . . I awoke at eight and took coffee and oranges, read letters, thought of my parents, sang, cried &c (O yes—the night before I heard Shubert's beautiful unfinished symphony. . . .). Then I wandered up to the reading room, then to the art gallery, then to a fine dinner. . . . Then went to Potsdam for coffee & saw a pretty girl. Then came back to the seminar, took a wander, supped on cocoa, wine, oranges and cake, wrote my year book & letters—and now I go to bed after one of the happiest days of my happy life.

Night—grand and wonderful. I am glad I am living. I rejoice as a strong man to run a race. And I am strong—is it egotism or is it assurance? . . . I know that I am either a genius or a fool. O I wonder what I am—I wonder what the world is—I wonder if life is worth the striving. I do not know—perhaps I never shall know; but this I do know: be the Truth what it may I shall seek it on the pure assumption that it is worth seeking— and Heaven nor Hell, God nor Devil shall turn me from my purpose till I die. . . .

I am striving to make my life all that life may be—and I am limiting that strife only in so far as that strife is incompatible with others of my brothers and sisters making their lives similar. The crucial question now is where that limit comes . . . God knows I am sorely puzzled. I am firmly convinced that my own best development is not one and the same with the best development of the world and here I am willing to sacrifice. . . . The general proposition of working for the world's good becomes too soon sickly sentimentality. I therefore take the world that the Unknown lay in my hands & work for the rise of the Negro people, taking for granted that their best development means the best development of the world. . . .

These are my plans: to make a name in science, to make a name in literature and thus to raise my race. . . .

I wonder what will be the outcome? Who knows?

I will go unto the King—which is not according to the law & if I perish—*I Perish.*

To a Schoolgirl, 1905

I wonder if you will let a stranger say a word to you about yourself? I have heard that you are a young woman of some ability but that you are neglecting your school work because you have become hopeless of trying to do anything in the world. I am very sorry for this. How any human being whose wonderful fortune it is to live in the 20th century should under ordinarily fair advantages despair of life is almost unbelievable. And if in addition to this that person is, as I am, of Negro lineage with all the hopes and yearnings of hundreds of millions of human souls dependent in some degree on her striving, then her bitterness amounts to crime.

There are in the U.S. today tens of thousands of colored girls who would be happy beyond measure to have the chance of educating themselves that you are neglecting. If you train yourself as you easily can, there are wonderful chances of usefulness before you: you can join the ranks of 15,000 Negro women teachers, of hundreds of nurses and physicians, of the growing number of clerks and stenographers, and above all of the host of homemakers. Ignorance is a cure for nothing. Get the very best training possible & the doors of opportunity will fly open before you as they are flying before thousands of your fellows. On the other hand every time a colored person neglects an opportunity, it makes it more difficult for others of the race to get such an opportunity. Do you want to cut off the chances of the boys and girls of tomorrow?

The Name "Negro"

This is an exchange of letters between Roland A. Barton, a high school student, and Dr. DuBois, concerning the use of the term "Negro" in describing black Americans. The letters originally appeared in the March, 1928, issue of Crisis, *the NAACP magazine which was edited by Dr. DuBois for twenty-three years. The debate over the relative merits of the terms "Negro," "black," "Afro-American," and others, still continues, and these letters were included in a 1967 article in* Ebony *magazine.*

South Bend, Indiana

DEAR SIR:

I am only a high school student in my sophomore year, and have not the understanding of you college educated men. It seems to me that since THE CRISIS is the Official Organ of the National Association for the Advancement of Colored People which stand for equality for all Americans, why would it designate, and segregate us as "Negroes", and not as "Americans".

W. E. B. DuBois

The most piercing thing that hurts me in this February CRISIS, which forced me to write, was the notice that called the natives of Africa, "Negroes", instead of calling them "Africans", or "natives".

The word, "Negro", or "nigger", is a white man's word to make us feel inferior. I hope to be a worker for my race, that is why I wrote this letter. I hope that by the time I become a man, that this word, "Negro", will be abolished.

ROLAND A. BARTON

MY DEAR ROLAND:

Do not at the outset of your career make the all too common error of mistaking names for things. Names are only conventional signs for identifying things. Things are the reality that counts. If a thing is despised, either because of ignorance or because it is despicable, you will not alter matters by changing its name. If men despise Negroes, they will not despise them less if Negroes are called "colored" or "Afro-Americans".

Moreover, you cannot change the name of a thing at will. Names are not merely matters of thought and reason; they are growths and habits. As long as the majority of men mean black or brown folk when they say "Negro", so long will Negro be the name of folks brown and black. And neither anger nor wailing nor tears can or will change the name until the name-habit changes.

But why seek to change the name? "Negro" is a fine word. Etymologically and phonetically it is much better and more logical than "African" or "colored" or any of the various hyphenated circumlocutions. Of course, it is not "historically" accurate. No name ever was historically accurate: neither "English," "French," "German," "White," "Jew," "Nordic" nor "Anglo-Saxon." They were all at first nicknames, misnomers, accidents, grown eventually to conventional habits and achieving accuracy because, and simply because, wide and continued usage rendered them accurate. In this sense "Negro" is quite as accurate, quite as old and quite as definite as any name of any great group of people.

Suppose now we could change the name. Suppose we arose

tomorrow morning and lo! instead of being "Negroes", all the world called us "Cheiropolidi",—do you really think this would make a vast and momentous difference to you and to me? Would the Negro problem be suddenly and eternally settled? Would you be any less ashamed of being descended from a black man, or would your schoolmates feel any less superior to you? The feeling of inferiority is in you, not in any name. The name merely evokes what is already there. Exorcise the hateful complex and no name can ever make you hang your head.

Your real work, my dear young man, does not lie with names. It is not a matter of changing them, losing them, or forgetting them. Names are nothing but little guideposts along the Way. The Way would be there and just as hard and just as long if there were no guideposts,—but not quite as easily followed! Your real work as a Negro lies in two directions: *First,* to let the world know what there is fine and genuine about the Negro race. And *secondly,* to see that there is nothing about that race which is worth contempt; your contempt, my contempt; or the contempt of the wide, wide world.

———

Get this then, Roland, and get it straight even if it pierces your soul: a Negro by any other name would be just as black and just as white; just as ashamed of himself and just as shamed by others, as today. It is not the name—it's the Thing that counts. Come on, Kid, let's go get the Thing!

W. E. B. DuBois.

From *The Souls of Black Folk*

The Souls of Black Folk *was published in 1903.*

THE BLACK BELT

Out of the North the train thundered, and we woke to see the crimson soil of Georgia stretching away bare and monotonous right and left. Here and there lay straggling, unlovely villages, and lean men loafed leisurely at the depots; then again came the stretch of pines and clay. Yet we did not nod, nor weary of the scene; for this is historic ground. Right across our track, three hundred and sixty years ago, wandered the cavalcade of Hernando de Soto, looking for gold and the Great Sea; and he and his foot-sore captives disappeared yonder in the grim forests to the west. Here sits Atlanta, the city of a hundred hills, with something Western, something Southern, and something quite its own, in its busy life. Just this side of Atlanta is the land of the Cherokees and to the southwest, not far from where Sam Hose was crucified, you may stand on a spot which is to-day the centre of the Negro problem,—the centre of those nine million men who are America's dark heritage from slavery and the slave-trade.

Not only is Georgia thus the geographical focus of our Negro population, but in many other respects, both now and yesterday, the Negro problems have seemed to be centered in this State. No other State in the Union can count a million Negroes among its citizens,—a population as large as the slave population of the whole Union in 1800; no other State fought so long and strenuously to gather this host of Africans. Oglethorpe thought slavery against law and gospel; but the circumstances which gave Georgia its first inhabitants were not calculated to furnish citizens over-nice in their ideas about rum and slaves. Despite the prohibitions of the trustees, these Georgians, like some of their descendants, proceeded to take the law into their own hands; and so pliant were the judges, and so flagrant the smuggling, and so earnest were the prayers of Whitefield, that by the middle of the eighteenth century all restrictions were swept away, and the slave-trade went merrily on for fifty years and more.

Down in Darien, where the Delegal riots took place some summers ago, there used to come a strong protest against slavery from the Scotch Highlanders; and the Moravians of Ebenezer did not like the system. But not till the Haitian Terror of Toussaint was the trade in men even checked; while the national statute of 1808 did not suffice to stop it. How the Africans poured in—fifty thousand between 1790 and 1810, and then, from Virginia and from smugglers, two thousand a year for many years more. So the thirty thousand Negroes of Georgia in 1790 doubled in a decade,—were over a hundred thousand in 1810, had reached two hundred thousand in 1820, and half a million at the time of the war. Thus like a snake the black population writhed upward. . . .

How curious a land is this,—how full of untold story, of tragedy and laughter, and the rich legacy of human life; shadowed with a tragic past, and big with future promise! This is the Black Belt of Georgia. Dougherty County is the west end of the Black Belt, and men once called it the Egypt of the Confederacy. It is full of historic interest. First there is the Swamp, to the west, where the Chickasawhatchee flows sullenly southward. The shadow of an old plantation lies at its edge, forlorn and dark. Then comes the pool; pendent gray moss and brackish waters appear, and forests filled with wildfowl. In one place the wood is on fire, smouldering in dull red anger; but nobody minds. Then the swamp grows beautiful; a raised road, built by chained Negro convicts, dips down into it, and forms a way walled and almost covered in living green. Spreading trees spring from a prodigal luxuriance of undergrowth; great dark green shadows fade into the black background, until all is one mass of tangled semi-tropical foliage, marvellous in its weird savage splendor. Once we crossed a black silent stream, where the sad trees and writhing creepers, all glinting fiery yellow and green, seemed like some vast cathedral,—some green Milan builded of wildwood. And as I crossed, I seemed to see again that fierce tragedy of seventy years ago. Osceola, the Indian-Negro chieftain, had risen in the swamps of Florida, vowing vengeance. His warcry reached the red Creeks of Dougherty, and their war-cry rang from the Chattahoochee to the sea. Men and women and children fled and fell before them as they swept into Dougherty. In yonder shadows a dark and hideously painted warrior glided stealthily on,—another and another, until three hundred had crept into the treacherous swamp. Then the false slime closing about them called the white men from the east. Waist-deep, they fought beneath the tall trees, until the war-cry was hushed and the Indians glided back into the west. Small wonder the wood is red.

Then came the black slaves. Day after day the clank of chained feet marching from Virginia and Carolina to Georgia was heard in these rich swamp lands. Day after day the songs of the callous, the wail of the motherless, and the muttered curses of the wretched echoed from the Flint to the Chickasawhatchee, until by 1860 there had risen in West Dougherty perhaps the richest slave kingdom the modern world ever knew. A hundred and fifty barons commanded the labor of nearly six thousand Negroes, held sway over farms with ninety thousand acres of tilled land, valued even in times of cheap soil at three millions of dollars. Twenty thousand bales of ginned cotton went yearly to England, New and Old; and men that came there bankrupt made money and grew rich. In a single decade the cotton output increased four-fold and the value of lands was tripled. It was the heyday of the *nouveau riche,* and a life of careless extravagance among the masters. Four and six bob-tailed thoroughbreds rolled their coaches to town; open hospitality and gay entertainment were the rule. Parks and groves were laid out, rich with flower and vine, and in the midst stood the low wide-halled "big house," with its porch and columns and great fire-places.

And yet with all this there was something sordid, something forced,—a certain feverish unrest and recklessness; for was not all this show and tinsel built upon a groan? "This land was a little Hell," said a ragged, brown, and grave-faced man to me. We were seated near a roadside blacksmith-shop, and behind was the bare ruin of some master's home. "I've seen niggers drop dead in the furrow, but they were kicked aside, and the plough never stopped. Down in the guard-house, there's where the blood ran."

With such foundations a kingdom must in time sway and fall. The masters moved to Macon and Augusta, and left only the irresponsible overseers on the land. And the result is such ruin as this, the Lloyd "home-place":—great waving oaks, a spread of lawn, myrtles and chestnuts, all ragged and wild; a solitary gate-post standing where once was a castle entrance; an old rusty anvil lying amid rotting bellows and wood in the ruins of a blacksmith shop; a wide rambling old mansion, brown and dingy, filled now with the grandchildren of the slaves who once waited on its tables; while the family of the master has dwindled to two lone women, who live in Macon and feed hungrily off the remnants of an earldom. So we ride on, past phantom gates and falling homes,—past the once flourishing farms of the Smiths, the Gandys, and the Lagores,—and find all dilapidated and half ruined, even there where a solitary white woman, a relic of other days, sits alone in state among miles of Negroes and rides to town in her ancient coach each day.

This was indeed the Egypt of the Confederacy,—the rich granary whence potatoes and corn and cotton poured out to the famished and ragged Confederate troops as they battled for a cause lost long before 1861. Sheltered and secure, it became the place of refuge for families, wealth, and slaves. Yet even then the hard ruthless rape of the land began to tell. The red-clay sub-soil already had begun to peer above the loam. The harder the slaves were driven the more careless and fatal was their farming. Then came the revolution of war and Emancipation, the bewilderment of Reconstruction,—and now, what is the Egypt of the Confederacy, and what meaning has it for the nation's weal or woe?

It is a land of rapid contrasts and of curiously mingled hope and pain. Here sits a pretty blue-eyed quadroon hiding her bare feet; she was married only last week, and yonder in the field is her dark young husband, hoeing to support her, at thirty cents a day without board. Across the way is Gatesby, brown and tall, lord of two thousand acres shrewdly won and held. There is a store conducted by his black son, a blacksmith shop, and a ginnery. Five miles below here is a town owned and controlled by one white New Englander. He owns almost a Rhode Island county, with thousands of acres and hundreds of black laborers. Their cabins look better than most, and the farm, with machinery and fertilizers, is much more business-like than any in the county, although the manager drives hard bargains in wages. When now we turn and look five miles above, there on the edge of town are five houses of prostitutes,—two of blacks and three of whites; and in one of the houses of the whites a worthless black boy was harbored too openly two years ago; so he was hanged for rape. And here, too, is the high whitewashed fence of the "stockade," as the county prison is called; the white folks say it is ever full of black criminals,—the black folks say that only colored boys are sent to jail, and they not because they are guilty, but because the State needs criminals to eke out its income by their forced labor.

Immigrants are heirs of the slave baron in Dougherty; and as we ride westward, by wide stretching cornfields and stubby orchards of peach and pear, we see on all sides within the circle of dark forest a Land of Canaan. Here and there are tales of projects for money-getting, born in the swift days of Reconstruction,—"improvement" companies, wine companies, mills and factories; most failed, and foreigners fell heir. It is a beautiful land, this Dougherty, west of the Flint. The forests are wonderful, the solemn pines have disappeared, and this is the "Oakey Woods," with its wealth of hickories, beeches, oaks and palmettos. But a pall of debt hangs over the beautiful land; the merchants are in debt to the wholesalers, the planters are in debt to the merchants, the tenants owe the planters, and laborers bow and bend beneath the burden of it all. Here and there a man has raised his head above these murky waters. We passed one fenced stock-farm with grass and grazing cattle, that looked very homelike after endless corn and cotton. Here and there are black freeholders: there is the gaunt dull-black Jackson, with his hundred acres. "I says, 'Look up! If you don't look up you can't get up,'" remarks Jackson, philosophically. And he's gotten up. Dark Carter's neat barns would do credit to New England. His master helped him to get a start, but when the black man died last fall the master's sons immediately laid claim to the estate. "And them white folks will get it, too," said my yellow gossip.

I turn from these well-tended acres with a comfortable feeling that the Negro is rising. Even then, however, the fields, as we proceed, begin to redden and the trees disappear. Rows of old cabins appear filled with renters and laborers,—cheerless, bare, and dirty, for the most part, although here and there the very age and decay makes the scene picturesque. A young black fellow greets us. He is twenty-two, and just married. Until last year he had good luck renting; then cotton fell, and the sheriff seized and sold all he had. So he moved here, where the rent is higher, the land poorer, and the owner inflexible; he rents a forty-dollar mule for twenty dollars a year. Poor lad!—a slave at twenty-two. This plantation, owned now by a foreigner, was a part of the famous Bolton estate. After the war it was for many years worked by gangs of Negro convicts,—and black convicts then were even more plentiful than now; it was a way of making Negroes work, and the question of guilt was a minor one. Hard tales of cruelty and mistreatment of the chained freemen are told, but the county authorities were deaf until the free-labor market was nearly ruined by wholesale migration. Then they took the convicts from the plantations, but not until one of the fairest regions of the "Oakey Woods" had been ruined and ravished into a red waste, out of which only a Yankee or an immigrant could squeeze more blood from debt-cursed tenants.

From *Dusk of Dawn*

Dusk of Dawn, an autobiography by Dr. DuBois, was published in 1940.

REVOLUTION

My leadership was a leadership solely of ideas. I never was, nor ever will be, personally popular. This was not simply because of my idiosyncrasies but because I despise the essential demagoguery of personal leadership; of that hypnotic ascendancy over men which carries out objectives regardless of their value or validity, simply by personal loyalty and admiration. In my case I withdrew sometimes ostentatiously from the personal nexus, but I sought all the more determinedly to force home essential ideas.

I think I may say without boasting that in the period from 1910 to 1930 I was a main factor in revolutionizing the attitude of the American Negro toward caste. My stinging hammer blows made Negroes aware of themselves, confident of their possibilities and determined in self-assertion. So much so that today common slogans among the Negro people are taken bodily from the words of my mouth.

But of course, no idea is perfect and forever valid. Always to be living and apposite and timely, it must be modified and adapted to changing facts. What I began to realize was that the heights and fastnesses which we black folk were assailing could not in America be gained by sheer force of assault, because of our relatively small numbers. They could only be gained as the majority of Americans were persuaded of the rightness of our cause and joined with us in demanding our recognition as full citizens. This process must deal not only with conscious rational action, but with irrational and unconscious habit, long buried in folkways and custom. Intelligent propaganda, legal enactment and reasoned action must attack the conditioned reflexes of race hate and change them.

Slowly but surely I came to see that for many years, perhaps many generations, we could not count on any such majority; that the whole set of the white world in America, in Europe and in the world was too determinedly against racial equality to give power and persuasiveness to our agitation. Therefore, I began to emphasize and restate certain implicit aspects of my former ideas. I tried to say to the American Negro: during the time of this frontal attack which you are making upon American and European prejudice, and with your unwavering statement and restatement of what is right and just, not only for us, but in the long run, for all men; during this time, there are certain things you must do for your own survival and self-preservation. You must put behind your demands, not simply American Negroes, but West Indians and Africans and all the colored races of the world. These things I began to say with no lessening, or thought of lessening of my emphasis upon the essential rightness of what we had been asking for a generation in the political and civic social equality.

It was clear to me that agitation against race prejudice and a planned economy for bettering the economic condition of the

American Negro were not antagonistic ideals but part of one ideal; that it did not increase segregation; the segregation was there and would remain for many years. But now I proposed that in economic lines, just as in lines of literature and religion, segregation should be planned and organized and carefully thought through. This plan did not establish a new segregation; it did not advocate segregation as the final solution of the race problem; exactly the contrary; but it did face the facts and faced them with thoughtfully mapped effort.

Of course I soon realized that in this matter of segregation I was touching an old and bleeding sore in Negro thought. From the eighteenth century down the Negro intelligentsia has regarded segregation as the visible badge of their servitude and as the object of their unceasing attack. The upper-class Negro has almost never been nationalistic. He has never planned or thought of a Negro state or a Negro church or a Negro school. This solution has always been a thought upsurging from the mass, because of pressure which they could not withstand and which compelled a racial institution or chaos. Continually such institutions were founded and developed, but this took place against the advice and best thought of the intelligentsia.

American Negroes have always feared with perfect fear their eventual expulsion from America. They have been willing to submit to caste rather than face this. The reasons have varied but today they are clear; Negroes have no Zion. There is no place where they can go today and not be subject to worse caste and greater disabilities from the dominant white imperialistic world than they suffer here today. On the other hand, there is no likelihood just now of their being forcibly expelled. So far as that is concerned, there was no likelihood ten years ago of the Jews being expelled from Germany. The cases are far from parallel. There is a good deal more profit in cheap Negro labor than in Jewish fellow citizens, which brings together strange bedfellows for the protection of the Negro. On the other hand, one must remember that this is a day of astonishing change, injustice and cruelty; and that many Americans of stature have favored the transportation of Negroes and they were not all of the mental caliber of the present junior senator from Mississippi. As the Negro develops from an easily exploitable, profit-furnishing laborer to an intelligent independent self-supporting citizen, the possibility of his being pushed out of his American fatherland may easily be increased rather than diminished. We may be expelled from the United States as the Jew is being expelled from Germany.

At any rate it is the duty of American Negroes today to examine this situation not with hysteria and anger but with calm forethought. Whether self-segregation for his protection, for inner development and growth in intelligence and social efficiency, will increase his acceptability to white Americans or not, that growth must go on. And whatever the event may bring, it must be faced as men face crises and not with surprise and helpless amazement.

WALTER WHITE

I Investigate Lynchings

Nothing contributes so much to the continued life of an investigator of lynchings and his tranquil possession of all his limbs as the obtuseness of the lynchers themselves. Like most boastful people who practice direct action when it involves no personal risk, they just can't help talk about their deeds to any person who manifests even the slightest interest in them.

Most lynchings take place in small towns and rural regions where the natives know practically nothing of what is going on outside their own immediate neighborhoods. Newspapers, books, magazines, theatres, visitors and other vehicles for the transmission of information and ideas are usually as strange among them as dry-point etchings. But those who live in so sterile an atmosphere usually esteem their own perspicacity in about the same degree as they are isolated from the world of ideas. They gabble on *ad infinitum,* apparently unable to keep from talking.

In any American village, North or South, East or West, there is no problem which cannot be solved in half an hour by the morons who lounge about the village store. World peace, or the lack of it, the tariff, sex, religion, the settlement of the war debts, short skirts, Prohibition, the carryings-on of the younger generation, the superior moral rectitude of country people over city dwellers (with a wistful eye on urban sins)—all these controversial subjects are disposed of quickly and finally by the bucolic

35

wise men. When to their isolation is added an emotional fixation, such as the rural South has on the Negro, one can sense the atmosphere from which spring the Heflins, the Ku Kluxers, the two-gun Bible-beaters, the lynchers and the anti-evolutionists. And one can see why no great amount of cleverness or courage is needed to acquire information in such a forlorn place about the latest lynching.

Professor Earle Fiske Young of the University of Southern California recently analyzed the lynching returns from fourteen Southern states for thirty years. He found that in counties of less than 10,000 people there was a lynching rate of 3.2 per 100,000 of population; that in those of from 10,000 to 20,000 the rate dropped to 2.4; that in those of from 20,000 to 30,000, it was 2.1 per cent; that in those of from 30,000 to 40,000, it was 1.7, and that thereafter it kept on going down until in counties with from 300,000 to 800,000 population it was only 0.05.

Of the forty-one lynchings and eight race riots I have investigated for the National Association for the Advancement of Colored People during the past ten years, all of the lynchings and seven of the riots occurred in rural or semi-rural communities. The towns ranged in population from around one hundred to ten thousand or so. The lynchings were not difficult to inquire into because of the fact already noted that those who perpetrated them were in nearly every instance simple-minded and easily fooled individuals. On but three occasions were suspicions aroused by my too definite questions or by informers who had seen me in other places. These three times I found it rather desirable to disappear slightly in advance of reception committees imbued with the desire to make an addition to the lynching record. One other time the possession of a light skin and blue eyes (though I consider myself a colored man) almost cost me my life when (it was during the Chicago race riots in 1919) a Negro shot at me, thinking me to be a white man.

II

In 1918 a Negro woman, about to give birth to a child, was lynched with almost unmentionable brutality along with ten

36

men in Georgia. I reached the scene shortly after the butchery and while excitement yet ran high. It was a prosperous community. Forests of pine trees gave rich returns in turpentine, tar and pitch. The small towns where the farmers and turpentine hands traded were fat and rich. The main streets of the largest of these towns were well paved and lighted. The stores were well stocked. The white inhabitants belonged to the class of Georgia crackers—lanky, slow of movement and of speech, long-necked, with small eyes set close together, and skin tanned by the hot sun to a reddish-yellow hue.

As I was born in Georgia and spent twenty years of my life there, my accent is sufficiently Southern to enable me to talk with Southerners and not arouse their suspicion that I am an outsider. (In the rural South hatred of Yankees is not much less than hatred of Negroes.) On the morning of my arrival in the town I casually dropped into the store of one of the general merchants who, I had been informed, had been one of the leaders of the mob. After making a small purchase I engaged the merchant in conversation. There was, at the time, no other customer in the store. We spoke of the weather, the possibility of good crops in the fall, the political situation, the latest news from the war in Europe. As his manner became more and more friendly I ventured to mention guardedly the recent lynchings.

Instantly he became cautious—until I hinted that I had great admiration for the manly spirit the men of the town had exhibited. I mentioned the newspaper accounts I had read and confessed that I had never been so fortunate as to see a lynching. My words or tone seemed to disarm his suspicions. He offered me a box on which to sit, drew up another one for himself, and gave me a bottle of Coca-Cola.

"You'll pardon me, Mister," he began, "for seeming suspicious but we have to be careful. In ordinary times we wouldn't have anything to worry about, but with the war there's been some talk of the Federal government looking into lynchings. It seems there's some sort of law during wartime making it treason to lower the man power of the country."

"In that case I don't blame you for being careful," I assured him. "But couldn't the Federal government do something if it wanted to when a lynching takes place, even if no war is going on at the moment?"

"Naw," he said, confidently, proud of the opportunity of displaying his store of information to one who he assumed knew nothing whatever about the subject. "There's no such law, in spite of all the agitation by a lot of fools who don't know the niggers as we do. States' rights won't permit Congress to meddle in lynching in peace time."

"But what about your State government—your Governor, your sheriff, your police officers?"

"Humph! Them? We elected them to office, didn't we? And the niggers, we've got them disfranchised, ain't we? Sheriffs and police and Governors and prosecuting attorneys have got too much sense to mix in lynching-bees. If they do they know they might as well give up all idea of running for office any more— if something worse don't happen to them—" This last with a tightening of the lips and a hard look in the eyes.

I sought to lead the conversation into less dangerous channels. "Who was the white man who was killed—whose killing caused the lynchings?" I asked.

"Oh, he was a hard one, all right. Never paid his debts to white men or niggers and wasn't liked much around here. He was a mean 'un all right, all right."

"Why, then, did you lynch the niggers for killing such a man?"

"It's a matter of safety—we gotta show niggers that they mustn't touch a white man, no matter how low-down and ornery he is."

Little by little he revealed the whole story. When he told of the manner in which the pregnant woman had been killed he chuckled and slapped his thigh and declared it to be "the best show, Mister, I ever did see. You ought to have heard the wench howl when we strung her up."

Covering the nausea the story caused me as best I could, I slowly gained the whole story, with the names of the other participants. Among them were prosperous farmers, business men, bankers, newspaper reporters and editors, and several law-enforcement officers.

My several days of discreet inquiry began to arouse suspicions in the town. On the third day of my stay I went once more into the store of the man with whom I had first talked. He asked me to wait until he had finished serving the sole customer. When she had gone he came from behind the counter and with secretive manner and lowered voice he asked, "You're a government man, ain't you?" (An agent of the Federal Department of Justice was what he meant.)

"Who said so?" I countered.

"Never mind who told me; I know one when I see him," he replied, with a shrewd harshness in his face and voice.

Ignorant of what might have taken place since last I had talked with him, I thought it wise to learn all I could and say nothing which might commit me. "Don't you tell anyone I am a government man; if I *am* one, you're the only one in town who knows it," I told him cryptically. I knew that within an hour everybody in town would share his "information."

An hour or so later I went at nightfall to the little but not uncomfortable hotel where I was staying. As I was about to enter a Negro approached me and, with an air of great mystery, told me that he had just heard a group of white men discussing me and declaring that if I remained in the town overnight "something would happen" to me.

The thought raced through my mind before I replied that it was hardly likely that, following so terrible a series of lynchings, a Negro would voluntarily approach a supposedly white man whom he did not know and deliver such a message. He had been sent, and no doubt the persons who sent him were white and for some reason did not dare tackle me themselves. Had they dared there would have been no warning in advance—simply an attack. Though I had no weapon with me, it occurred to me that there was no reason why two should not play at the game of bluffing. I looked straight into my informant's eyes and said: "You go back to the ones who sent you and tell them this: that I have a damned good automatic and I know how to use it. If anybody attempts to molest me tonight or any other time, somebody is going to get hurt."

39

That night I did not take off my clothes nor did I sleep. Ordinarily in such small Southern towns everyone is snoring by nine o'clock. That night, however, there was much passing and re-passing of the hotel. I learned afterward that the merchant had, as I expected, told generally that I was an agent of the Department of Justice, and my empty threat had served to reinforce his assertion. The Negro had been sent to me in the hope that I might be frightened enough to leave before I had secured evidence against the members of the mob. I remained in the town two more days. My every movement was watched, but I was not molested. But when, later, it became known that not only was I not an agent of the Department of Justice but a Negro, the fury of the inhabitants of the region was unlimited—particularly when it was found that evidence I gathered had been placed in the hands of the Governor of Georgia. It happened that he was a man genuinely eager to stop lynching—but restrictive laws against which he had appealed in vain effectively prevented him from acting upon the evidence. And the Federal government declared itself unable to proceed against the lynchers.

LANGSTON HUGHES

In Love with Harlem

"In Love with Harlem" was written by Mr. Hughes for the Summer, 1963, issue of Freedomways *magazine, which was devoted to Harlem.*

On a bright September morning in 1921, I came up out of the subway at 135th and Lenox into the beginnings of the Negro Renaissance. I headed for the Harlem Y.M.C.A. down the block, where so many new, young, dark, male arrivals in Harlem have spent early days. The next place I headed to that afternoon was the Harlem Branch Library just up the street. There, a warm and wonderful librarian, Miss Ernestine Rose, white, made newcomers feel welcome, as did her assistant in charge of the Schomburg Collection, Catherine Latimer, a luscious café au lait. That night I went to the Lincoln Theatre across Lenox Avenue where maybe one of the Smiths—Bessie, Clara, Trixie, or Mamie—was singing the blues. And as soon as I could I made a beeline for *Shuffle Along*, the all-colored hit musical playing on 63rd Street in which Florence Mills came to fame.

I had come to New York to enter Columbia College as a freshman, but really why I had come to New York was to see Harlem. I found it hard a week or so later to tear myself away from Harlem when it came time to move up the hill to the dormitory at Columbia. That winter I spent as little time as possible on the campus. Instead, I spent as much time as I could

41

in Harlem, and this I have done ever since. I was in love with Harlem long before I got there, and I still am in love with it. Everybody seemed to make me welcome. The sheer dark size of Harlem intrigued me. And the fact that at that time poets and writers like James Weldon Johnson and Jessie Fauset lived there, and Bert Williams, Duke Ellington, Ethel Waters, and Walter White, too, fascinated me. Had I been a rich young man, I would have bought a house in Harlem and built musical steps up the front door, and installed chimes that at the press of a button played Ellington tunes.

After a winter at Columbia, I moved back down to Harlem. Everywhere I roomed, I had the good fortune to have lovely landladies. If I did not like a landlady's looks, I would not move in with her, maybe that is why. But at finding work in New York, my fortune was less than good. Finally, I went to sea— Africa, Europe—then a year in Paris working in a night club where the band was from Harlem. I was a dishwasher, later bus boy, listening every night to the music of Harlem transplanted to Montmartre. And I was on hand to welcome Bricktop when she came to sing for the first time in Europe, bringing with her news of Harlem.

When I came back to New York in 1925 the Negro Renaissance was in full swing. Countee Cullen was publishing his early poems, Aaron Douglas was painting, Zora Neale Hurston, Rudolph Fisher, Jean Toomer, and Wallace Thurman were writing, Louis Armstrong was playing, Cora La Redd was dancing, and the Savoy Ballroom was open with a specially built floor that rocked as the dancers swayed. Alain Locke was putting together *The New Negro*. Art took heart from Harlem creativity. Jazz filled the night air—but not everywhere—and people came from all around after dark to look upon our city within a city, Black Harlem. Had I not had to earn a living, I might have thought it even more wonderful than it was. But I could not eat the poems I wrote. Unlike the whites who came to spend their money in Harlem, only a few Harlemites seemed to live in even a modest degree of luxury. Most rode the subway downtown every morning to work or to look for work.

Downtown! I soon learned that it was seemingly impossible for black Harlem to live without white downtown. My youthful illusion that Harlem was a world unto itself did not last very long. It was not even an area that ran itself. The famous night clubs were owned by whites, as were the theatres. Almost all the stores were owned by whites, and many at that time did not even (in the very middle of Harlem) employ Negro clerks. The books of Harlem writers all had to be published downtown, if they were to be published at all. Downtown: white. Uptown: black. White downtown pulling all the strings in Harlem. Moe Gale, Moe Gale, Moe Gale, Lew Leslie, Lew Leslie, Lew Leslie, Harper's, Knopf, *The Survey Graphic,* the Harmon Foundation, the racketeers who kidnapped Casper Holstein and began to take over the numbers for whites. Negroes could not even play their own numbers with their own people. And almost all the policemen in Harlem were white. Negroes couldn't even get graft from themselves for themselves by themselves. Black Harlem really was in white face, economically speaking. So I wrote this poem:

Because my mouth
Is wide with laughter
And my throat
Is deep with song,
You do not think
I suffer after
I have held my pain
So long?

Because my mouth
Is wide with laughter,
You do not hear
My inner cry?
Because my feet
Are gay with dancing,
You do not know
I die?

Harlem, like a Picasso painting in his cubistic period. Harlem —Southern Harlem—the Carolinas, Georgia, Florida—looking for the Promised Land—dressed in rhythmic words, painted in bright pictures, dancing to jazz—and ending up in the subway at morning rush time—headed downtown. West Indian Harlem —warm rambunctious sassy remembering Marcus Garvey. Haitian Harlem, Cuban Harlem, little pockets of tropical dreams in alien tongues. Magnet Harlem, pulling an Arthur Schomburg from Puerto Rico, pulling an Arna Bontemps all the way from California, a Nora Holt from way out West, an E. Simms Campbell from St. Louis, likewise a Josephine Baker, a Charles S. Johnson from Virginia, an A. Philip Randolph from Florida, a Roy Wilkins from Minnesota, an Alta Douglas from Kansas. Melting pot Harlem—Harlem of honey and chocolate and caramel and rum and vinegar and lemon and lime and gall. Dusky dream Harlem rumbling into a nightmare tunnel where the subway from the Bronx keeps right on downtown, where the money from the nightclubs goes right on back downtown, where the jazz is drained to Broadway, whence Josephine goes to Paris, Robeson to London, Jean Toomer to a Quaker Meeting House, Garvey to the Atlanta Federal Penitentiary, and Wallace Thurman to his grave; but Duke Ellington to fame and fortune, Lena Horne to Broadway, and Buck Clayton to China.

Before it was over—our NEW NEGRO RENAISSANCE—poems became placards: Don't buy where you can't work! Adam Powell with a picket sign; me, too. BUY BLACK! Sufi long before the Black Muslims. FIRST TO BE FIRED, LAST TO BE HIRED! The Stock Market crash. The bank failures. Empty pockets. God Bless The Child That's Got His Own. Depression, Federal Theatre in Harlem, the making of Orson Welles, WPA, CCC, the Blue Eagle, Father Divine. In the midst of the Depression I got a cable from Russia inviting me to work on a motion picture there. I went to Moscow. That was the end of the early days of Langston Hughes in Harlem.

From *The Big Sea*

NEGRO

You see, unfortunately, I am not black. There are lots of different kinds of blood in our family. But here in the United States, the word "Negro" is used to mean anyone who has *any* Negro blood at all in his veins. In Africa, the word is more pure. It means *all* Negro, therefore *black*.

I am brown. My father was a darker brown. My mother an olive-yellow. On my father's side, the white blood in his family came from a Jewish slave trader in Kentucky, Silas Cushenberry, of Clark County, who was his mother's father; and Sam Clay, a distiller of Scotch descent, living in Henry County, who was his father's father. So on my father's side both male great-grandparents were white, and Sam Clay was said to be a relative of the great statesman, Henry Clay, his contemporary.

On my mother's side, I had a paternal great-grandfather named Quarles—Captain Ralph Quarles—who was white and who lived in Louisa County, Virginia, before the Civil War, and who had several colored children by a colored housekeeper, who was his slave. The Quarles traced their ancestry back to Francis Quarles, famous Jacobean poet, who wrote *A Feast for Wormes*.

On my maternal grandmother's side, there was French and Indian blood. My grandmother looked like an Indian—with very long black hair. She said she could lay claim to Indian land, but that she never wanted the government (or anybody else) to give her anything. She said there had been a French trader who came down the St. Lawrence, then on foot to the Carolinas, and mated with her grandmother, who was a Cherokee —so all her people were free. During slavery, she had free papers in North Carolina, and traveled about free, at will. Her name was Mary Sampson Patterson, and in Oberlin, Ohio, where she went to college, she married a free man named Sheridan Leary.

She was with child in Oberlin when Sheridan Leary went away, and nobody knew where he had gone, except that he told her he was going on a trip. A few weeks later his shawl came back to her full of bullet holes. He had been killed following John Brown in that historic raid at Harper's Ferry. They did not hang him. He had been killed that first night in the raid—shot attacking, believing in John Brown. My grandmother said Sheridan Leary always did believe people should be free.

She married another man who believed the same thing. His name was Charles Langston, my grandfather. And in the 70's the Langstons came out to Kansas where my mother was born on a farm near Lawrence.

My grandfather never made much money. But he went into

politics, looking for a bigger freedom than the Emancipation Proclamation had provided. He let his farm and his grocery store in Lawrence run along, and didn't much care about making money. When he died, none of the family had any money. But he left some fine speeches behind him.

His brother, John Mercer Langston, left a book of speeches, too, and an autobiography, *From a Virginia Plantation to the National Capital*. But he was much better than Charles at making money, so he left a big house as well, and I guess some stocks and bonds. When I was small, we had cousins in Washington, who lived a lot better than we did in Kansas. But my grandmother never wrote them for anything. John Mercer Langston had been a Congressman from Virginia, and later United States Minister to Haiti, and Dean of the first Law School at Howard University. He had held many high positions—very high positions for a Negro in his day, or any day in this rather difficult country. And his descendants are still in society.

We were never very much "in society" in Kansas, because we were always broke, and the families of the Negro doctors and lawyers lived much better than we did. One of the first things I remember is my grandmother worrying about the mortgage on our house. It was always very hard for her to raise the money to pay the interest. And when my grandmother died, the house went right straight to the mortgage man, quickly.

I was born in Joplin, Missouri, in 1902, but I grew up mostly in Lawrence, Kansas. My grandmother raised me until I was twelve years old. Sometimes I was with my mother, but not often. My father and mother were separated. And my mother, who worked, always traveled about a great deal, looking for a better job. When I first started to school, I was with my mother a while in Topeka. (And later, for a summer in Colorado, and another in Kansas City.) She was a stenographer for a colored lawyer in Topeka, named Mr. Guy. She rented a room near his office, downtown. So I went to a "white" school in the downtown district.

At first, they did not want to admit me to the school, because there were no other colored families living in that neighborhood. They wanted to send me to the colored school, blocks away down across the railroad tracks. But my mother, who was always ready to do battle for the rights of a free people, went directly to the school board, and finally got me into the Harrison Street School —where all the teachers were nice to me, except one who sometimes used to make remarks about my being colored. And after such remarks, occasionally the kids would grab stones and tin cans out of the alley and chase me home.

But there was one little white boy who would always take up for me. Sometimes others of my classmates would, as well. So I learned early not to hate *all* white people. And ever since, it has seemed to me that *most* people are generally good, in every race and every country where I have been.

The room my mother lived in in Topeka was not in a house. It was in a building, upstairs over a plumbing shop. The other rooms on that floor facing a long hall were occupied by a white architect and a colored painter. The architect was a very old man, and very kind. The colored painter was young, and used to paint marvelous lions and tigers and jungle scenes. I don't know where he saw such things in Topeka, but he used to paint them. Years later, I saw him paint them on the walls of cheap barrooms in Chicago and New York. I don't know where he is now.

My mother had a small monkey-stove in our room for both heating and cooking. You could put only one pot on the stove at a time. She used to send me through the downtown alleys every day after the stores closed to pick up discarded boxes to burn in our stove. Sometimes we would make a great racket, cutting kindling with a hatchet in our room at night. If it was a tough box we could not break up, we would put a whole piece of board in the stove, and it would stick out through the top, and my mother would call it "long-branch kindling." When she would go away and leave me alone, she would warn me about putting "long-branch kindling" in the stove, because it might burn until it broke off, and fall, and catch the rug on fire.

My mother used to take me to see all the plays that came to Topeka like *Buster Brown*, *Under Two Flags*, and *Uncle Tom's Cabin*. We were very fond of plays and books. Once we heard *Faust*.

When I was about five or six years old, my father and mother

47

decided to go back together. They had separated shortly after I was born, because my father wanted to go away to another country, where a colored man could get ahead and make money quicker, and my mother did not want to go. My father went to Cuba, and then to Mexico, where there wasn't any color line, or any Jim Crow. He finally sent for us, so we went there, too.

But no sooner had my mother, my grandmother, and I got to Mexico City than there was a big earthquake, and people ran out from their houses into the Alameda, and the big National Opera House they were building sank down into the ground, and tarantulas came out of the walls—and my mother said she wanted to go back home at once to Kansas, where people spoke English or something she could understand and there were no earthquakes. So we went. And that was the last I saw of my father until I was seventeen.

When I was in the second grade, my grandmother took me to Lawrence to raise me. And I was unhappy for a long time, and very lonesome, living with my grandmother. Then it was that books began to happen to me, and I began to believe in nothing but books and the wonderful world in books—where if people suffered, they suffered in beautiful language, not in monosyllables, as we did in Kansas. And where almost always the mortgage got paid off, the good knights won, and the Alger boy triumphed.

Our mortgage never got paid off—for my grandmother was not like the other colored women of Lawrence. She didn't take in washing or go out to cook, for she had never worked for anyone. But she tried to make a living by renting rooms to college students from Kansas University; or by renting out half her house to a family; or sometimes she would move out entirely and go to live with a friend, while she rented the whole little house for ten or twelve dollars a month, to make a payment on the mortgage. But we were never quite sure the white mortgage man was not going to take the house. And sometimes, on that account, we would have very little to eat, saving to pay the interest.

I remember one summer a friend of my mother's in Kansas City sent her son to pass a few weeks with me at my grandmother's home in Lawrence. But the little boy only stayed a few days, then wrote his mother that he wanted to leave, because we had nothing but salt pork and wild dandelions to eat. The boy was right. But being only eight or nine years old, I cried when he showed me the letter he was writing his mother. And I never wanted my mother to invite any more little boys to stay with me at my grandmother's house.

You see, my grandmother was very proud, and she would never beg or borrow anything from anybody. She sat, looking very much like an Indian, copper-colored with long black hair, just a little gray in places at seventy, sat in her rocker and read the Bible, or held me on her lap and told me long, beautiful stories about people who wanted to make the Negroes free, and how her father had had apprenticed to him many slaves in Fayetteville, North Carolina, before the War, so that they could work out their freedom under him as stone masons. And once they had worked out their purchase, he would see that they reached the North, where there was no slavery.

Through my grandmother's stories always life moved, moved heroically toward an end. Nobody ever cried in my grandmother's stories. They worked, or schemed, or fought. But no crying. When my grandmother died, I didn't cry, either. Something about my grandmother's stories (without her ever having said so) taught me the uselessness of crying about anything.

She was a proud woman—gentle, but Indian and proud. I remember once she took me to Osawatomie, where she was honored by President Roosevelt—Teddy—and sat on the platform with him while he made a speech; for she was then the last surviving widow of John Brown's raid.

I was twelve when she died. I went to live with a friend of my grandmother's named Auntie Reed. Auntie Reed and her husband had a little house a block from the Kaw River, near the railroad station. They had chickens and cows. Uncle Reed dug ditches and laid sewer pipes for the city, and Auntie Reed sold milk and eggs to her neighbors. For me, there have never been any better people in the world. I loved them very much. Auntie Reed let me set the hens, and Uncle Reed let me drive the cows to pasture. Auntie Reed was a Christian and made me go to church and Sunday school every Sunday. But Uncle Reed was a sinner and never went to church as long as he lived, nor cared anything about it. In fact, he washed his overalls every Sunday morning (a grievous sin) in a big iron pot in the back yard, and then just sat and smoked his pipe under the grape arbor in summer, in winter on a bench behind the kitchen range. But both of them were very good and kind—the one who went to church and the one who didn't. And no doubt from them I learned to like both Christians and sinners equally well.

RICHARD WRIGHT

From *Black Boy*

"WHEN I HAD LEARNED TO RECOGNIZE . . ."

In the immediate neighborhood there were many school children who, in the afternoons, would stop and play en route to their homes; they would leave their books upon the sidewalk and I would thumb through the pages and question them about the baffling black print. When I had learned to recognize certain words, I told my mother that I wanted to learn to read and she encouraged me. Soon I was able to pick my way through most of the children's books I ran across. There grew in me a consuming curiosity about what was happening around me and, when my mother came home from a hard day's work, I would question her so relentlessly about what I had heard in the streets that she refused to talk to me.

One cold morning my mother awakened me and told me that, because there was no coal in the house, she was taking my brother to the job with her and that I must remain in bed until the coal she had ordered was delivered. For the payment of the coal, she left a note together with some money under the dresser scarf. I went back to sleep and was awakened by the ringing of the doorbell. I opened the door, let in the coal man, and gave him the money and the note. He brought in a few bushels of coal, then lingered, asking me if I were cold.

"Yes," I said, shivering.

He made a fire, then sat and smoked.

"How much change do I owe you?" he asked me.

"I don't know," I said.

"Shame on you," he said. "Don't you know how to count?"

"No, sir," I said.

"Listen and repeat after me," he said.

He counted to ten and I listened carefully; then he asked me to count alone and I did. He then made me memorize the words twenty, thirty, forty, etc., then told me to add one, two, three, and so on. In about an hour's time I had learned to count to a hundred and I was overjoyed. Long after the coal man had gone I danced up and down on the bed in my nightclothes, counting again and again to a hundred, afraid that if I did not keep repeating the numbers I would forget them. When my mother returned from her job that night I insisted that she stand still and listen while I counted to one hundred. She was dumfounded. After that she taught me to read, told me stories. On Sundays I would read the newspapers with my mother guiding me and spelling out the words.

I soon made myself a nuisance by asking far too many questions of everybody. Every happening in the neighborhood, no matter how trivial, became my business. It was in this manner that I first stumbled upon the relations between whites and blacks, and what I learned frightened me. Though I had long known that there were people called "white" people, it had never meant anything to me emotionally. I had seen white men and women upon the streets a thousand times, but they had never looked particularly "white." To me they were merely people like other people, yet somehow strangely different because I had never come in close touch with any of them. For the most part I never thought of them; they simply existed somewhere in the background of the city as a whole. It might have been that my tardiness in learning to sense white people as "white" people came from the fact that many of my relatives were "white"-looking people. My grandmother, who was white as any "white" person, had never looked "white" to me. And when word circulated among the black people of the neighborhood that a "black" boy had been severely beaten by a "white" man, I felt that the "white" man had had a right to beat the "black" boy, for I naïvely assumed that the "white" man must have been the "black" boy's father. And did not all fathers, like my father, have the right to beat their children? A paternal right was the only right, to my understanding, that a man had to beat a child. But when my mother told me that the "white" man was not the father of the "black" boy, was no kin to him at all, I was puzzled.

"Then why did the 'white' man whip the 'black' boy?" I asked my mother.

"The 'white' man did not *whip* the 'black' boy," my mother told me. "He *beat* the 'black' boy."

"But why?"

"You're too young to understand."

"I'm not going to let anybody beat me," I said stoutly.

"Then stop running wild in the streets," my mother said.

I brooded for a long time about the seemingly causeless beating of the "black" boy by the "white" man and the more questions I asked the more bewildering it all became. Whenever I saw "white" people now I stared at them, wondering what they were really like.

"REMEMBER YOU'RE BLACK"

I held a series of petty jobs for short periods, quitting some to work elsewhere, being driven off others because of my attitude, my speech, the look in my eyes. I was no nearer than ever to my goal of saving enough money to leave. At times I doubted if I could ever do it.

One jobless morning I went to my old classmate, Griggs, who worked for a Capitol Street jeweler. He was washing the windows of the store when I came upon him.

"Do you know where I can find a job?" I asked.

He looked at me with scorn.

"Yes, I know where you can find a job," he said, laughing.

"Where?"

"But I wonder if you can hold it," he said.

"What do you mean?" I asked. "Where's the job?"

"Take your time," he said. "You know, Dick, I know you. You've been trying to hold a job all summer, and you can't. Why? Because you're impatient. That's your big fault."

I said nothing, because he was repeating what I had already heard him say. He lit a cigarette and blew out smoke leisurely.

"Well," I said, egging him on to speak.

"I wish to hell I could talk to you," he said.

"I think I know what you want to tell me," I said.

He clapped me on the shoulder; his face was full of fear, hate, concern for me.

"Do you want to get killed?" he asked me.

"Hell, no!"

"Then, for God's sake, learn how to live in the South!"

"What do you mean?" I demanded. "Let white people tell me that. Why should you?"

"See?" he said triumphantly, pointing his finger at me. "There it is, *now!* It's in your face. You won't let people tell you things. You rush too much. I'm trying to help you and you won't let me." He paused and looked about; the streets were filled with white people. He spoke to me in a low, full tone. "Dick, look, you're black, black, *black*, see? Can't you understand that?"

"Sure. I understand it," I said.

"You don't act a damn bit like it," he spat.

He then reeled off an account of my actions on every job I had held that summer.

"How did you know that?" I asked.

"White people make it their business to watch niggers," he explained. "And they pass the word around. Now, my boss is a Yankee and he tells me things. You're marked already."

Could I believe him? Was it true? How could I ever learn this strange world of white people?

"Then tell me how must I act?" I asked humbly. "I just want to make enough money to leave."

"Wait and I'll tell you," he said.

At that moment a woman and two men stepped from the jewelry store; I moved to one side to let them pass, my mind intent upon Griggs's words. Suddenly Griggs reached for my arm and jerked me violently, sending me stumbling three or four feet across the pavement. I whirled.

"What's the matter with you?" I asked.

Griggs glared at me, then laughed.

"I'm teaching you how to get out of white people's way," he said.

I looked at the people who had come out of the store; yes, they were *white,* but I had not noticed it.

"Do you see what I mean?" he asked. "White people want you out of their way." He pronounced the words slowly so that they would sink into my mind.

"I know what you mean," I breathed.

"Dick, I'm treating you like a brother," he said. "You act around white people as if you didn't know that they were white. And they *see* it."

"Oh, Christ, I can't be a slave," I said hopelessly.

"But you've got to eat," he said.

"Yes, I got to eat."

"Then start acting like it," he hammered at me, pounding his fist in his palm. "When you're in front of white people, *think* before you act, *think* before you speak. Your way of doing things is all right among *our* people, but not for *white* people. They won't stand for it."

I stared bleakly into the morning sun. I was nearing my seventeenth birthday and I was wondering if I would ever be free of this plague. What Griggs was saying was true, but it was simply utterly impossible for me to calculate, to scheme, to act, to plot all the time. I would remember to dissemble for short periods, then I would forget and act straight and human again, not with the desire to harm anybody, but merely forgetting the artificial status of race and class. It was the same with whites as with blacks; it was my way with everybody. I sighed, looking at the glittering diamonds in the store window, the rings and the neat rows of golden watches.

"I guess you're right," I said at last. "I've got to watch myself, break myself . . ."

55

"No," he said quickly, feeling guilty now. Someone—a white man—went into the store and we paused in our talk. "You know, Dick, you may think I'm an Uncle Tom, but I'm not. I hate these white people, hate 'em with all my heart. But I can't show it; if I did, they'd kill me." He paused and looked around to see if there were any white people within hearing distance. "Once I heard an old drunk nigger say:

> *All these white folks dressed so fine*
> *Their ass-holes smell just like mine . . ."*

I laughed uneasily, looking at the white faces that passed me. But Griggs, when he laughed, covered his mouth with his hand and bent at the knees, a gesture which was unconsciously meant to conceal his excessive joy in the presence of whites.

"That's how I feel about 'em," he said proudly after he had finished his spasm of glee. He grew sober. "There's an optical company upstairs and the boss is a Yankee from Illinois. Now, he wants a boy to work all day in summer, mornings and evenings in winter. He wants to break a colored boy into the optical trade. You know algebra and you're just cut out for the work. I'll tell Mr. Crane about you and I'll get in touch with you."

"Do you suppose I could see him now?" I asked.

"For God's sake, take your *time!*" he thundered at me.

"Maybe that's what's wrong with Negroes," I said. "They take too much time."

I laughed, but he was disturbed. I thanked him and left. For a week I did not hear from him and I gave up hope. Then one afternoon Griggs came to my house.

"It looks like you've got a job," he said. "You're going to have a chance to learn a trade. But remember to keep your head. Remember you're black. You start tomorrow."

"What will I get?"

"Five dollars a week to start with, they'll raise you if they like you," he explained.

My hopes soared. Things were not quite so bad, after all. I would have a chance to learn a trade. And I need not give up

56

school. I told him that I would take the job, that I would be humble.

"You'll be working for a Yankee and you ought to get along," he said.

The next morning I was outside the office of the optical company long before it opened. I was reminding myself that I must be polite, must think before I spoke, must think before I acted, must say "yes sir, no sir," that I must so conduct myself that white people would not think that I thought I was as good as they. Suddenly a white man came up to me.

"What do you want?" he asked me.

"I'm reporting for a job, sir," I said.

"O.K. Come on."

I followed him up a flight of steps and he unlocked the door of the office. I was a little tense, but the young white man's manner put me at ease and I sat and held my hat in my hand. A white girl came and began punching the typewriter. Soon another white man, thin and gray, entered and went into the rear room. Finally a tall, red-faced white man arrived, shot me a quick glance and sat at his desk. His brisk manner branded him a Yankee.

"You're the new boy, eh?"

"Yes, sir."

"Let me get my mail out of the way and I'll talk with you," he said pleasantly.

"Yes, sir."

I even pitched my voice to a low plane, trying to rob it of any suggestion or overtone of aggressiveness.

Half an hour later Mr. Crane called me to his desk and questioned me closely about my schooling, about how much mathematics I had had. He seemed pleased when I told him that I had had two years of algebra.

"How would you like to learn this trade?" he asked.

"I'd like it fine, sir. I'd like nothing better," I said.

He told me that he wanted to train a Negro boy in the optical trade; he wanted to help him, guide him. I tried to answer in a way that would let him know that I would try to be worthy of what he was doing. He took me to the stenographer and said:

"This is Richard. He's going to be with us."

He then led me into the rear room of the office, which turned out to be a tiny factory filled with many strange machines smeared with red dust.

"Reynolds," he said to a young white man, "this is Richard."

"What you saying there, boy!" Reynolds grinned and boomed at me.

Mr. Crane took me to the older man.

"Pease, this is Richard, who'll work with us."

Pease looked at me and nodded. Mr. Crane then held forth to the two white men about my duties; he told them to break me in gradually to the workings of the shop, to instruct me in the mechanics of grinding and polishing lenses. They nodded their assent.

"Now, boy, let's see how clean you can get this place," Mr. Crane said.

"Yes, sir."

I swept, mopped, dusted, and soon had the office and the shop clean. In the afternoons, when I had caught up with my work, I ran errands. In an idle moment I would stand and watch the two white men grinding lenses on the machines. They said nothing to me and I said nothing to them. The first day passed, the second, the third, a week passed and I received my five dollars. A month passed. But I was not learning anything and nobody had volunteered to help me. One afternoon I walked up to Reynolds and asked him to tell me about the work.

"What are you trying to do, get smart, nigger?" he asked me.

"No, sir," I said.

I was baffled. Perhaps he just did not want to help me. I went to Pease, reminding him that the boss had said that I was to be given a chance to learn the trade.

"Nigger, you think you're white, don't you?"

"No, sir."

"You're acting mighty like it," he said.

"I was only doing what the boss told me to do," I said.

Pease shook his fist in my face.

"This is a *white* man's work around here," he said.

From then on they changed toward me; they said good morning no more. When I was just a bit slow in performing some duty, I was called a lazy black sonofabitch. I kept silent, striving to offer no excuse for worsening of relations. But one day Reynolds called me to his machine.

"Nigger, you think you'll ever amount to anything?" he asked in a slow, sadistic voice.

"I don't know, sir," I answered, turning my head away.

"What do niggers think about?" he asked.

"I don't know, sir," I said, my head still averted.

"If I was a nigger, I'd kill myself," he said.

I said nothing. I was angry.

"You know why?" he asked.

I still said nothing.

"But I don't reckon niggers mind being niggers," he said suddenly and laughed.

I ignored him. Mr. Pease was watching me closely; then I saw them exchange glances. My job was not leading to what Mr. Crane had said it would. I had been humble, and now I was reaping the wages of humility.

"Come here, boy," Pease said.

I walked to his bench.

"You didn't like what Reynolds just said, did you?" he asked.

"Oh, it's all right," I said smiling.

"You didn't like it. I could see it on your face," he said.

I stared at him and backed away.

"Did you ever get into any trouble?" he asked.

"No, sir."

"What would you do if you got into trouble?"

"I don't know, sir."

"Well, watch yourself and don't get into trouble," he warned.

I wanted to report these clashes to Mr. Crane, but the thought of what Pease or Reynolds would do to me if they learned that I had "snitched" stopped me. I worked through the days and tried to hide my resentment under a nervous, cryptic smile.

59

The climax came at noon one summer day. Pease called me to his workbench; to get to him I had to go between two narrow benches and stand with my back against a wall.

"Richard, I want to ask you something," Pease began pleasantly, not looking up from his work.

"Yes, sir."

Reynolds came over and stood blocking the narrow passage between the benches; he folded his arms and stared at me solemnly. I looked from one to the other, sensing trouble. Pease looked up and spoke slowly, so there would be no possibility of my not understanding.

"Richard, Reynolds here tells me that you called me Pease," he said.

I stiffened. A void opened up in me. I knew that this was the showdown.

He meant that I had failed to call him Mr. Pease. I looked at Reynolds; he was gripping a steel bar in his hand. I opened my mouth to speak, to protest, to assure Pease that I had never called him simply *Pease,* and that I had never had any intention of doing so, when Reynolds grabbed me by the collar, ramming my head against a wall.

"Now, be careful, nigger," snarled Reynolds, baring his teeth. "I heard you call 'im *Pease.* And if you say you didn't, you're calling me a liar, see?" He waved the steel bar threateningly.

If I had said: No, sir, Mr. Pease, I never called you *Pease,* I would by inference have been calling Reynolds a liar; and if I had said: Yes, sir, Mr. Pease, I called you *Pease,* I would have been pleading guilty to the worst insult that a Negro can offer to a southern white man. I stood trying to think of a neutral course that would resolve this quickly risen nightmare, but my tongue would not move.

"Richard, I asked you a question!" Pease said. Anger was creeping into his voice.

"I don't remember calling you *Pease,* Mr. Pease," I said cautiously. "And if I did, I sure didn't mean . . ."

"You black sonofabitch! You called me *Pease,* then!" he spat, rising and slapping me till I bent sideways over a bench.

Reynolds was up on top of me demanding:

"Didn't you call him *Pease*? If you say you didn't, I'll rip your gut string loose with this f--k--g bar, you black granny dodger! You can't call a white man a liar and get away with it!"

I wilted. I begged them not to hit me. I knew what they wanted. They wanted me to leave the job.

"I'll leave," I promised. "I'll leave right now!"

They gave me a minute to get out of the factory, and warned me not to show up again or tell the boss. Reynolds loosened his hand on my collar and I ducked out of the room. I did not see Mr. Crane or the stenographer in the office. Pease and Reynolds had so timed it that Mr. Crane and the stenographer would be out when they turned on the terror. I went to the street and waited for the boss to return. I saw Griggs wiping glass shelves in the jewelry store and I beckoned to him. He came out and I told him what had happened.

"Then what are you standing there like a fool for?" he demanded. "Won't you ever learn? Get home! They might come down!"

I walked down Capitol Street feeling that the sidewalk was unreal, that I was unreal, that the people were unreal, yet expecting somebody to demand to know what right I had to be on the streets. My wound went deep; I felt that I had been slapped out of the human race. When I reached home, I did not tell the family what had happened; I merely told them that I had quit, that I was not making enough money, that I was seeking another job.

That night Griggs came to my house; we went for a walk.

"You got a goddamn tough break," he said.

"Can you say it was my fault?" I asked.

He shook his head.

"Well, what about your goddamn philosophy of meekness?" I asked him bitterly.

"These things just happen," he said, shrugging.

"They owe me money," I said.

"That's what I came about," he said. "Mr. Crane wants you to come in at ten in the morning. Ten sharp, now, mind you, because he'll be there and those guys won't gang up on you again."

The next morning at ten I crept up the stairs and peered into the office of the optical shop to make sure that Mr. Crane was in. He was at his desk. Pease and Reynolds were at their machines in the rear.

"Come in Richard," Mr. Crane said.

I pulled off my hat and walked into the office; I stood before him.

"Sit down," he said.

I sat. He stared at me and shook his head.

"Tell me, what happened?"

An impulse to speak rose in me and died with the realization that I was facing a wall that I would never breech. I tried to speak several times and could make no sounds. I grew tense and tears burnt my cheeks.

"Now, just keep control of yourself," Mr. Crane said.

I clenched my fists and managed to talk.

"I tried to do my best here," I said.

"I believe you," he said. "But I want to know what happened. Which one bothered you?"

"Both of 'em," I said.

Reynolds came running to the door and I rose. Mr. Crane jumped to his feet.

"Get back in there," he told Reynolds.

"That nigger's lying!" Reynolds said. "I'll kill 'im if he lies on me!"

"Get back in there or get out," Mr. Crane said.

Reynolds backed away, keeping his eyes on me.

"Go ahead," Mr. Crane said. "Tell me what happened."

Then again I could not speak. What could I accomplish by telling him? I was black; I lived in the South. I would never learn to operate those machines as long as those two white men in there stood by them. Anger and fear welled in me as I felt what I had missed; I leaned forward and clapped my hands to my face.

"No, no, now," Mr. Crane said. "Keep control of yourself. No matter what happens, keep control . . ."

"I know," I said in a voice not my own. "There's no use of my saying anything."

"Do you want to work here?" he asked me.

I looked at the white faces of Pease and Reynolds; I imagined their waylaying me, killing me. I was remembering what had happened to Ned's brother.

"No, sir," I breathed.

"Why?"

"I'm scared," I said. "They would kill me."

Mr. Crane turned and called Pease and Reynolds into the office.

"Now, tell me which one bothered you. Don't be afraid. Nobody's going to hurt you," Mr. Crane said.

I stared ahead of me and did not answer. He waved the men inside. The white stenographer looked at me with wide eyes and I felt drenched in shame, naked to my soul. The whole of my being felt violated, and I knew that my own fear had helped to violate it. I was breathing hard and struggling to master my feelings.

"Can I get my money, sir?" I asked at last.

"Just sit a minute and take hold of yourself," he said.

I waited and my roused senses grew slowly calm.

"I'm awfully sorry about this," he said.

"I had hoped for a lot from this job," I said. "I'd wanted to go to school, to college . . ."

"I know," he said. "But what are you going to do now?"

My eyes traveled over the office, but I was not seeing.

"I'm going away," I said.

"What do you mean?"

"I'm going to get out of the South," I breathed.

"Maybe that's best," he said. "I'm from Illinois. Even for me, it's hard here. I can do just so much."

He handed me my money, more than I had earned for the week. I thanked him and rose to leave. He rose. I went into the hallway and he followed me. He reached out his hand.

"It's tough for you down here," he said.

I barely touched his hand. I walked swiftly down the hall, fighting against crying again. I ran down the steps, then paused and looked back up. He was standing at the head of the stairs, shaking his head. I went into the sunshine and walked home like a blind man.

From *White Man, Listen!*

THE PSYCHOLOGICAL REACTIONS OF OPPRESSED PEOPLE

Published in 1957, White Man, Listen! *is a collection of essays which were originally delivered as lectures in Europe between 1950 and 1956.*

Buttressed by their belief that their God had entrusted the earth into their keeping, drunk with power and possibility, waxing rich through trade in commodities, human and non-human, with awesome naval and merchant marines at their disposal, their countries filled with human debris anxious for any adventures, psychologically armed with new facts, white Western Christian civilization during the fourteenth, fifteenth, sixteenth, and seventeenth centuries, with a long, slow, and bloody explosion, hurled itself upon the sprawling masses of colored humanity in Asia and Africa.

I say to you white men of the West: Don't be too proud of how easily you conquered and plundered those Asians and Africans. You had unwitting allies in your campaigns; you had Fifth Columns in the form of indigenous cultures to facilitate your military, missionary, and mercenary efforts. Your collaborators in those regions consisted of the mental habits of the people, habits for which they were in no way responsible, no more than you were responsible for yours. Those habits constituted corps of saboteurs, of spies, if you will, that worked in the interests of European aggression. You must realize that it was not your courage or racial superiority that made you win, nor was it the racial inferiority or cowardice of the Asians and Africans that made them lose. This is an important point that you must grasp, or your concern with this problem will be forever wide of the facts. How, then, did the West, numerically the minority, achieve, during the last four centuries, so many dazzling victories over the body of colored mankind? Frankly, it took you centuries to do a job that could have been done in fifty years! You had the motive, the fire power, the will, the religious spur, the superior organization, but you dallied. Why? You were not aware exactly of what you were doing. You didn't suspect your impersonal strength, or the impersonal weakness on the other side. You were as unconscious, at bottom, as were your victims about what was really taking place.

Your world of culture clashed with the culture-worlds of colored mankind, and the ensuing destruction of traditional beliefs among a billion and a half of black, brown, and yellow men has set off a tide of social, cultural, political, and economic revolution that grips the world today. That revolution is assuming many forms, absolutistic, communistic, fascistic, theocratistic etc.—all marked by unrest, violence, and an astounding emotional thrashing about as men seek· new objects about which they can center their loyalties.

It is of the reactions, tortured and turbulent, of those Asians and Africans, in the New and Old World, that I wish to speak to you. Naturally I cannot speak for those Asians and Africans who are still locked in their mystical or ancestor-worshiping traditions. They are the voiceless ones, the silent ones. Indeed, I think that they are the doomed ones, men in a tragic trap. Any attempt on their part to wage a battle to protect their outmoded traditions and religions is a battle that is lost before it starts. And I say frankly that I suspect any white man who loves to dote upon those "naked nobles," who wants to leave them as they are, who finds them "primitive and pure," for such mystical hankering is, in my opinion, the last refuge of reactionary racists and psychological cripples tired of their own civilization. My remarks will, of necessity, be confined to those Asians and Africans who, having been partly Westernized, have a quarrel with the West. They are the ones who feel that they are oppressed. In a sense, this is a fight of the West with *itself,* a fight that the West blunderingly began, and the West does not to this day realize that it is the sole responsible agent, the sole instigator. For the West to disclaim responsibility for what it so clearly did is to make every white man alive on earth today a criminal. In history as in law, men must be held strictly responsible for the consequences of their historic actions, whether they intended those consequences or not. For the West to accept its responsibility is to create the means by which white men can liberate themselves from their fears, panic, and terror while they confront the world's colored majority of men who are also striving for liberation from the irrational ties which the West prompted them to disown—ties of which the West has partially robbed them.

Let's imagine a mammoth flying saucer from Mars landing, say, in a peasant Swiss village and debouching swarms of fierce-looking men whose skins are blue and whose red eyes flash lightning bolts that deal instant death. The inhabitants are all the more terrified because the arrival of these men had been predicted. The religious myths of the Western world—the Second Coming of Christ, the Last Judgment, etc., have conditioned Europeans for just such an improbable event. Hence, those Swiss natives will feel that resistance is useless for a while. As long as the blue strangers are casually kind, they are obeyed and served. They become the Fathers of the people. Is this a fragment of paperback science fiction? No. It's more prosaic than that. The image I've sketched above is the manner, by and large, in which white Europe overran Asia and Africa. (Remember the Cortés-Montezuma drama!)

But why did Europe do this? Did it only want gold, power, women, raw materials? It was more complicated than that.

The fifteenth-, sixteenth-, and seventeenth-century neurotic European, sick of his thwarted instincts, restless, filled with self-disgust, was looking for not only spices and gold and slaves when he set out; he was looking for an Arcadia, a Land's End, a Shangri-la, a world peopled by shadow men, a world that would permit free play for his repressed instincts. Stripped of tradition, these misfits, adventurers, indentured servants, convicts and freebooters were the most advanced individualists of their time. Rendered socially superfluous by the stifling weight of the Church and nobility, buttressed by the influence of the ideas of Hume and Descartes, they had been brutally molded toward attitudes of emotional independence and could doff the cloying ties of custom, tradition, and family. The Asian-African native, anchored in family-dependence systems of life, could not imagine why or how these men had left their homelands, could not conceive of the cold, arid emotions sustaining them. . . . Emotional independence was a state of mind not only utterly inconceivable, but an attitude toward life downright evil to the Asian-African native—something to be avoided at all costs. Bound by a charged array of humble objects that made up an emotionally satisfying and exciting world, they, trapped by their limited mental horizon, could not help thinking that the white men invading their lands had been driven forcibly from their homes!

Living in a waking dream, generations of emotionally impoverished colonial European whites wallowed in the quick gratification of greed, reveled in the cheap superiority of racial domination, slaked their sensual thirst in illicit sexuality, draining off the dammed-up libido that European morality had condemned, amassing through trade a vast reservoir of economic fat, thereby establishing vast accumulations of capital which spurred the industrialization of the West. Asia and Africa thus became a neurotic habit that Europeans could forgo only at the cost of a powerful psychic wound, for this emotionally crippled Europe had, through the centuries, grown used to leaning upon this black crutch.

But what of the impact of those white faces upon the personalities of the native? Steeped in dependence systems of family life and anchored in ancestor-worshiping religions, the native was prone to identify those powerful white faces falling athwart his existence with the potency of his dead father who had sustained him in the past. Temporarily accepting the invasion, he transferred his loyalties to those white faces, but, because of the psychological, racial, and economic luxury which those faces derived from their domination, the native was kept at bay.

Today, as the tide of white domination of the land mass of Asia and Africa recedes, there lies exposed to view a procession of shattered cultures, disintegrated societies, and a writhing sweep of more aggressive, irrational religion than the world has known for centuries. And, as scientific research, partially freed from the blight of colonial control, advances, we are witnessing the rise of a new genre of academic literature dealing with colonial and post-colonial facts from a wider angle of vision than ever possible before. The personality distortions of hundreds of millions of black, brown, and yellow people that are being revealed by this literature are confounding and will necessitate drastic alteration of our past evaluations of colonial rule. In this new literature one enters a universe of menacing shadows where disparate images coalesce —white turning into black, the dead coming to life, the top becoming the bottom—until you think you are seeing Biblical beasts with seven heads and ten horns rising out of the sea. Imperialism turns out to have been much more morally foul a piece of business than even Marx and Lenin imagined!

An agony was induced into the native heart, rotting and pulverizing it as it tried to live under a white domination with which it could not identify in any real sense, a white domination that mocked it. The more Westernized that native heart became, the more anti-Western it had to be, for that heart was now weighing itself in terms of white Western values that made it feel degraded. Vainly attempting to embrace the world of white faces that rejected it, it recoiled and sought refuge in the ruins of moldering tradition. But it was too late; it was trapped; it found haven in neither. This is the psychological stance of the elite of the populations, free or still in a state of subjection, of present-day Asia and Africa; this is the profound revolution that the white man cast into the world; this is the revolution (a large part of which has been successfully captured by the Communists) that the white man confronts today with fear and paralysis.

TED POSTON

The Revolt of the Evil Fairies

The grand dramatic offering of the Booker T. Washington Colored Grammar School was the biggest event of the year in our social life in Hopkinsville, Kentucky. It was the one occasion on which they let us use the old Cooper Opera House, and even some of the white folks came out yearly to applaud our presentation. The first two rows of the orchestra were always reserved for our white friends, and our leading colored citizens sat right behind them—with an empty row intervening, of course.

Mr. Ed Smith, our local undertaker, invariably occupied a box to the left of the house and wore his cutaway coat and striped breeches. This distinctive garb was usually reserved for those rare occasions when he officiated at the funerals of our most prominent colored citizens. Mr. Thaddeus Long, our colored mailman, once rented a tuxedo and bought a box too. But nobody paid him much mind. We knew he was just showing off.

The title of our play never varied. It was always "Prince Charming and the Sleeping Beauty," but no two presentations were ever the same. Miss H. Belle LaPrade, our sixth-grade teacher, rewrote the script every season, and it was never like anything you read in the story books.

Miss LaPrade called it "a modern morality play of conflict between the forces of good and evil." And the forces of evil, of course, always came off second best.

69

Ted Poston

The Booker T. Washington Colored Grammar School was in a state of ferment from Christmas until February, for this was the period when parts were assigned. First there was the selection of the Good Fairies and the Evil Fairies. This was very important, because the Good Fairies wore white costumes and the Evil Fairies black. And strangely enough most of the Good Fairies usually turned out to be extremely light in complexion, with straight hair and white folks' features. On rare occasions a dark-skinned girl might be lucky enough to be a Good Fairy, but not one with a speaking part.

There never was any doubt about Prince Charming and the Sleeping Beauty. They were *always* light-skinned. And though nobody ever discussed those things openly, it was an accepted fact that a lack of pigmentation was a decided advantage in the Prince Charming and Sleeping Beauty sweepstakes.

And therein lay my personal tragedy. I made the best grades in my class, I was the leading debater, and the scion of a respected family in the community. But I could never be Prince Charming, because I was black.

In fact, every year when they started casting our grand dramatic offering my family started pricing black cheesecloth at Franklin's Department Store. For they knew that I would be leading the forces of darkness and skulking back in the shadows—waiting to be vanquished in the third act. Mamma had experience with this sort of thing. All my brothers had finished Booker T. before me.

Not that I was alone in my disappointment. Many of my classmates felt it too. I probably just took it more to heart. Rat Joiner, for instance, could rationalize the situation. Rat was not only black; he lived on Billy Goat Hill. But Rat summed it up like this:

"If you black, you black."

I should have been able to regard the matter calmly too. For our grand dramatic offering was only a reflection of our daily community life in Hopkinsville. The yallers had the best of everything. They held most of the teaching jobs in Booker T. Washington Colored Grammar School. They were the Negro doctors, the lawyers, the insurance men. They even had a "Blue Vein Society," and if your dark skin obscured your throbbing pulse you were hardly a member of the élite.

Yet I was inconsolable the first time they turned me down for Prince Charming. That was the year they picked Roger Jackson. Roger was not only dumb; he stuttered. But he was light enough to pass for white, and that was apparently sufficient.

In all fairness, however, it must be admitted that Roger had other qualifications. His father owned the only colored saloon in town and was quite a power in local politics. In fact, Mr. Clinton Jackson had a lot to say about just who taught in the Booker T. Washington Colored Grammar School. So it was understandable that Roger should have been picked for Prince Charming.

My real heartbreak, however, came the year they picked Sarah Williams for Sleeping Beauty. I had been in love with Sarah since kindergarten. She had soft light hair, bluish gray eyes, and a dimple which stayed in her left cheek whether she was smiling or not.

Of course Sarah never encouraged me much. She never answered any of my fervent love letters and Rat was very scornful of my one-sided love affair. "As long as she don't call you a black baboon," he sneered, "you'll keep on hanging around."

After Sarah was chosen for Sleeping Beauty, I went out for the Prince Charming role with all my heart. If I had declaimed boldly in previous contests, I was matchless now. If I had bothered Mamma with rehearsals at home before, I pestered her to death this time. Yes, and I purloined my sister's can of Palmer's Skin Success.

I knew the Prince's role from start to finish, having played the Head Evil Fairy opposite it for two seasons. And Prince Charming was one character whose lines Miss LaPrade never varied much in her many versions. But although I never admitted it, even to myself, I knew I was doomed from the start. They gave the part to Leonardius Wright. Leonardius, of course, was yaller.

The teachers sensed my resentment. They were almost apologetic. They pointed out that I had been such a splendid Head Evil Fairy for two seasons that it would be a crime to let anybody else try the role. They reminded me that Mamma wouldn't have to buy any more cheesecloth because I could use my same old costume. They insisted that the Head Evil Fairy was even more important than Prince Charming because he was the one who cast the spell on Sleeping Beauty. So what could I do but accept?

I had never liked Leonardius Wright. He was a goody-goody, and even Mamma was always throwing him up to me. But above all, he too was in love with Sarah Williams. And now he got a chance to kiss Sarah every day in rehearsing the awakening scene.

Well, the show must go on, even for little black boys. So I threw my soul into my part and made the Head Evil Fairy a character to be remembered. When I drew back from the couch of Sleeping Beauty and slunk away into the shadows at the approach of Prince Charming, my facial expression was indeed something to behold. When I was vanquished by the shining sword of Prince Charming in the last act, I was a little hammy perhaps—but terrific!

The attendance at our grand dramatic offering that year was the best in its history. Even the white folks overflowed the two rows reserved for them and a few were forced to sit in the intervening one. This created a delicate situation, but everybody tactfully ignored it.

When the curtain went up on the last act, the audience was in fine fettle. Everything had gone well for me too—except for one spot in the second act. That was where Leonardius unexpectedly rapped me over the head with his sword as I slunk off into the shadows. That was not in the script, but Miss LaPrade quieted me down by saying it made a nice touch anyway. Rat said Leonardius did it on purpose.

The third act went on smoothly though until we came to the vanquishing scene. That was where I slunk from the shadows for the last time and challenged Prince Charming to mortal combat. The hero reached for his shining sword—a bit unsportsmanlike I always thought, since Miss LaPrade consistently left the Head Evil Fairy unarmed—and then it happened!

Later, I protested loudly—but in vain—that it was a case of self-defense. I pointed out that Leonardius had a mean look in his eye. I cited the impromptu rapping he had given my head in the second act. But nobody would listen. They just wouldn't believe that Leonardius really intended to brain me when he reached for his sword.

Anyway he didn't succeed. For the minute I saw that evil gleam in his eye—or was it my own?—I cut loose with a right to the chin, and Prince Charming dropped his shining sword and staggered back. His astonishment lasted only a minute though, for he lowered his head and came charging in, fists flailing. There was nothing yellow about Leonardius but his skin.

The audience thought the scrap was something new Miss LaPrade had written in. They might have kept on thinking so if Miss LaPrade hadn't been screaming so hysterically from the sidelines. And if Rat Joiner hadn't decided that this was as good a time as any to settle old scores. So he turned around and took a sock at the male Good Fairy nearest him.

When the curtain rang down, the forces of Good and Evil were locked in combat. And Sleeping Beauty was wide awake, and streaking for the wings.

They rang the curtain back up fifteen minutes later, and we finished the play. I lay down and expired according to specifications, but Prince Charming will probably remember my sneering corpse to his dying day. They wouldn't let me appear in the grand dramatic offering at all the next year. But I didn't care. I couldn't have been Prince Charming anyway.

GORDON PARKS

From *A Choice of Weapons*

A little after mid-December an order came from the Pentagon halting all furloughs. We knew what this meant. Any day now we would be going overseas. A new tempo hit the base; the men rushed about, restless, patting one another's backs, awaiting moving orders. They came one morning about a week before Christmas. That afternoon Colonel Davis called me to headquarters. "We're about to pull out," he said, "and your traveling papers are not in order."

"What's wrong with them?" I asked.

"You'll have to take that up with Washington. I'd advise you to fly there. We'll probably be leaving before they can get word back here to you."

I packed the battle gear that had been issued to me that morning, took a bus to Detroit, then a plane to Washington; I arrived there late that evening. Stryker had left the OWI [Office of War Information, the branch of the Army to which Mr. Parks was assigned in World War II] by now and had gone to work in New York for the Standard Oil Co. In fact, just about everyone I knew there had gone; the rest were preparing to leave. Besides, it was a weekend and no officials were around. I didn't know where to turn. The one man I did reach had developed a strange case of laryngitis, and was unable to talk, he said. Finally in desperation I tried to reach Elmer Davis, head of the OWI, but he was away on a trip. I fretted through Saturday and Sunday. Then the first

74

thing Monday morning I went to see Ted Poston, a friend of mine in the OWI press section. He had heard the rumors. And Ted put things in their true perspective: "There's some Southern gentlemen and conservative Republicans on Capitol Hill who don't like the idea of giving this kind of publicity to Negro soldiers."

I was shocked—and so was Ted—but there wasn't much we could do about it. The next day I reached Elmer Davis by telephone and told him my story. He listened attentively. When I finished he said, "Don't worry, Gordon, I'll be in touch with the Pentagon this afternoon. You report there tomorrow. I'm sure everything will be all right."

That night, on the Howard University campus, I met Captain Lee Rayford and Lieutenant Walter Lawson, two pilots from the 99th Fighter Squadron. They had returned to the States after completing their required number of missions. Captain Rayford was the holder of the Purple Heart, the Distinguished Flying Cross, the Croix de Guerre, the Air Medal, and the Yugoslav Red Star. He had been shot up over Austria by a Messerschmitt 109. Both of them could have remained Stateside as instructors. Instead they had volunteered to go back to the war zone. We ate dinner together, and since they had to go to the Pentagon the next day we agreed to meet and go together.

We had no sooner boarded the bus and seated ourselves behind the driver than his voice came at us, metallic and demanding. "If you fellas wanta ride into Virginyuh, you gotta go to the rear." We looked at one another questioningly, deciding in our silence not to move. The driver stood up and faced us, a scrawny disheveled man with tobacco-stained teeth and a hawk nose. The armpits of his uniform were discolored from sweat. "You all heard what I said. This bus ain't goin' nowhere till you all go to the back where you belong."

"We intend going to Virginia in the seats we're in," Lee said with finality.

"Okay, if you ain't back there in one minute I'm callin' the MP's and havin' you put off."

"You'd better start calling right now," Lee replied.

Two white Air Force captains and a major were seated across

the aisle from us and I noticed that they stirred uncomfortably. Several other whites were scattered in the near-empty bus and an elderly Negro woman sat at the rear. I watched her through the rear-view mirror. She had half risen from her seat; there was courage, dignity and anger in every line of her small body. Her look demanded that we stay there, and I was determined not to disappoint her. The bus had become dead quiet while the driver stood glowering at us.

"Fellows." One of the young white captains was speaking now. "We know how you feel about this," he said, his voice cloaked in false camaraderie, "but the major has an appointment at the Pentagon in a half hour. He wonders if you would mind moving back so that we can be on our way?"

My two friends were outranked. But there were no bars on my shoulders. The American eagle on my officer's cap was as large and significant as his or the major's. I took a good look at the old woman in the rear. She was standing now, gripping the seat ahead of her. Then, borrowing the captain's icy politeness, I stood and addressed the major. "Sir," I said, "as you can see, these men are fighter pilots. They have completed their missions but they have volunteered for more duty at the front. Would you like to order your fellow officers to the rear? They have no intention of moving otherwise." My anger was rising, so I sat back down.

The bus driver stood watching us until the major finally spoke to him. "Drive on," he said. "Can't you tell when you're licked?" The driver cursed under his breath, threw himself into the seat and slammed in the gears and we lurched off toward Virginia. "Hallelujah!" the Negro woman shouted from the rear. "Hallelujah!" Her voice rang with pathos and triumph. "Thank God we don't have to sit in the back of our P-38's," Lawson sighed as we got off the bus.

The three of us parted soon after. "We'll see you on the other side somewhere," Rayford said cheerfully. And I watched the two young men walk away from me at the entrance to the Pentagon, hoping that I would meet up with them again. Our thoughts were already separated from the incident on the bus. We had won; our anger was dead.

The officer in charge of overseas traffic was drinking a Coca-Cola when I entered. I handed him my papers and explained my situation. He scanned them without speaking—all the time sipping the Coke. He took one long swallow, smacked his lips and belched. "Far as I can see, your travelin' papers are in order," he finally said, opening another bottle.

"Then why was I sent back here?"

"Beats me, fellow. I'm just tellin' you far as this office is concerned they're in order."

"Thank you. Now where will I contact the fighter group?" I waited. He was gurgling Coke again.

"I can only give you directions as far as Newport News, Virginia. You'll have to play it by ear from there."

"But if everything is in order why can't you be more specific?"

"I'm being as specific as I can. I'm not allowed to give out the exact location; and that's that." He belched again.

I thanked him as coldly as he had received me and left, feeling that only luck could get me to the group before it sailed.

Our plane took off in a blinding rainstorm—and it landed in another one at Norfolk, Virginia. A taxi took me to the ferry landing where I would cross over into Newport News. I sat there in the waiting room for an hour on top of my battle gear among a boisterous group of white enlisted men. Four Negro soldiers were huddled in a nearby corner. Two of them were propped against each other sleeping. Most of the white boys seemed to be making a festivity of these last hours. But there was a sort of emptiness attached to their laughing and drinking. Obviously they were headed for some departure point. It's all to hide the fear, I thought. Their faces were so young.

We filed out when the ferry whistled. It was still raining and we stood near the edge of the dock watching the boat fasten into the slip. Through the wetness I noticed a sign reading COLORED PASSENGERS and another one reading WHITES ONLY. The four black soldiers moved automatically to the colored side, and so did I. How ironic, I thought; such nonsense would not stop until we were in enemy territory.

After all the outgoing passengers were off and the trucks and cars had rumbled past, we started forward. Then I saw a Negro girl step from the ferry. She had been standing in the section marked for cars; now she was in the direct line of the white enlisted men, who stampeded to the boat screaming at the tops of their voices. I saw the girl fall beneath them into the mud and water. The four Negro soldiers also saw her go down. The five of us rushed to her rescue. She was knocked down several times before we could get to her to pull her out of the scrambling mob.

"You lousy white bastards!" one of the Negro soldiers yelled. "If I only had a gun!" Tears were in his eyes, hysteria in his voice. A long knife was glistening in his hand.

"Soldier!" I shouted above the noise, letting him get a look at my officer's cap. "Put that knife away!"

He glared at me fiercely for a second. "But you saw what they did!"

"Yes, I saw, but we're outnumbered ten to one! You can't fight all of them. Get on the boat!" He looked at me sullenly for another moment, then moved off. We cleaned the mud from the girl's coat and she walked away without a word. Only proud anger glistened on her black face. Then the four of us joined the soldier I had ordered away. He was standing still tense beneath the sign reading "colored passengers."

"Sorry, soldier," I said. "We wouldn't have had a chance against a mob like that. You realize that, don't you?"

"If I've gotta die, I'd just as soon do it where I got real cause to." His tone was resolute. I had no answer. I was tempted to hand him the bit about the future and all that, but the future was too uncertain. The yelling was even louder now on the other side of the boat. "Sons-of-bitches," he muttered under his breath.

"Good luck," I said to them as we parted on the other shore. "So long," they said—except the one I had spoken to—then they moved off into the darkness and rain again. I turned away, feeling I had somehow let him down.

"Colored move to the rear!" The voice met me again when I got on the bus with some of the white enlisted men. Sick of trouble, I made my way to the back and sat down; I was the only Negro aboard. Some of the whites were standing, but I had four empty seats around me. "Gordy! My God, it's Gordy!" a voice rang out above the noise. And suddenly a soldier was rushing back toward me. "Bud!" I shouted, getting to my feet only to be knocked back to my seat by his bear hug. It was Bud Hallender, a husky man I had played basketball with back in St. Paul. Now he was down beside me, slapping my back and wringing my hands.

"You all cain't ride back there with that nigra! Move back up front where you belong!" Bud ignored the command; now he was telling the others I was the co-captain of his basketball team, his friend.

"You all hear me? You cain't ride back there with that nigra!"

"Go screw yourself!" Bud shouted back. "Drive on or we'll throw you off this goddamned crate and drive it ourselves!" Laughter rocked the bus. The driver plopped down into his seat without another word and drove off toward the heart of town. And Bud and I talked excitedly of a time and place where things had been different. Finally, at the terminal we wished each other a jovial goodbye.

I made a thorough check of my map; and, riding a hunch, I wrote out a government order for a bus ticket to a point where I suspected the pilots would be camped. The agent at the window examined it and looked at me suspiciously. "Where'd you get this?" he said.

"It's a government issue slip, for travel."

"I know what it is, fellow, but I ain't neva heard of a nigra writin' one of these things out. I ain't givin' you no ticket. Not me."

"I'm attached to the Office of War Information. I'm my own issuing officer," I explained.

"I don't care what you are. I just don't believe no nigra can write out one of these things without a white man signing it."

"I'm en route overseas. I've got to meet my group before sailing time. I've got to catch the next bus!" My voice had risen now.

"Well, I ain't givin' you no ticket unless you got cash!" His

79

voice was raised one notch higher than mine, and people were gathering around the window. We stood glaring at each other when a door opened on my right. "Can I be of any help to you, sir?" A young man with a pleasant face confronted me. I explained my problem and he asked me to step into his office. "Are you with an air group?" he asked after I had taken a seat.

"Yes. That's right," I answered cautiously.

"I thought so. You don't need that ticket. I have to make a telephone call. Excuse me for a moment." He came back after a few minutes. "It's all arranged. You walk straight down the main street for three blocks, turn left for two more blocks and wait there on the corner. Someone will pick you up within the next half hour."

I thanked him and went out to follow his directions, wondering whether this was a subterfuge of some kind, a way of evicting me from the terminal peacefully. I doubted it; yet such chicanery would come as no surprise now.

It was twenty minutes before an army command car rolled up beside me. A Wac stuck her head out the window and checked my description. "OWI?" she asked.

"That's right," I answered.

"Hop in," she said cheerfully. Another Wac drove the car and they whisked me off to a military barracks where my papers were thoroughly checked again, this time by an army captain.

"Have to be sure," he said; "once you're in there's no getting out." He finally handed them back with a smile. "They're okay. Good luck. Have a safe trip. The Wacs will drive you out to the embarkation base." My spirits leaped ahead of the car as we sped toward Camp Patrick Henry.

The pilots of the 332nd stopped their gambling, letter writing and drinking long enough to give me a rousing welcome. They were all genuinely happy that I had made it. My bunk had been made up and was waiting. And I showed my appreciation with two bottles of Scotch and several cartons of cigarettes which I had wrapped in my battle gear. Aside from women, I knew these were the things they would crave most. Money was useless now. They gambled it away with abandon. The noise kept up far into the night, then into morning. But I slept well, knowing the first leg of my mission had been accomplished. Now, if luck held, I would be at sea within four days.

Tony and I went out for some fresh air the next night. "It's hard to believe but we've had trouble right here on this base," he said as we walked along, "so we'd better stay in this area."

"What kind of trouble?"

"The same old jazz. One of our ground crewmen was beaten up by some white paratroopers night before last. Then they've tried to segregate us at the base's movie house. Everyone's in a hell of a mood." We became suddenly quiet as we circled the area.

A shot sounded nearby and the two of us stopped in our tracks. Then there was another shot. Someone seemed to be returning the fire. "We'd better get in. Sounds like trouble," Tony said. Our barracks had already gone dark when we entered it. Several men were at the windows with guns looking out cautiously into the night. When all was quiet again, the lights went back on and the gambling and the letter writing and the drinking started again. New orders came the following morning. We would take to the boat two days earlier than had been proposed. I was happy about this. There seemed to be less danger at sea than on this troubled base.

Colonel Davis sent for me just before noon. I hurried anxiously to his office. No more trouble, I hoped; it was too close to sailing time. But when he looked up at me his face was calm. It was, after all, some routine matter he would speak about, I thought.

"I'm sorry. Your papers are not in order. A final call from the Pentagon has come through. You will not be able to embark with us."

"This is ridiculous," I said. "Can't you do anything? Someone in Washington is trying to prevent coverage of your group overseas, Colonel. This is the first Negro fighter group. It's history. It has to be covered. Can't you protest in some way, Colonel?"

"There's nothing, absolutely nothing I can do. The orders are from the Pentagon. They cannot be rescinded. I'm terribly sorry."

I had lost. And suddenly anesthetized to the colonel and all that was around him, I turned and started out. "You are aware that you are sworn to the strictest of secrecy about what you have seen or learned here," he was saying as he followed me to the door. "You realize the dangers of any slip."

"Yes. I understand, Colonel."

"It is even possible to detain you until we are overseas under such conditions. But I am sure you won't discuss our movements with anyone."

"I won't. Don't worry. I want to forget the whole thing as quickly as possible." I rushed back toward the barracks, angry and disgusted. I couldn't bring myself to say goodbye to the pilots again. I packed quickly and waited for the command car the colonel had ordered for me.

The pilots were readying themselves for the boat when the car arrived; and I slipped through the rear door without even a backward glance. At five o'clock the next morning after wiring Sally, I boarded a plane for Washington. I would change planes there and go on in to New York, where I would wait for my wife and children. The thought of even stopping in this city irked me. I wouldn't live there again if they gave me the White House rent free, I thought as the plane roared down the runway.

We began circling over Washington at dawn; and far below I could see the landing field, lying like small strips of cardboard under a wispy patch of cloud. Further out in the distance the monuments of the city shone milk-white in the winter sunlight and the water in the mall sparkled like an oblong jewel between the sculptured trees; there was the Capitol standing quiet and strong on one end and the Lincoln Memorial set on the high quarter of the opposite slope. What a beautiful sight to be wed to such human ugliness, I thought. And as we dropped lower I could see the tops of the stores, theaters and restaurants whose doors were still closed to me.

I thought back to the fighter pilots. They would soon be far out to sea, sailing toward war and death, ignoring, at least temporarily, their differences with the land they were leaving to defend. This was the price for a questionable equality.

We were landing, and the intolerance of Washington came rushing up toward me as the plane roared down toward the strip. There would only be an hour's wait before I took off again. And I would hate that hour; the memories here had been too searing. I just wanted to get out.

I strode into the air terminal, tired, hungry and irritated to a point of fury, my nerves stretched raw. Everyone in the place looked as if he were a member of the Klan. My whole body seemed to be itching for a fight—a last physical protest against the frustrations of these past six days. I walked toward the lunch counter, where only one seat remained unoccupied. The man next to it had a red creased neck, thin lips; his beady eyes, manner and clothing spoke of the deep South. I detested the very sight of him; I knew he would say the words that would set me upon him. I threw my gear on the floor, clenched my fists and sat down beside him—waiting. He was turning now, looking me over. My body tensed. And then he said easily, casually, "Good morning, soldier. Looks like it's going to be a nice day for flying." He pulled out a pack of cigarettes and offered me one, then lit it.

With some difficulty I came to terms with myself. Then I blew out the smoke and confusion in one long breath. "You're right— it looks like a good day for flying," I said, "a very good day." And the two of us ate in peace.

I didn't ask him where he was from or where he was going. It didn't make any difference. It was a nice day for flying. And I said this to the stewardess when I boarded the plane for New York and I said this to the old lady who sat beside me in the plane and I said this to the skycap who helped me with my bags at La Guardia Field and to the cabby who drove me up to Harlem.

A friendly word from a stranger, and a cigarette, had lifted me temporarily from the darkness. As I settled back into the cab, I linked him in my mind with the old trolley conductor who had befriended me on that cold and lonely morning twenty years before, moments after I had thought of robbing him. With a few kind words these two men, like all the others who had helped me, had pushed me a few more inches down the road.

Harvey Goldstein, for instance, had given me more than I expected—more, probably, than he could afford. Bill Hunter showed me the value of initiative and of receptiveness to other people. Roy Stryker, with patience and foresight, had given me discipline and a sense of direction. I could, in a way, even be thankful to my brother-in-law and to Barnes, the dining-car steward. Their actions had also propelled me to the point at which I now found myself. It was sad to think that somewhere they still wallowed in unhappiness. My experience had left me scarred and angry at times, but now I was bringing my hopes back to the shadowy ghetto, to see if they would take root in the asphalt of the city streets, would sprout in the smoke and soot, grow in barren days and nights—and at last know fruition. If so, the hunger, hardship and disillusion would have served me well. My mother had freed me from the curse of inferiority long before she died by not allowing me to take refuge in the excuse that I had been born black. She had given me ambition and purpose, and set the course I had since traveled.

As we reached the high point of the bridge, a stretch of dreary rooftops widened on the horizon. I didn't know what lay ahead of me, but I believed in myself. My deepest instincts told me I would not perish. Poverty and bigotry would still be around, but at last I could fight them on even terms. The significant thing was a choice of weapons with which to fight them most effectively. That I would accept those of a mother who placed love, dignity and hard work over hatred was a fate that had accompanied me from her womb.

We left the bridge and rolled into Harlem; and I was among the tired tenements and garbage cans again. They didn't seem strange to me now. When we crossed Lenox Avenue an icy wind was swirling trash up from the gutters. The hawk was over the ghetto—and all around me, black people were buttoned up and hurrying against its fury.

LOFTEN MITCHELL

From *Black Drama*

When I was a boy in Harlem, the ten-cent movie houses were my windows to the world. But the movies did not project the stories I heard from older people—from Southern Negroes, West Indians and Northerners. Therefore, I found my visits to Harlem's vaudeville houses—the Lafayette, the Lincoln and the Alhambra—much more rewarding than moviegoing. At these theatres I saw vaudeville sketches, dramatic sketches and musical revues performed by black people. I identified with these artists and grew to love them.

The depression of 1929 ended my theatrical visits. Dimes were hard to get. My brother, Clayton, and I heard stories of boys buying daily newspapers for a penny, then selling them for a nickel. We went into the streets to sell papers.

I found my best sales backstage at Harlem's theatres. I met such artists as Ethel Waters, Fredi Washington, Dick Campbell, Muriel Rahn, Ralph Cooper, George Wiltshire, Juano Hernandez, John Bunn and Canada Lee. Invariably, I got into long discussions with them, and they were very good to me. They bought newspapers, then gave them back for me to sell elsewhere.

Those were difficult, depression years; yet these artists encouraged me to go into the theatre. And they told me wonderful stories of other black writers—of Bob Cole, Jesse Shipp and Paul Laurence Dunbar. They spoke, too, of Bert Williams, George

Walker, Florence Mills, Bessie Smith and Josephine Baker. From them, too, I first heard of Ira Aldridge and James Hewlett. Anyone who believes the Negro theatre artist of those or earlier days was a handkerchief-head, a shuffling person of little education, should have known these proud, literate artists. The one thing these men and women did not tell me was the reason they were not truthfully presented in motion pictures. They didn't have to. I already knew that.

And so I set out to become a playwright, largely because I dared to dream the long dream and others dared to encourage me. I read every play I could get my hands on, and many of them were worthless. Later I discovered the plays of Shakespeare, O'Casey and Synge and the poems of Langston Hughes, Countee Cullen, Arna Bontemps and Paul Laurence Dunbar. I saw in the theatre the elevation of human life and the hopes, the aspirations and image of the people I knew being projected to the world. I saw hope in the midst of hopelessness, progress in the place of frutration.

I saw, too, that some of the so-called finest plays in Western history contradicted everything I knew about black people. And insulted them. People seeing those plays on stage or screen or reading them could get angry enough to kill Negroes—just as I was angry enough to kill some white folks.

My father didn't shuffle to punch a white schoolteacher who had mistreated my brother. And he actually ran after a car in trying to catch a white driver who had yelled insulting remarks at my mother. My mother didn't wear bandannas, nor did she bow and bend to the whites for whom she managed an apartment building. I heard her use some language with them that would have shocked her church sisters—unless they used that language, too. And we youngsters didn't allow white gangs to attack us without retaliating with fists, sticks, rocks and lead pipes.

Andrew Burris, and later Zell Ingram and Glenn Carrington— leaders of boys' clubs to which I belonged—were no drawling characters. They and other dedicated Negroes were in the streets, building clubs, organizing meetings and bringing celebrated

86

Negro figures to speak to us. We went to excellent concerts and lectures in Harlem. Contrary to a lot of present-day thinking, we knew of the Negro's participation in this nation's history long before we were out of our teens.

We knew, too, that Harlem was Africa-conscious. Anyone who states otherwise is ignorant and insulting to the nationalist leader Marcus Garvey, to J. A. Rogers, Claude McKay, Richard Moore, and the whole West Indian group that revitalized the black American's interest in Africa. Men like Frederick Douglass, W. E. B. DuBois, Carter Woodson, and groups like the Association for the Study of Negro Life and History resisted distorted views of the mother continent. The *New York Age* of 1906 used the term "Afro-American" consistently in referring to black people.

We knew, despite Hollywood, that while Europe was still a "barbaric land," Africans had learned to smelt iron, build monuments and record human history. The oldest university in the world was at Timbuktu, and its scholars were experts in mathematics, astronomy and other sciences. One, Ahmed Baba, wrote forty-seven books, all on different subjects. His personal library of sixteen hundred books was destroyed when the Moors invaded Timbuktu.

We knew, too, that Africans were welcomed in Europe as possessors of numerous skills. Historians—among them J. A. Rogers and John Henrik Clarke—suggest that Columbus' knowledge of a land to the west was due to his contact with Africans. They cite the Africanesque features of many Mexican statues as evidence of Africa's contact with the Americas long before 1492.

The suggestion that Negroes first reached America in 1619 is a deliberate lie, created by those who would perpetuate the non-truth that the *only* black people to come to this continent were slaves. Pietro, who captained one of Columbus' ships, was of African origin, and so were many crewmen. Ponce De Leon had a Negro with him when he landed in Florida on Easter Sunday, 1512. Balboa had Pedro Mexia with him when he discovered the Pacific. A Negro named Estevanico was with De Narváez' expedition in 1527. He crossed the continent to Lower California, and he later led an expedition that discovered what is now Arizona and New Mexico. And Negroes either discovered or helped discover San Francisco, Los Angeles, Chicago, Wisconsin, Denver and Pike's Peak.

The image of a people depends not only upon the prejudices of others but also upon projection. These images shift as the community shifts. In the nineteen-twenties and nineteen-thirties, our community was seen by outsiders as a showplace, a center of night life, a place for discovering "exotic Negroes" and new art. In the nineteen-sixties Harlem is projected by well-intentioned white and Negro artists as a slum, crowded with winos, addicts, pushers, muggers, thugs and impoverished, angry, depraved, rioting Negroes. Harlem certainly has more than its share of these, but it also has doctors, lawyers, artists, writers, cultural groups and ordinary working people. You can't get into a Harlem bank without standing in long lines. Obviously *somebodies* there work for a living. In fact, the reason the Bowery Savings Bank opened a branch there is because the management learned there were more postal savings in that area than in any other postal district. The reality is that, like all places, Harlem has many sides.

RALPH ELLISON

From *Paris Review* Interview

In 1963, Ralph Ellison was interviewed by Paris Review *magazine for its series, "Writers at Work," and a portion of that interview is presented here.*

ELLISON: If the Negro, or any other writer, is going to do what is expected of him, he's lost the battle before he takes the field. I suspect that all the agony that goes into writing is borne precisely because the writer longs for acceptance—but it must be acceptance on his own terms. Perhaps, though, this thing cuts both ways: the Negro novelist draws his blackness too tightly around him when he sits down to write—that's what the anti-protest critics believe—but perhaps the white reader draws his whiteness around himself when he sits down to read. He doesn't want to identify himself with Negro characters in terms of our immediate racial and social situation, though on the deeper human level identification can become compelling when the situation is revealed artistically. The white reader doesn't want to get too close, not even in an imaginary re-creation of society. Negro writers have felt this, and it has led to much of our failure.

Too many books by Negro writers are addressed to a white audience. By doing this the authors run the risk of limiting themselves to the audience's presumptions of what a Negro is or should be; the tendency is to become involved in polemics, to plead the Negro's humanity. You know, many white people question that humanity, but I don't think that Negroes can afford to indulge in such a false issue. For us the question should be, what are the specific *forms* of that humanity, and what in our background is worth preserving or abandoning. The clue to this can be found in folklore, which offers the first drawings of any group's character. It preserves mainly those situations which have repeated themselves again and again in the history of any given group. It describes those rites, manners, customs, and so forth, which insure the good life, or destroy it; and it describes those boundaries of feeling, thought, and action which that particular group has found to be the limitation of the human condition. It projects this wisdom in symbols which express the group's will to survive; it embodies those values by which the group lives and dies. These drawings may be crude but they are nonetheless profound in that they represent the group's attempt to humanize the world. It's no accident that great literature, the product of individual artists, is erected upon this humble base. The hero of Dostoevski's *Notes from Underground* and the hero of Gogol's "The Overcoat" appear in their rudimentary forms far back in Russian folklore. French literature has never ceased exploring the nature of the Frenchman. Or take Picasso—

INTERVIEWERS: How does Picasso fit into all this?

ELLISON: Why, he's the greatest wrestler with forms and techniques of them all. Just the same, he's never abandoned the old symbolic forms of Spanish art: the guitar, the bull, daggers, women, shawls, veils, mirrors. Such symbols serve a dual function: they allow the artist to speak of complex experiences and to annihilate time with simple lines and curves; and they allow the viewer an orientation, both emotional and associative, which goes so deep that a total culture may resound in a simple rhythm, an image. It has been said that Escudero could recapitulate the history and spirit of the Spanish dance with a simple arabesque of his fingers.

INTERVIEWERS: But these are examples from homogeneous cultures. How representative of the American nation would you say Negro folklore is?

ELLISON: The history of the American Negro is a most intimate part of American history. Through the very process of slavery came the building of the United States. Negro folklore, evolving within a larger culture which regarded it as inferior, was an especially courageous expression. It announced the Negro's willingness to trust his own experience, his own sensibilities as to the definition of reality, rather than allow his masters to define these crucial matters for him. His experience is that of America and the West, and is as rich a body of experience as one would find anywhere. We can view it narrowly as something exotic, folksy, or "low-down," or we may identify ourselves with it and recognize it as an important segment of the larger American experience—not lying at the bottom of it, but intertwined, diffused in its very texture. I can't take this lightly or be impressed by those who cannot see its importance; it is important to *me*. One ironic witness to the beauty and the universality of this art is the fact that the descendants of the very men who enslaved us can now sing the spirituals and find in the singing an exaltation of their own humanity. Just take a look at some of the slave songs, blues, folk ballads; their possibilities for the writer are infinitely suggestive. Some of them have named human situations so well that a whole corps of writers could not exhaust their universality. For instance, here's an old slave verse:

Ole Aunt Dinah, she's just like me
She work so hard she want to be free
But ole Aunt Dinah's gittin' kinda ole
She's afraid to go to Canada on account of the cold.

Ole Uncle Jack, now he's a mighty "good nigger"
You tell him that you want to be free for a fac'
Next thing you know they done stripped the skin off your back.

Now ole Uncle Ned, he want to be free
He found his way north by the moss on the tree
He cross that river floating in a tub
The patateroller¹ give him a mighty close rub.

¹ Patroller.

91

It's crude, but in it you have three universal attitudes toward the problem of freedom. You can refine it and sketch in the psychological subtleties and historical and philosophical allusions, action and whatnot, but I don't think its basic definition can be exhausted. Perhaps some genius could do as much with it as Mann has done with the Joseph story.

INTERVIEWERS: Can you give us an example of the use of folklore in your own novel?

ELLISON: Well, there are certain themes, symbols, and images which are based on folk material. For example, there is the old saying among Negroes: If you're black, stay back; if you're brown, stick around; if you're white, you're right. And there is the joke Negroes tell on themselves about their being so black they can't be seen in the dark. In my book this sort of thing was merged with the meanings which blackness and light have long had in Western mythology: evil and goodness, ignorance and knowledge, and so on. In my novel the narrator's development is one through blackness to light; that is, from ignorance to enlightenment: invisibility to visibility. He leaves the South and goes North; this, as you will notice in reading Negro folk tales, is always the road to freedom—the movement upward. You have the same thing again when he leaves his underground cave for the open.

It took me a long time to learn how to adapt such examples of myth into my work—also ritual. The use of ritual is equally a vital part of the creative process. I learned a few things from Eliot, Joyce and Hemingway, but now how to adapt them. When I started writing, I knew that in both *The Waste Land* and *Ulysses* ancient myth and ritual were used to give form and significance to the material; but it took me a few years to realize that the myths and rites which we find functioning in our everyday lives could be used in the same way. In my first attempt at a novel—which I was unable to complete—I began by trying to manipulate the simple structural unities of *beginning, middle,* and *end,* but when I attempted to deal with the psychological strata—the images, symbols, and emotional configurations—of the experience at hand, I discovered that the unities were simply cool points of stability on which one could suspend the narrative line—but beneath the surface of apparently rational human relationships there seethed a chaos before which I was helpless. People rationalize what they shun or are incapable of dealing with; these superstitions and their rationalizations become ritual as they govern behavior. The rituals become social forms, and it is one of the functions of the artist to recognize them and raise them to the level of art.

I don't now whether I'm getting this over or not. Let's put it this way: Take the "Battle Royal" passage in my novel, where the boys are blindfolded and forced to fight each other for the amusement of the white observers. This is a vital part of behavior pattern in the South, which both Negroes and whites thoughtlessly accept. It is a ritual in preservation of caste lines, a keeping of taboo to appease the gods and ward off bad luck. It is also the initiation ritual to which all greenhorns are subjected. This passage states what Negroes will see I did not have to invent; the patterns were already there in society so that all I had to do was present them in a broader context of meaning. In any society there are many rituals of situation which, for the most part, go unquestioned. They can be simple or elaborate but they are the connective tissue between the work of art and the audience.

INTERVIEWERS: Do you think a reader unacquainted with this folklore can properly understand your work?

ELLISON: Yes, I think so. It's like jazz; there's no inherent problem which prohibits understanding but the assumptions brought to it. We don't all dig Shakespeare uniformly, or even "Little Red Riding Hood." The understanding of art depends finally upon one's willingness to extend one's humanity and one's knowledge of human life. I noticed, incidentally, that the Germans, having no special caste assumptions concerning American Negroes, dealt with my work simply as a novel. I think the Americans will come to view it that way in twenty years—if it's around that long.

INTERVIEWERS: Don't you think it will be?

ELLISON: I doubt it. It's not an important novel. I failed of eloquence and many of the immediate issues are rapidly fading away. If it does last, it will be simply because there are things going on in its depth that are of more permanent interest than on its surface. I hope so, anyway.

JAMES BALDWIN

Unnameable Objects, Unspeakable Crimes

I have often wondered, and it is not a pleasant wonder, just what white Americans talk about with one another. I wonder this because they do not, after all, seem to find very much to say to *me,* and I concluded long ago that they found the color of my skin inhibitory. This color seems to operate as a most disagreeable mirror, and a great deal of one's energy is expended in reassuring white Americans that they do not see what *they* see. This is utterly futile, of course, since *they do* see what *they* see. And what they see is an appallingly oppressive and bloody history, known all over the world. What they see is a disastrous, continuing, present, condition which menaces them, and for which they bear an inescapable responsibility. But since, in the main, they appear to lack the energy to change this condition, they would rather not be reminded of it. Does this mean that, in their conversations with one another, they merely make reassuring sounds? It scarcely seems possible, and yet, on the other hand, it seems all too likely.

Whatever they bring to one another, it is certainly not *freedom from guilt.*

The guilt remains, more deeply rooted, more securely lodged, than the oldest of old trees; and it can be unutterably exhausting to deal with people who, with a really dazzling ingenuity, a tireless agility, are perpetually defending themselves against charges which one has not made.

94

One does not have to make them. The record is there for all to read. It resounds all over the world. It might as well be written in the sky.

One wishes that Americans, white Americans, would read, for their own sakes, this record, and stop defending themselves against it. Only then will they be enabled to change their lives. The fact that Americans, white Americans, have not yet been able to do this—to face their history, to change their lives—hideously menaces this country. Indeed, it menaces the entire world.

For history, as nearly no one seems to know, is not merely something to be read. And it does not refer merely, or even principally, to the past. On the contrary, the great force of history comes from the fact that we carry it within us, are unconsciously controlled by it in many ways, and history is literally *present* in all that we do. It could scarcely be otherwise, since it is to history that we owe our frames of reference, our identities, and our aspirations.

And it is with great pain and terror that one begins to realize this. In great pain and terror, one begins to assess the history which has placed one where one is, and formed one's point of view. In great pain and terror, because, thereafter, one enters into battle with that historical creation, oneself, and attempts to re-create oneself according to a principle more humane and more liberating; one begins the attempt to achieve a level of personal maturity and freedom which robs history of its tyrannical power, and also changes history.

But, obviously, I am speaking as an historical creation which has had bitterly to contest its history, to wrestle with it and finally accept it, in order to bring myself out of it. My point of view is certainly formed by my history and it is probable that only a creature despised by history finds history a questionable matter. On the other hand, people who imagine that history flatters them (as it does, indeed, since they wrote it) are impaled on their history like a butterfly on a pin and become incapable of seeing or changing themselves or the world.

This is the place in which, it seems to me, most white Americans find themselves. They are dimly, or vividly, aware that the history they have fed themselves is mainly a lie, but they do not know how to release themselves from it, and they suffer enormously from the resulting personal incoherence. This incoherence is heard nowhere more plainly than in those stammering, terrified dialogues white Americans sometimes entertain with that black conscience, the black man in America.

The nature of this stammering can be reduced to a plea: Do not blame *me*. I was not there. I did not do it. My history has nothing to do with Europe or the slave trade. Anyway, it was *your* chiefs who sold *you* to *me*. I was not present on the middle passage. I am not reponsible for the textile mills of Manchester, or the cotton fields of Mississippi. Besides, consider how the English, too, suffered in those mills and in those awful cities! I, also, despise the governors of Southern states and the sheriffs of Southern counties; and I also want your child to have a decent education and rise as high as his capabilities will permit. I have nothing against you, *nothing!* What have *you* got against *me? What do you want?*

But, on the same day, in another gathering, and in the most private chamber of his heart always, he, the white man, remains proud of that history for which he does not wish to pay, and from which, materially, he has profited so much. On that same day, in another gathering, and in the most private chamber of the black man's heart always, he finds himself facing the terrible roster of the lost: the dead, black junkie; the defeated, black father; the unutterably weary, black mother; the unutterably ruined black girl. And one begins to suspect an awful thing: that people believe that they *deserve* their history and that when they operate on this belief, they perish. But they can scarcely avoid believing that they deserve it—one's short time on this earth is very mysterious and very dark and hard. I have known many black men and women and black boys and girls, who really believed that it was better to be white than black, whose lives were ruined or ended by this belief; and I myself carried the seeds of this destruction within me for a long time.

Now, if I, as a black man, profoundly believe that I deserve my history and deserve to be treated as I am, then I must also, fatally, believe that white people deserve their history and deserve the power and the glory which their testimony and the evidence of my own senses assure me that they have. And if black people fall into this trap, the trap of believing that they deserve their fate, white people fall into the yet more stunning and intricate trap of believing that they deserve *their* fate, and their comparative safety; and that black people, therefore, need only do as white people have done to rise to where white people now are. But this simply cannot be said, not only for reasons of politeness or charity, but also because white people carry in them a carefully muffled fear that black people long to do to others what has been done to them. Moreover, the history of white people has led them to a fearful, baffling place where they have begun to lose touch with reality—to lose touch, that is, with themselves—and where they certainly are not happy. They do not know how this came about; they do not dare examine how this came about. On the one hand, they can scarcely dare to open a dialogue which must, if it is honest, become a personal confession—a cry for help and healing, which is really, I think, the basis of all dialogues—and, on the other hand, the black man can scarcely dare to open a dialogue which must, if it is honest, become a personal confession which, fatally, contains an accusation. And yet, if we cannot do this, each of us will perish in those traps in which we have been struggling for so long.

The American situation is very peculiar, and it may be without precedent in the world. No curtain under heaven is heavier than that curtain of guilt and lies behind which Americans hide: it may prove to be yet more deadly to the lives of human beings than that iron curtain of which we speak so much—and know so little. The American curtain is color. We have used this word, this concept, to justify unspeakable crimes, not only in the past, but in the present. One can measure very neatly the white American's distance from his conscience—from himself—by observing the distance between himself and black people. One has only to ask oneself who established this distance. Who is this distance designed to protect? And from what is this distance designed to protect him?

I have seen this very vividly, for example, in the eyes of

97

Southern law enforcement officers barring, let us say, the door to the courthouse. There they stand, comrades all, invested with the authority of the community, with helmets, with sticks, with guns, with cattle prods. Facing them are unarmed black people— or, more precisely, they are faced by a group of unarmed people arbitrarily called black, whose color really ranges from the Russian steppes to the Golden Horn, to Zanzibar. In a moment, because he can resolve the situation in no other way, this sheriff, this deputy, this honored American citizen, must begin to club these people down. Some of these people may be related to him by blood; they are assuredly related to the black Mammy of his memory, and the black playmates of his childhood. And for a moment, therefore, he seems nearly to be pleading with the people facing him not to force him to commit yet another crime and not to make yet deeper that ocean of blood in which his conscience is drenched, in which his manhood is perishing. The people do not go away, of course; once a people arise, they never go away, a fact which should be included in the Marine hand- book; and the club rises, the blood comes down, and our crimes and our bitterness and our anguish are compounded. Or, one sees it in the eyes of rookie cops in Harlem, who are really among the most terrified people in the world, and who must pretend to themselves that the black mother, the black junkie, the black father, the black child are of a different human species than themselves. They can only deal with their lives and their duties by hiding behind the color curtain. This curtain, indeed, eventu- ally becomes their principal justification for the lives they lead.

But it is not only on this level that one sees the extent of our disaster. Not so very long ago, I found myself in Mont- gomery, with many, many thousands, marching to the Capitol. Much has been written about this march—for example, the Confederate flag was flying from the Capitol dome; the Federal- ized National Guard, assigned to protect the marchers, wore Confederate flags on their jackets; if the late Mrs. Viola Liuzzo was avoiding the patrols on that deadly stretch of road that night, she had far sharper eyesight than mine, for I did not see any. Well, there we were, marching to that mansion from which authority had fled. All along that road—I pray that my country-men will hear me—old, black men and women, who have en-dured an unspeakable oppression for so long, waved and cheered and sang and wept. They could not march, but they had done something else: they had brought us to the place where we could march. How many of us, after all, were brought up on the white folks leavings, and how mighty a price those old men and women paid to bring those leavings home to us!

We reached the white section of town. There the business-men stood, on balconies, jeering; there stood their maids, in back doors, silent, not daring to wave, but nodding. I watched a black, or rather, a beige-colored woman, standing in the street, watching us thoughtfully; she looked as though she probably held a clerical job in one of those buildings; proof, no doubt, to the jeering white businessmen that the South was making prog-ress. This woman decided to join us, for when we reached the Capitol, I noticed that she was there. But, while we were still marching, through the white part of town, the watching, the waiting, the frightened part of town, we lifted our small Ameri-can flags, and we faced those eyes—which could not face ours—and we sang. I was next to Harry Belafonte. From upstairs office windows, white American secretaries were leaning out of win-dows, jeering and mocking, and using the ancient Roman sentence of death: thumbs down. Then they saw Harry, who is my very dear friend and a beautiful cat, and who is also, in this most desperately schizophrenic of republics, a major, a reigning matinée idol. One does not need to be a student of Freud to understand what buried forces create a matinée idol, or what he represents to that public which batters down doors to watch him (one need only watch the rise and fall of American politicians. This is a sinister observation. And I mean it very seriously). The secre-taries were legally white—it was on that basis that they lived their lives, from this principle that they took, collectively, their values; which is, as I have tried to indicate, an interesting spirit-ual condition. But they were also young. In that ghastly town, they were certainly lonely. They could only, after all, look forward to an alliance, by and by, with one of the jeering businessmen; their boyfriends could only look forward to becoming one of them. And they were also female, a word, which, in the context of the color curtain, has suffered the same fate as the word, "male": it has become practically obscene. When the girls saw Harry Belafonte, a collision occurred in them so visible as to be at once hilarious and unutterably sad. At one moment, the thumbs were down, they were barricaded within their skins, at the next moment, those downturned thumbs flew to their mouths, their fingers pointed, their faces changed, and exactly like bobby-soxers, they oohed, and aahed and moaned. God knows what was happening in the minds and hearts of those girls. Perhaps they would like to be free.

The white man's guilt, which he pretends is due to the fact that the world is a place of many colors, has nothing to do with color. If one attempts to reduce his dilemma to its essence, it really does not have much to do with his crimes, except in the sense that he has locked himself into a place where he is doomed to continue repeating them. The great, unadmitted crime is what he has done to himself. A man is a man, a woman is a woman, and a child is a child. To deny these facts is to open the doors on a chaos deeper and deadlier, and, within the space of a man's lifetime, more timeless, more eternal, than the medieval vision of Hell. And we have arrived at this unspeakable blasphemy in order to acquire things, in order to make money. We cannot endure the things we acquire—the only reason we continually acquire them, like junkies on a hundred dollar a day habit—and our money exists mainly on paper. God help us on that day when the population demands to know what is behind the paper. But, beyond all this, it is terrifying to consider the precise nature of the things we buy with the flesh we sell.

In Henry James' novel *The Ambassadors* published not long before World War I, and not long before his death, he recounts the story of a middle-aged New Englander, assigned by his middle-aged bride-to-be—a widow—the task of rescuing from the flesh-pots of Paris her only son. She wants him to come home to take over the direction of the family factory. In the event, it is the middle-aged New Englander—*The Ambassador*—who is seduced, not so much by Paris, as by a new and less utilitarian view of life. He counsels the young man to "live. Live all you can. It is a mistake not to." Which I translate as meaning "Trust life, and it will teach you, in joy and sorrow, all you need to know." Jazz musicians know this. Those old men and women who waved and sang and wept as we marched in Montgomery know this. White Americans, in the main, do not know this. They are still trapped in that factory to which, in Henry James' novel, the son returns. We never know what this factory produces, for James never tells us. He only conveys to us that the factory, at an unbelievable human expense, produces unnameable objects.

LERONE BENNETT, Jr.

The White Problem in America

Lerone Bennett was an editor of The White Problem in America, *a collection of essays by a number of well-known Negro American writers. Mr. Bennett's title piece from that volume appears here.*

There is no Negro problem in America.

The problem of race in America, insofar as that problem is related to packets of melanin in men's skins, is a white problem. And in order to solve that problem we must seek its source, not in the Negro but in the white American (in the process by which he was educated, in the needs and complexes he expresses through racism) and in the structure of the white community (in the power arrangements and the illicit uses of racism in the scramble for scarce values: power, prestige, income).

The depth and intensity of the race problem in America is, in part, a result of a 100-year flight from that unpalatable truth. It was a stroke of genius really for white Americans to give Negro Americans the name of their problem, thereby focusing attention on symptoms (the Negro and the Negro community) instead of causes (the white man and the white community).

When we say that the causes of the race problem are rooted in the white American and the white community, we mean that the power is the white American's and so is the responsibility. We mean that the white American created, *invented* the race problem and that his fears and frailties are responsible for the urgency of the problem.

When we say that the fears of white Americans are at the root of the problem, we mean that the white American is a problem to himself and that because he is a problem to himself he has made others problems to themselves.

When we say that the white American is a problem to himself, we mean that racism is a reflection of personal and collective anxieties lodged deep in the hearts and minds of white Americans.

By all this, we must understand that Harlem is a white-made thing and that in order to understand Harlem we must go not to Harlem but to the conscience of white Americans and we must ask not what is Harlem but what have you made of Harlem. Why did you create it? And why do you need it?

The validity of this approach has been underlined by many experts, including Gunnar Myrdal, who began his massive work on the Negro (*An American Dilemma*) by admitting, in so many words, that he had studied the wrong people. "Although the Negro problem is a moral issue both to Negroes and to whites in America," he wrote, "we shall in this book have to give *primary* attention to what goes on in the minds of white Americans. . . . When the present investigator started his inquiry, his preconception was that it had to be focused on the Negro people and their peculiarities. . . . But as he proceeded in his studies into the Negro problem, it became increasingly evident that little, if anything, could be scientifically explained in terms of the peculiarities of the Negroes themselves. . . . It is thus the white majority group that naturally determines the Negro's 'place.' All our attempts to reach scientific explanations of why the Negroes are what they are and why they live as they do have regularly led to determinants on the white side of the racial line. In the practical and political struggles of affecting changes, the views and attitudes of the white Americans are likewise strategic. The Negro's entire life, and, consequently, also his opinions on the Negro problem, are, in the main, to be considered as secondary reactions to more primary pressures from the side of the dominant white majority."

Lerone Bennett, Jr.

Scores of investigators have reached the same conclusions: namely, that the peculiarities of white folk are the primary determinants of the American social problem.

Consider, for example, the testimony of James Weldon Johnson, the great Negro leader:

". . . the main difficulty of the race question does not lie so much in the actual condition of the blacks as it does in the mental attitude of the whites."

Johnson also said:

"The race question involves the saving of black America's body and white America's soul."

White Americans have perceived the same truth. Author Ray Stannard Baker wrote:

"It keeps coming to me that this is more a white man's problem than it is a Negro problem."

So it seemed also to Thomas P. Bailey, a Southern white.

"The real problem," he wrote, "is not the Negro but the white man's attitude toward the Negro."

And again:

"Yes, we Southerners need a freedom from suspicion, fear, anxiety, doubt, unrest, hate, contempt, disgust, and all the rest of the race-feeling-begotten brood of vituperation."

Ralph McGill, another Southerner, made a similar observation.

"We do not have a minority problem," he said, "but a majority problem."

Of like tone and tenor was the perceptive statement of Thomas Merton, the Trappist monk.

"The purpose of non-violent protest, in its deepest and most spiritual dimension is then to awaken the conscience of the white man to the awful responsibility of his injustice and sin, so that he will be able to see that the Negro problem is really a *White* problem: that the cancer of injustice and hate which is eating white society and is only partly manifested in racial segregation with its consequences, *is rooted in the heart of the white man himself.* [Merton's emphasis.]

It is there, "in the heart of the white man himself," in his peculiarities, in his mental attitudes, in his need for "a freedom

104

from suspicion, fear, anxiety, doubt, unrest, hate, contempt, disgust," that we must situate the racial problem. For here, as elsewhere, the proper statement of the problem, though not a solution, is at least a strong step in the right direction. For too long now, we have focused attention on the Negro, forgetting that the Negro is who he is because white people are what they are. In our innocence—and in our guile—we have spoken of Negro crime, when the problem is white crime; we have spoken of the need for educating Negroes, when the problem is the education of whites; we have spoken of the lack of responsible Negro leadership, when the problem is the lack of responsible white leadership.

The premise of this special issue is that America can no longer afford the luxury of ignoring its real problem: the white problem. To be sure, Negroes are not blameless. It takes two to tango and the Negro, at the very least, is responsible for accepting the grapes of degradation. But that, you see, has nothing to do with the man who is responsible for the degradation. The prisoner is always free to try to escape. What the jailer must decide is whether he will help escaping prisoners over the wall or shoot them in the back. And the lesson of American life is that no Negro—no matter how much money he accumulated, no matter how many degrees he earned—has ever crossed completely the wall of color-caste, except by adopting the expedient of passing. Let us come to that point and stand on it: Negroes are condemned in America, not because they are poor, not because they are uneducated, not because they are brown or black—Negroes are condemned in America because they are Negroes, i.e., because of an idea of the Negro and of the Negro's place in the white American's mind.

When we say that the race problem in America is a white problem, we mean that the real problem is an irrational and antiscientific idea of race in the minds of white Americans. Let us not be put off by recitations of "social facts." Social facts do not make Negroes; on the contrary, it is the idea of the Negro which organizes and distorts social facts in order to make "Negroes." Hitler, who had some experience in the matter, said social facts are sustainers and not creators of prejudice. In other words: If we assume that Negroes are inferior and if we use that assumption as a rationale for giving Negroes poor schools, poor jobs, and poor housing, we will sooner or later create a condition which "confirms" our assumption and "justifies" additional discrimination.

No: social facts are not at the heart of the problem. In fact, social facts tell us more about whites, about their needs, insecurities, and immaturities, than about Negroes. Many Negroes are poor, but so are forty to fifty million American whites. Some Negro women have babies out of wedlock, but so do millions of middle-class American white women. Racists and millions of "normal" white Americans know this; but they are not and cannot be convinced *for their knowledge precedes facts.* Because the *idea of race* intervenes between the concrete Negro and the social fact, Negro intellectuals and white racists rarely, if ever, understand each other. What the white racist means by social facts is that there are "Negro social facts," that Negroes, by virtue of their birth, have within them a magical substance that gives facts a certain quality. He means by that that there is a Negro and a white way of being poor, that there is a Negro and white way of being immoral, that, in his mind, white people and black people are criminals in different ways. As a result of this magical thinking, millions on millions of white Americans are unable to understand that slums, family disorganization and illiteracy are not the causes of the racial problem, but the end product of the problem.

That problem, in essence, is racism. But we misunderstand racism completely if we do not understand that racism is a mask for a much deeper problem involving not the victims of racism but the perpetrators. We must come to see that racism in America is the poor man's way out and the powerful man's way in: *a way in* for the powerful who derive enormous profits from the divisions in our society; *a way out* for the frustrated and frightened who excuse economic, social, and sexual failure by convincing themselves that no matter how low they fall they are still higher and better than Harry Belafonte, Ralph Bunche, Cassius Clay and Martin Luther King Jr., all rolled up into one.

We must realize also that prejudice on all levels reflects a high level of personal and social disorganization in the white community. On a personal level, particularly among lower-income and middle-income whites, prejudice is an avenue of flight, a cry for help from desperate men stifling in the prisons of their skins. Growing up in a culture permeated with prejudice, imbibing it, so to speak, with their milk, millions of white Americans find that Negroes are useful screens to hide themselves from themselves. Repeated studies have shown that Negro hate is, in part, a socially-sanctioned outlet for personal and social anxieties and frustrations. From this standpoint, racism is a flight from the self, a flight from freedom, a flight from the intolerable burdens of being a man in a menacing world.

Not all white Americans are biased, of course, but all white Americans and all Americans have been affected by bias. This issue suggests that we need to know a great deal more about how white Americans exist with their whiteness, and how some white Americans, to a certain extent, rise above early conditioning through non-Communist radicalism or liberalism.

The racist impulse, which white Americans express in different ways but which almost all do express, either by rebelling against it or by accepting it, reflects deep forces in the dominant community. There is considerable evidence, for example, that the culture's stress on success and status induces exaggerated anxieties and fears which are displaced onto the area of race relations. The fear of failure, the fear of competitors, the fear of losing status, of not living in the "right" neighborhood, of not having the "right" friends or the "right" gadgets: these fears weigh heavily on the minds of millions of white Americans and lead to a search for avenues of escape. And so the second- or third-generation factory worker or the poor white farmer who finds himself at a dead end with a nagging wife, a problem child, and a past-due bill may take out his aggressive feelings and his frustrations in race hatred.

Lerone Bennett, Jr.

The concept of the Negro problem as a white problem suggests that there is a need for additional research to determine
to what extent Negro hate is a defense against self-hate. It also
suggests that attention should be directed to the power gains of
highly-placed politicians and businessmen who derive direct
power gains from the division of our population into mutually
hostile groups. By using racism, consciously or unconsciously, to
divert public discontent and to boost the shaky egos of white
groups on or near the bottom, men of power in America have
played a key role in making racism a permanent structure of our
society.

It is fashionable nowadays to think of racism as a vast impersonal system for which no one is responsible. But this is still
another evasion. Racism did not fall from the sky; it was not
secreted by insects. No: racism in America was made by men,
neighborhood by neighborhood, law by law, restrictive covenant
by restrictive covenant, deed by deed.

It is not remembered often enough today that the color-caste
vise, which constricts both Negroes and whites, was created by
men of power who artificially separated Negroes and whites who
got on famously in Colonial America. This is a fact of capital
importance in considering the white problem. The first black
immigrants in America were not slaves; nor, for the most part,
were the first white immigrants free. Most of the English colo-
nists, in the beginning, were white indentured servants possessing
remarkably little racial prejudice.

Back there, in the beginning, Negro and white indentured
servants worked together in the same fields, lived together in
the same huts and played together after working hours. And,
of course, they also mated and married. So widespread was inter-
mingling during this period that Peter Fontaine and other
writers said the land "swarmed with mulatto" children.

From 1619 to about 1660, a period of primary importance
in the history of America, America was not ruled by color. Some,
perhaps all, of the first group of African-Americans worked out
their terms of servitude and were freed. Within a few years.
Negroes were accumulating property, pounds, and indentured

servants. One Negro immigrant, Richard Johnson, even imported a white man and held him in servitude.

The breaking of the developing bonds of community between Negro and white Americans began with a conscious decision by the power structures of Colonial America. In the 1660s, men of power in the colonies decided that human slavery, based on skin color, was to be the linchpin of the new society. Having made this decision, they were forced to take another, more ominous step. Nature does not prepare men for the roles of master or racist. It requires rigid training, long persisted in, to make men and women deny other men and women and themselves. Men must be carefully taught to hate, and the lessons learned by one generation must be relearned by the next.

The Negro and white working class of the 1660s, the bulk of the population, had not been prepared for the roles outlined in the new script of statutes. It was necessary, therefore, to teach them that they could not deal with each other as fellow human beings.

How was this done?

It was done by an assault on the Negro's body and the white man's soul.

Legislatures ground out laws of every imaginable description and vigilantes whipped the doubtful into line. Behind the night-riders, of course, stood God himself in the person of parsons who blessed the rupture in human relations with words from the Bible.

Who was responsible for this policy?

The planters, the aristocrats, the parsons, the lawyers, the Founding Fathers—*the good people:* they created the white problem.

Men would say later that there is a natural antipathy between Negro and white Americans. But the record belies them. Negro and white Americans were taught to hate and fear each other by words, sermons, whips, and signed papers. The process continued over a period of more than 100 years, a period which saw the destruction of the Negro family and the exclusion of Negro workers from one skilled trade after another. Nor did white men escape. They saw, dimly, what they were doing to themselves and to others and they drew back from themselves, afraid. But they did not stop; perhaps they could not stop. For, by now, racism had become central to their needs and to their identity. Moreover, they were moved by dark and turbulent forces within. The evidence of their deeds bred fear and guilt which, in turn, led to more anxiety and guilt and additional demands for exclusion and aggression. Propelled by this dynamic, the whole process of excluding and fearing reached something of a peak in the first decade of the Twentieth Century with a carnival of Jim Crow in the South and a genteel movement which blanketed the North with restrictive covenants. The net result was a system of color-caste which divided communities, North and South, into mutually hostile groups.

Since that time, investigators have focused almost all of their attention on the Negro community, with the resulting neglect of primary determinants on the white side of the racial line. By asserting that the Negro problem is predominantly a white problem, this issue summons us to a new beginning and suggests that anything that hides the white American from a confrontation with himself and with the fact that he must change before the Negro can change is a major part of the problem.

DICK GREGORY

From *nigger*

Dick Gregory's autobiography, nigger, *was written with Robert Lipsyte and published in 1964.*

NOT POOR, JUST BROKE

I never learned hate at home, or shame. I had to go to school for that. I was about seven years old when I got my first big lesson. I was in love with a little girl named Helene Tucker, a light-complected little girl with pigtails and nice manners. She was always clean and she was smart in school. I think I went to school then mostly to look at her. I brushed my hair and even got me a little old handkerchief. It was a lady's handkerchief, but I didn't want Helene to see me wipe my nose on my hand. The pipes were frozen again, there was no water in the house, but I washed my socks and shirt every night. I'd get a pot, and go over to Mister Ben's grocery store, and stick my pot down into his soda machine. Scoop out some chopped ice. By evening the ice melted to water for washing. I got sick a lot that winter because the fire would go out at night before the clothes were dry. In the morning I'd put them on, wet or dry, because they were the only clothes I had.

Everybody's got a Helene Tucker, a symbol of everything you want. I loved her for her goodness, her cleanness, her popularity. She'd walk down my street and my brothers and sisters would yell, "Here comes Helene," and I'd rub my tennis sneakers on the back of my pants and wish my hair wasn't so nappy and the white folks' shirt fit me better. I'd run out on the street. If I knew my place and didn't come too close, she'd wink at me and say hello. That was a good feeling. Sometimes I'd follow her all the way home, and shovel the snow off her walk and try to make friends with her Momma and her aunts. I'd drop money on her stoop late at night on my way back from shining shoes in the taverns. And she had a Daddy, and he had a good job. He was a paper hanger.

I guess I would have gotten over Helene by summertime, but something happened in that classroom that made her face hang in front of me for the next twenty-two years. When I played the drums in high school it was for Helene and when I broke track records in college it was for Helene and when I started standing behind microphones and heard applause I wished Helene could hear it, too. It wasn't until I was twenty-nine years old and married and making money that I finally got her out of my system. Helene was sitting in that classroom when I learned to be ashamed of myself.

It was on a Thursday. I was sitting in the back of the room, in a seat with a chalk circle drawn around it. The idiot's seat, the troublemaker's seat.

The teacher thought I was stupid. Couldn't spell, couldn't read, couldn't do arithmetic. Just stupid. Teachers were never interested in finding out that you couldn't concentrate because you were so hungry, because you hadn't had any breakfast. All you could think about was noontime, would it ever come? Maybe you could sneak into the cloakroom and steal a bite of some kid's lunch out of a coat pocket. A bite of something. Paste. You can't really make a meal of paste, or put it on bread for a sandwich, but sometimes I'd scoop a few spoonfuls out of the paste jar in the back of the room. Pregnant people get strange tastes. I was pregnant with poverty. Pregnant with dirt and pregnant with smells that made people turn away, pregnant with cold and pregnant with shoes that were never bought for me, pregnant with five other people in my bed and no Daddy in the next room, and pregnant with hunger. Paste doesn't taste too bad when you're hungry.

The teacher thought I was a troublemaker. All she saw from the front of the room was a little black boy who squirmed in his idiot's seat and made noises and poked the kids around him. I guess she couldn't see a kid who made noises because he wanted someone to know he was there.

It was on a Thursday, the day before the Negro payday. The eagle always flew on Friday. The teacher was asking each student how much his father would give to the Community Chest. On Friday night, each kid would get the money from his father, and on Monday he would bring it to the school. I decided I was going to buy me a Daddy right then. I had money in my pocket from shining shoes and selling papers, and whatever Helene Tucker pledged for her Daddy I was going to top it. And I'd hand the money right in. I wasn't going to wait until Monday to buy me a Daddy.

I was shaking, scared to death. The teacher opened her book and started calling out names alphabetically.

"Helene Tucker?"

"My Daddy said he'd give two dollars and fifty cents."

"That's very nice, Helene. Very, very nice indeed."

That made me feel pretty good. It wouldn't take too much to top that. I had almost three dollars in dimes and quarters in my pocket. I stuck my hand in my pocket and held onto the money, waiting for her to call my name. But the teacher closed her book after she called everybody else in the class.

I stood up and raised my hand.

"What is it now?"

"You forgot me."

She turned toward the blackboard. "I don't have time to be playing with you, Richard."

"My Daddy said he'd . . ."

"Sit down, Richard, you're disturbing the class."

"My Daddy said he'd give . . . fifteen dollars."

113

She turned around and looked mad. "We are collecting this money for you and your kind, Richard Gregory. If your Daddy can give fifteen dollars you have no business being on relief."

"I got it right now, I got it right now, my Daddy gave it to me to turn in today, my Daddy said . . ."

"And furthermore," she said, looking right at me, her nostrils getting big and her lips getting thin and her eyes opening wide, "we know you don't have a Daddy."

Helene Tucker turned around, her eyes full of tears. She felt sorry for me. Then I couldn't see her too well because I was crying, too.

"Sit down, Richard."

And I always thought the teacher kind of liked me. She always picked me to wash the blackboard on Friday, after school. That was a big thrill, it made me feel important. If I didn't wash it, come Monday the school might not function right.

"Where are you going, Richard?"

I walked out of school that day, and for a long time I didn't go back very often. There was shame there.

Now there was shame everywhere. It seemed like the whole world had been inside that classroom, everyone had heard what the teacher had said, everyone had turned around and felt sorry for me. There was shame in going to the Worthy Boys Annual Christmas Dinner for you and your kind, because everybody knew what a worthy boy was. Why couldn't they just call it the Boys Annual Dinner, why'd they have to give it a name? There was shame in wearing the brown and orange and white plaid mackinaw the welfare gave to 3,000 boys. Why'd it have to be the same for everybody so when you walked down the street the people could see you were on relief? It was a nice warm mackinaw and it had a hood, and my Momma beat me and called me a little rat when she found out I stuffed it in the bottom of a pail full of garbage way over on Cottage Street. There was shame in running over to Mister Ben's at the end of the day and asking for his rotten peaches, there was shame in asking Mrs. Simmons for a spoonful of sugar, there was shame in running out to meet the relief truck. I hated that truck, full of food for you and your kind. I ran into the house and hid when it came. And then I started to sneak through alleys, to take the long way home so the people going into White's Eat Shop wouldn't see me. Yeah, the whole world heard the teacher that day, we all know you don't have a Daddy.

From ONE LESS DOOR

A scared Negro is one thing. A mad Negro is something else. I had always gone down South scared. But in September, when I went down to Selma, Alabama, Whitey had a mad Negro on his hands.

Those brave, beautiful kids from SNCC had started their big voter registration drive in Selma, and had asked me to help them. I was too sick to travel, but I didn't want to let them down. I sent Lillian in my place. She was pregnant again. We didn't know it at the time, but she was carrying twin girls. Lillian was in jail a week before I was able to get to Selma.

It was a Friday night. I talked to Lillian through a jailhouse window, and she said everything was all right. Then I went to speak at a rally. I walked through a deputized posse of 200 rednecks, into a church that had been tear-gassed a few days before. I got up on stage in front of a crowd of scared Negroes. They needed some courage. Courage to go out and buck the system, courage to let their children demonstrate, courage to stand up and be counted in a town where the front row of their church was filled that night with policemen pretending to be newspaper reporters and taking notes. I directed my speech at those cops in the front row. I was mad. I told that audience how surprised I was to see a dumb Southern cop who knew how to write. The crowd was nervous. They had never heard such talk in front of a white man before.

It always amazes me to see how the Southern white folks will knock themselves out, pose as all kinds of things to slip into a Negro meeting, and we haven't gotten around to wanting to slip into a Ku Klux Klan meeting. I think that speaks for itself. The whole world wants to slip in and be around right and good and Godliness, but only fools want to be around filth.

They looked at each other and giggled nervously, but they sat up a little straighter.

A Southern white man. Only thing he has to be able to identify with is a drinking fountain, a toilet, and the right to call me nigger.

They liked that. A few people clapped, and somebody yelled: "You tell 'em, brother."

Every white man in America knows we are Americans, knows we are Negroes, and some of them know us by our names. So when he calls us a nigger, he's calling us something we are not, something that exists only in his mind. So if nigger exists only in his mind, who's the nigger?

They laughed and they clapped.

Now let's take it one step further. This is a Bible here. We know it's a book. Now if I sat here and called it a bicycle, I have called it something it is not. So where does the bicycle exist? In my mind. I'm the sick one, right?

And they were cheering now, and screaming and laughing and the white cops up front looked pale. The crowd wasn't afraid of them.

I talked for about an hour that Friday night. I told them how important it was for them to get out and support the voter registration drive on Monday. If they registered, they could vote, and if they voted the politicians would represent their interests, too.

Saturday, Lillian came out of jail, and Saturday night I went back to the church to speak again. Before I began, I asked the audience to sing, "Were You There When They Crucified the Lord?" Then I started, and I wasn't mad any more, and I laid it down to them.

It's amazing how we come to this church every Sunday and cry over the crucifixion of Christ, and we don't cry over these things that are going on around and among us. If He was here now and saw these things, He would cry. And He would take those nails again. For us. For this problem.

It just so happened that in His day and time, religion was the big problem. Today, it is color.

What do you think would happen to Christ tonight if He arrived in this town a black man and wanted to register to vote on Monday? What do you think would happen? Would you be there? You would? Then how come you're not out there with these kids, because He said that whatever happens to the least, happens to us all . . .

Let's analyze the situation.

We're not saying, "Let's go downtown and take over City Hall."

We're not saying, "Let's stand on the rooftops and throw bricks at the white folks."

We're not saying, "Let's get some butcher knives and some guns and make them pay for what they've done."

We're talking to the white man, and this is what we're saying.

We're saying, "We want what you said belongs to us. You have a constitution. I'm a black man, and you make me sit down in a black school and take a test on the United States Constitution, a constitution that hasn't worked for anyone but you. And you expect me to learn it from front to back. So I learned it.

"You made me stand up as a little kid and sing 'God Bless America,' and 'America the Beautiful,' and all those songs the white kids were singing. I Pledge Allegiance to the Flag. That's all I'm asking you for today."

Something important happened in 1963, and the sooner we wake up and realize it, the better off this whole world is going to be. Because for some reason God has put in your hands the salvation of not just America—this thing is bigger than just this country—but the salvation of the whole world. . . .

The Negro in America has the highest standard of living, the highest educational standard, the highest medical standard of any black man the world over and of most white men outside America. And yet there are backward countries getting more

117

respect from this American white man than you people could ever command. Do you know why?

It's because we grinned when he wanted us to grin. We cried when he wanted us to cry. We've spent money when he wanted us to spend money. And we've done without when he said do without.

He owns all the missiles in the world, and when he talks to you about owning a switchblade you become ashamed.

He started all the wars, and when he talks to you about cutting somebody on Saturday night you become ashamed.

He makes me feel small. He calls me everything on the job but my name, so I'm aggravated before I get home.

Then he tells me about my education. Well, if it takes education his-style to produce a clown that would throw dynamite in a church, I hope we never get that.

I have a newspaper and I wish I brought it tonight. It embarrasses me just to look at it. It's a newspaper from 1848, a New Orleans newspaper.

On the back page are ads offering rewards for the return of runaway slaves. Can you believe in 1848 we were running away, rebelling, and we didn't have any place to run to? 1848. Slaves were running away.

Can you imagine what this old Negro had to go through? Can you imagine the day a Negro woman went to a black man and said: "Honey, I'm pregnant," and both of them fell on their knees and prayed that their baby would be born deformed? Can you imagine what this Negro went through, hoping his baby is born crippled?

Because if he was born crippled, he would have less chance of being a slave and more chance of having freedom.

Think about that. Think about the women you love coming to you and saying she's pregnant with your baby and you both pray the baby is born crippled.

This is what the slaves went through. And a hundred years later, we have parallels.

A hundred years later and you people are worrying about your kids being in jail overnight, being in jail because they demon-

strated for freedom. So many parents who don't even know where their kids are, for the first time they'll know where their kids are twenty-four hours a day. In jail. And know that they're there for a good cause and a good reason.

How many mothers let their sons play football, and all he can get from that is a chance to help his team win a victory. A victory that will be forgotten tomorrow. So can't you let your son fight for freedom, something that the whole world will profit from, forever?

Sometimes I wonder how much this system has corrupted us. Sometimes I wonder when we will wake up to see that the day is over when we can say: "I'm not involved."

Those four kids who were killed in that church in Birmingham, they weren't demonstrating.

You don't have to participate. Just be black. Or be white, and for our cause. When the bomb is thrown, somebody has to die.

And do you know that 50 per cent of the killings are our fault? That's right. We let this white man go crazy on us, instead of straightening him out when we should have.

Each one of us scratched our heads five years too long.

Sure, tomming was good once upon a time. That's how we got here. The old folks knew that was the only way they could raise you. What we call Uncle Tomism today was nothing but finesse and tact then. The old folks had to scratch their heads and grin their ways into a white man's heart. A white man who wouldn't accept them any other way.

But at what point do we stop tomming?

A Negro is better off going to a foreign country fighting for America than he is coming to the South fighting for the Negro cause. When he's in a foreign country, fighting to give those people rights he doesn't even get, the whole of America is behind him. When he comes down here, there are only a few behind him.

So it's coming down to this. You have to commit. You're going through the same thing today that the folks went through when the Lord was crucified.

"Who else is with Christ?" the Romans asked.

And everybody just stood there. And prayed silently. And they went back and said: "I prayed."

No, sister, I didn't even see your lips move.

Were you there when they crucified the Lord? It's a nice song to sing. But this time, you have an opportunity to be there.

Sure would be a heck of a thing, twenty, thirty years from now when they're singing a song about these days, and your grand-kids and great-grand-kids can stand up and say: "Yeah, baby, he was there, my grandfather was there."

And when they ask you, you can nod your head and say: "Yeah, I was there."

I'd like to tell you a story before I leave. I talked to the father of one of the kids who died in that church in Birmingham. He said to me: "You know, Gregory, my daughter begged me to let her demonstrate, and I told her no. I told her she was too young. And she looked at me, and she said: 'Then you do it, Daddy.' " . . .

And that's what that man will have to live with for the rest of his life. Because if Birmingham had had enough Negroes be-hind them, there wouldn't have been a bombing. . . .

These kids here in Selma aren't doing anything just for them-selves. There's nothing selfish about what they're doing here. Freedom will run all over this town. But you have to get behind them. Because there are too many white folks in front of them.

Get behind your kids in this town.

Good-by and God Bless You and Good Night.

The next morning Lil and I went home. It's hard to say good-by to people in the South, people you're leaving behind on the battle line. They have that look in their eyes, thanks a million, please don't go. They were singing "We Shall Overcome," as we drove out of Selma, and somehow we could still hear them on the plane back to Chicago.

That Sunday we took the kids to a drive-in movie. Michele and Lynne sat in the back of the car, one on each side of Lil. On the way, Michele pointed out the window.

"What's that, Mommy?"

"That's a filling station, Michele, it sells gasoline. Daddy's car runs on gasoline, all cars run on gasoline. Look over there, Michele, across the street. That's another filling station. You see, honey, there are different kinds of gas, there's Shell, and over there, that's Standard, and now, look over there. . . ."

I'm driving with tears in my eyes. Here's a woman who just spent eight days in jail, and she's able to sit back there, so patient and kind, and tell her kids about the different kinds of gasoline. I wish I had that kind of beauty. I wish the world was that free from malice and hate.

They burst into my hotel room, a dozen of them, laughing and screaming and singing, and for a moment all I saw were the flickering flames the first one was carrying in his hands. I jumped up and my stomach turned over and then I was angry because they had scared me, and then I cried. It was a cake with candles. It was my first birthday party. I was thirty-one.

Jim Sanders was there, and his new wife, Jackie, and my managers and agents and writers and some of the other performers from the night club. We drank and we talked and they didn't believe this was my first real party. And I told them about Richard, the kid I once knew in St. Louis who used to buy himself a Twinkie Cupcake and steal a little pink candle and pretend he was having a party.

Oh, Momma, I wish you could see your little Richard now. He's all right. I didn't lie to you, Momma, about people buying me birthday presents, about people inviting me over to their houses. It's true now, so it's no lie any more. And you know, Momma, that old lady who saw a star in the middle of my forehead, she was right. We thought I was going to be a great athlete, and we were wrong, and I thought I was going to be a great entertainer, and that wasn't it, either. I'm going to be an American citizen. First-class.

Hot damn, we're going to bust this thing. I feel it when I stand in front of a crowd of people hungry for freedom, and I feel it when we march down a street for our rights. Hot water seeping up into a cold body, that dry taste in my mouth. The monster. But it's not content to beat some mother's son in a foot race any more, and it's not satisfied to make people laugh and love me. Now it wants some respect and dignity, and it wants freedom. It's willing to die for freedom.

It's getting stronger every day. It would frighten you, Momma. But now it has truth and justice and the Constitution of the greatest country in the world on its side.

It's not just a Negro monster. I saw it in a Northern white boy who marched with us for freedom through the snow in Georgia. He had no soles on his shoes, and his feet were blue and he never said a word. I asked him why he didn't go home and take that big engineering job he had been offered. He said that there would be nothing to build on unless every American citizen got his rights first.

When I saw him, Momma, I laughed at every Northern liberal who ever said: "Slow down, you people, don't alienate your friends." Yeah, baby, were you there when they crucified the Lord? Or were you just singing?

Yeah, that monster's growing stronger, Momma, I saw it in New York where we marched against school segregation, Northern-style, marched to give little black kids a chance for a better education and college and good jobs. And a chance for little white kids to sit with us and know us and learn to love and hate us as individuals, not just fear and hate us as a color like their parents do.

I saw it in Chester, Pennsylvania, with Stanley Branche where we marched for equal opportunities, a chance to be ordinary if we wanted, to be great if we could. Just a chance to be Americans.

I saw it in Atlanta where we marched against segregation in restaurants. I was in my first sit-in there, and I did my first official negotiating. I learned that when honesty sits around a conference table, black men and white men can understand and feel each other's problems, and help each other.

I saw the monster in Mississippi where we marched for voter registration, so a Negro can cast his ballot for the government he lives under and supports with his tax money, and dies for in wars.

I saw it in San Francisco where white doctors and lawyers marched on the lines with us and went to jail with us and showed the world that this isn't a revolution of black against white, this is a revolution of right against wrong. And right has never lost.

This is a revolution. It started long before I came into it, and I may die before it's over, but we'll bust this thing and cut out this cancer. America will be as strong and beautiful as it should be, for black folks and white folks. We'll all be free then, free from a system that makes a man less than a man, that teaches hate and fear and ignorance.

You didn't die a slave for nothing, Momma. You brought us up. You and all those Negro mothers who gave their kids the strength to go on, to take that thimble to the well while the whites were taking buckets. Those of us who weren't destroyed got stronger, got calluses on our souls. And now we're ready to change a system, a system where a white man can destroy a black man with a single word. Nigger.

When we're through, Momma, there won't be any niggers any more.

BILL RUSSELL

From *Go Up for Glory*

Go Up for Glory *was written with William McSweeney.*

"BE INCONSPICUOUS"

One major incident during my years with the Celtics came during a non-Celtic NBA All Star exhibition tour after the 1958 playoffs. We were being paid in good, cold cash per game so don't think that I only do this when I'm already on a seasonal payroll.

Dallas was on the schedule and we were told Negro members of the team would be treated as much like Americans as anyone else.

We flew from Louisville to Dallas in a DC-3 on a particularly bad day. The plane almost crashed. We were late getting in. When we arrived, the promoter still said everything was all right, although I wanted to call the hotel from the airport. But we went and played because we were late.

When we finally got to the hotel, the promoter and his local aide said: "You're going to stay at. . . ."

No thanks, baby. Money never meant that much to me.

They protested it wasn't their fault. The man put out his hand for me to shake. I spat at it. I went back to the airport and flew home. It cost me several thousand dollars. About one quarter of what I was earning that year. I was broke. But I was a man. I would do it again. It is the people who say they're not responsible who are just as responsible as anyone else.

The only thing you can do is make the cost of being a bigot just that—costly. I try. It cost them on the tour. Regrettably, it cost me, too. But it was worth it. Success in having all Americans just that—all Americans—will only come when the cost of being a bigot becomes too high to pay.

Another time, I was going to Miami for an exhibition. They told me the hotel was all right. I called up and the guy said: "Yes."

I didn't believe it. I stayed on him. Finally, he said, "Oh yes. You can stay here. You may use the dining room and the swimming pool. We ask only one thing. Be inconspicuous."

I broke up in laughter and in anger.

Six-10. A Negro. Wearing a beard. Can you just see me using the swimming pool and being inconspicuous?

I checked into a Negro hotel, instead. It wasn't like the one in North Carolina. I had a ball.

And got a suntan.

The other time "it" happened with the Celtics was in Lexington, Kentucky.

Ramsay was an All-American graduate of the University of Kentucky and it was a Homecoming Day Exhibition with St. Louis for Rams and his Kentucky teammate (then with the Hawks) Cliff Hagan.

We flew all day from Wichita to Lexington and had no breakfast or lunch. We checked into the hotel.

I was just leaving my room to eat when Sam Jones and Tom Sanders came down the hall and met K.C. and me.

"Where are you going?" they asked.

"To get something to eat in the coffee-shop," K.C. said.

"Not down there you're not," said Sam.

They had gone in to eat and the waitress refused to serve them.

I just went back in the room and called the airport. "I would like a plane," I said.

"To where?" asked the girl.

"Whichever is the next plane going to Washington, New York or Chicago," I said.

I told "you guys" that I was leaving. They could guide themselves accordingly.

They all wanted to leave.

Al Butler, another teammate, was absent from the hotel and we couldn't find him. We did see Woody Sauldsberry and Cleo Hill of St. Louis and informed them of the circumstances of our "residence" in this palatial hostelry for Americans and they left as well.

Next, we called Auerbach who tried to convince us that it was better for our race, better for all Negroes, if we stayed. I was sick and tired of that argument. I believe, most sincerely, that for decades a proud race—the American Negro—has attempted to make it better "for your people" by playing the game of life with bigots by maintaining the status quo. It never worked. The only way to gain rights is to fight for them. Regardless of whether I was suspended, fined, or whatever, I was going to fight.

"I speak for no one but myself, Red," I said. "I'm leaving. I've gone through all the arguments. I am simply no longer satisfied to go along with the status quo."

The others agreed. Auerbach took us to the airport.

Later, Ramsay sided with us and there were many apologies. We were not condemning one waitress, one person, but rather the climate which makes such a thing possible.

The people of Lexington, who had a double standard at that time, were not offended at the game that evening. They got just what they apparently wanted—a lily-white basketball game.

A St. Louis sportswriter, Bob Burns, insisted in his column that I should be suspended and fined for insulting two such fine gentlemen as Ramsay and Hagan.

I wondered then and I wonder now—what about me being insulted? Or am I a person?

Success rode easily with the Celtics. I do not believe we ever became swell-headed. God knows, we had to fight for everything.

More often than not crucial series went to the final, gasping minute. Sometimes into overtime.

But, black, white, religious, irreligious, we somehow put together a rather unique example of Americans—a mixed team of men who in forty-eight tumultuous minutes of play could survive it all to go on and win championship after championship.

There were Jews, Catholics, Protestants, agnostics, white men, black men. The one thing we had in common was an Irish name. The Celtics.

Believe me. We did the Irish name proud. Through it all—though I tell truths which may nip occasionally at the heels and the hearts of some members—we never had a clique, we never had a quarrel. A man might be a black super star or a white super star. It made no difference. You might see me, the bomb-thrower, out one night with whites, another night with Negroes, a third night with whites and Negroes. We never considered it unusual. We simply considered ourselves a proud group of men who bore the distinction of being something no one else could be in our sport—the champions of the world.

FELTON X

When you become a so-called "name" athlete, you get involved in many State Department trips overseas.

Mine started before the Olympics when we went to South America. After the 1959 season, I went to Africa alone.

My first stop was Tripoli where a large press conference had been arranged. I was warned to be careful. Communist writers were present. They would try to embarrass the United States.

The first question was: "Why are you really here?"

I said: "I am here to play basketball and to show the people of Tripoli something about a sport which I love because I believe they will love it, too."

The Communist writer now threw his bomb and I saw our State people flinch: "What's the name of the King?"

What do you do now, baby?

Bill Russell

No one had thought to brief me on the political aspects of Tripoli and I didn't have the vaguest idea of the name of the King, or even if there was one.

I figured truth was a better answer than a stutter, so I said:

"I don't know the name of the King. I am not a politician. I am not interested in politics. I'm interested only in teaching basketball. Were I a spy then I would be very well-informed. I have come here only to work with kids."

Suddenly all the press corps were on their feet and giving me a cheer and they were even throwing a few barbed chuckles at the Communist. No one bothered me any more in press conferences.

From Tripoli, I flew to Ethiopia.

The State Department has been labelled "Ugly" in some countries. In Ethiopia, they did not make a strong impression on me.

I was met at the airport by the cultural attaché. I knew he was there by the yell:

"Hey, Bill . . . Hey, Bill . . . Hey, Boy . . ."

Along came this charging American. "You're a big boy, aren't you? Yeh, Bill Boy, you're a big one."

How to make friends.

No Negro man likes to be called "Boy."

We are men . . . not boys. Not some dumb backwoods slave . . . the connotation of "boy" to the Negro is of servitude . . . of being less than a man.

Then he told me: "You'd better apply for your exit visa two weeks in advance. Their system is so bad it will take that long."

Later, when the time came, I got my exit visa in five minutes.

Then they pulled the really classic boner. In the province of Harra, old tribalism is still very much existent. There were two schools and they were separate entities. One tribe, one school, would not talk to the other.

So, the State Department invited them both to a clinic I was conducting.

Talk about a rumble. You should have been there. Stones. Clubs. Fists.

128

Where was Russell? Where do you think. I was running as fast as anyone else. The only guy who passed me was the charging American from State. Cultural advisor.

There was one memorable experience. I was giving a clinic one day when an escorted limousine drove up. In it was the Lion himself, Haile Selassie. I was invited to join him in the back seat of the car.

The tiny little giant of a man apologized to me for requiring the conference in the automobile, but explained that it simply would not do to have the Emperor looking up at someone 6-10.

Giant? I felt like a pygmy beside him.

We talked on and on for about ten minutes. He spoke impeccable English. Our State people had told me he did not understand the language. Years later, I watched him being interviewed on television. All the questions went through an interpreter and it was explained that he did not speak English.

Yeah.

It was on this first trip to Africa that I was confronted with the deep emotional feeling of returning to a homeland. I was overwhelmed with the beauty and the depth of the land.

I finally found the most beautiful of all in Liberia.

It crystallized in a schoolroom far upcountry. A question and answer period was held and a child asked me: "Why are you here?"

Without even thinking, I answered: "I came here because I believe that somewhere in Africa is my ancestral home. I came here because I am drawn here, like any man, drawn to seek the land of my ancestors."

The kids stood up and cheered. The demonstration touched me so deeply I began to cry and was unable to continue. In that one short statement I had expressed, poured forth a deep, inner feeling I had never previously recognized.

It welled up from deep inside me like something clean and beautiful and new and it is a feeling I have had ever since. America is my native land. To it I owe my fidelity, my trust, my loyalty. Yet, like any man, I am moved to great emotion by the

129

memory of my ancestors and of their triumphs and their despairs.

Perhaps that was one major reason why I invested in Liberia. Mr. Buchanan, the Commissioner of the Department of Public Works, took me on a tour of the countryside and showed me the excellent economic opportunities in Liberia. Indeed, many U.S. firms have deep investments. Later I found some acreage and I thought, "This is it. This is the place." I obtained it. We started with investments in rubber. Since then the plantation has grown considerably and after six years of worrying and pouring in money and frustrations, and learning about business and rubber, we now appear to be on the verge of making a success of it.

Believe me, however. It wasn't a present. And it didn't come easy.

Things didn't come easy when I returned to the United States either. There was speculation about my investments in Liberia and my statements about my ancestral home. Was I planning to reject the United States and live in Liberia? Being the usual grouchy guy I can be when pestered with questions which are patently ridiculous—and being deeply frustrated by the continuing unequal (at that time, 1959) struggle for equality—I answered: "Yeah. Maybe I will. I'll get away from you, anyway."

The reporter left out the last sentence. The story just read that I was planning to move to Liberia.

No one could understand that a man can be caught between two worlds. West Africa is my ancestral home. The United States is my native land.

But because of what I said, the avalanche began. From there, it went on and at one point I was being labeled a Black Muslim.

"Felton X" they called me.

For the record—I am not a Black Muslim.

For the record, I am a proud, reasonably happy man, who was blessed by God in being born a Negro. I am happy to be a Negro. I am happy to share in the problems of the Negro here in America. I hope to do more about it. I understand that the Irish are proud of Ireland, the Italians are proud of Italy and the Jews are proud of Israel. Just like them, I am proud of my ancestral home—West Africa.

And as far as being a Black Muslim goes, let me phrase it this way:

Someone asked me if I was in favor of Muslimism. I answered: "I don't know, because I don't know enough about it."

They wrote: Felton X.

A man should not be against something until he has studied it. I was not against Communism until I thoroughly studied it and recognized that the whole theory was not for me.

I am not a Muslim because I cannot intellectually follow their line of reasoning, although I agree with some of the points they make and honor their right to their philosophy.

But a man cannot be against a name. He cannot just be "anti-Muslim." Or "anti-Communist." He must be against the philosophy, having understood it.

Because I am what I am, it was easy for some persons to fail to accept the true answer and instead dismiss it with: "He's a Muslim."

That is their prerogative but, in turn, any thoughtful person must agree that the basic problems of our society which have created an organization such as Muslimism cannot be answered if people react with "He's a Muslim" when confronted with the naked facts of the human rights issue here in the United States.

And if people don't really realize what Black Muslimism was caused by.

If nothing else, it served a unique purpose. It was so far out—so desperately far out—that it caused more people to move towards the center, to move towards a rational way of thought about civil rights.

Yet, for some, Black Muslimism was an answer. It served as a focal point for the torments of men who needed a far out proposal to shock them from their depravity. Men who were dope addicts, drunks, wife beaters, jailbirds, who had fought all their lives against a society they could not comprehend in a manner they could not comprehend, were attracted to Black Muslimism and embraced it.

They didn't realize it, but they were seeking their manhood . . . the manhood so many Negroes have been deprived of.

But for the record . . . Bill Russell already had his manhood. The name is Felton, yes.

But not Felton X.

THE BATTLEGROUND

It was July 1963, and the phone rang at my home in Reading, Massachusetts.

Charlie Evers was on the phone from Jackson, Mississippi.

He said: "When Medgar was shot you told me you'd do anything you could to help. I can use some help right now. But you may get killed."

He wanted me in Mississippi two days later to give basketball clinics. The City of Jackson was torn with violence. Other towns came later. Selma . . . Birmingham . . . Bogalusa . . . Oxford . . . the roll-call of the battles of our generation in the 1960s.

I didn't want to go to Mississippi. I was like anyone else. I was afraid to get killed.

My wife asked me not to go. Some friends said the same thing. A man must do what he thinks is right. I called Eastern Airlines and ordered my ticket.

Thirty-six hours later I was playing for a different kind of championship in Jackson, Mississippi. The baggage agent at Eastern couldn't find my suitcase. "You sure you had one, boy?"

I had one, baby.

I had been forewarned. I knew what I was getting into. Jackson was another skirmish in a long battle. The red-necks were out to fight one more delaying action, one more last stand.

Men like Medgar Evers were dead and other men had taken up his flag. Charlie Evers was a man marked for death, who slept with a pistol in his hand. The first night in Jackson I had no pistol, but I stayed with a friend with the door bolted. It would be rattled once in a while. There were noises in the alley. My friend couldn't sleep. "They're coming for us, they're after us," he said.

The kind of men who come after you in the darkness do not frighten me I went to sleep.

The next day I started giving my basketball clinics. They were the first integrated clinics ever held in the Jackson Auditorium.

There was no trouble in the Auditorium. The Mayor was even pleased, proud, that Jackson could hold such an event.

I was not proud or pleased. It was a century in coming. I could hold clinics anywhere in the world—except in certain places in the United States.

But I was in Jackson to stay for three days. No one was going to drive me out. And no papers were going to print big stories about Bill Russell. It was just something I had to do. Not for credit. Just because I was a man.

At night, darkness came down on the no-man's land which is the Negro segment of the world south of Washington, D.C. Cars followed us down the road. Full of drunken red-necks. Later, they would shoot a soldier, a lady, a kid. They would shoot the unarmed ones. They would lose their taste for it when they came abreast of our car. They would see guns and they would pull back and fall away, the headlights fading into the background.

A coward will never fight a man who is equal. The sadness is that in the darkness of Jackson it had to be men who were equal only with guns.

I was having dinner in Jackson with two priests. Four red-necks came in. Paunchy, sick, loudmouth men who were drinking. They showed their guns as they took the table next to us. They began talking about the priests. I am not overly religious, but they were good men. I said: "I know how you are at praying, but can you fight?" I laughed. They laughed back. The red-necks kept on our backs.

I stood up and went to their table. My knees were shaking. Was it anger? Was it fear?

I stood beside the big one. "Baby," I said, "I am a peaceful man. But to me life is a jungle. When people threaten me or mine, then I go back to the law of the jungle. Now I tell you— which law are we living by here? Because if this is the jungle then I am going to start killing."

They jumped up and left. The priests and I went back to our supper.

Was it hatred?

Was it bitter anger?

Bill Russell

Who am I?
Why should I go through this?

I am, in the final sense, just a man. I am neither all right nor all wrong. I was born in this nation, in this century. I was born to be a member of the nation, a member of the century, a member of the world.

A man, nothing more.

Neither right nor wrong.

Maybe I've soured on life, or maybe I'm a cynic, but I wasn't born that way. Maybe, I am an idealist—a frustrated idealist—but I wasn't born that way either. Things that I have experienced have made me what I am.

All I have finally asked is for everybody to succeed or fail on their own merits. I have tried to have a difference in values as values are computed in our modern society. I have worked hard for money. But I have not worshiped it.

I have never worked to be well-liked or well-loved, but only to be respected. I have fought a problem the only way I know how. Maybe it was right or wrong in the approach, but a man can only ultimately be counted if he thinks he is doing right. Then, at least, he is a man.

In this book, I think that some of the problems of being a man, being a super star, being a Negro in the United States today have been pointed out.

I have my own ideas for the future.

I have my own hopes and my own dreams.

I believe that I can contribute something far more important than mere basketball.

I said before three emotions have always been very real to me—fear, prejudice and bitterness.

It is the reactions to these emotions that make a man.

In the end, I live with the hopes that when I die, it will be inscribed for me:

Bill Russell.

He was a man.

JOHN OLIVER KILLENS

From *Black Man's Burden*

THE BLACK MYSTIQUE

James Baldwin made one of the sharpest observations he has made in his short, illustrious life one Sunday over television, when he stared long and hard at John Kilpatrick, Southern genteel aristocrat from old Virginia, and stated matter-of-factly:

"You're not worried about me marrying *your* daughter. You're worried about me marrying your *wife's* daughter. I've been marrying your daughter ever since the days of slavery."

In the whole body of Negro-white dialogue, which has collected for over a hundred years, this bugaboo about marrying Mister Charlie's daughter is the *non sequitur* to end all *non sequiturs*. Indeed it would be ludicrous if white Americans had not made into a subjective reality what was historically an objective irrelevance. The fact of the matter is that the American Negro is the most multi-colored people on this planet, not because Old Black Joe married Missy Ann, nor did we become these many colors because Uncle Tom raped Little Eva. So let us try to put some of these myths to rest once and for all. Let us, at the very least, place things in their perspective.

During slavery old Massa put his white wife on a pedestal and threw Aunt Jemima in the Big House bed, or went down into the cabins and raped Aunt Hagar's defenseless young-uns. So that while old Missus was withering on the vine like a raisin in the sun, the kindly master was sowing black oats and making heaps of yaller chilluns. And that's how the American black race became so many colors, from coal-ebony all the way across the spectrum to blond and pinkish white. Thus we have to say, old Massa and his Caucasian heirs are the "Last of the Great Miscegenators."

Frances Anne Kimbel, a famous English actress who married a slaveholding Georgia plantation owner, describes in a letter to a friend a conversation she had had with Sophy, a slave. It was not an unusual conversation within the context of the Southern slavery system, but it serves to demonstrate this aspect of that peculiar institution:

Sophy went on to say that Isaac was her son by driver Morris [white], who had forced her while she was in her miserable exile at Five Pound. Almost beyond my patience with this string of detestable details, I exclaimed—foolishly enough, heavens knows: "Ah! but don't you know—did nobody ever tell you that it is a sin to live with men who are not your husband?"

Alas, Elizabeth, what could the poor creature answer but what she did, seizing me at the same time vehemently by the wrist: "Oh yes, Missis, we know—we know all about dat well enough; but we do anything to get our poor flesh some rest from the whip; when he made me follow him into the bush, what use me tell him no? He has the strength to make me."[1]

Or lend your ears to Mary Boykin Chesnut, a great white Southern lady, speaking of slavery as she knew it:

God forgive us, but ours is a monstrous system, a wrong and an iniquity! Like the patriarchs of old, our men live all in one house with their wives and their concubines; and the mulattoes one sees in every family partly resemble the white children. Any lady is ready to tell you who is the father of all mulatto children in everybody's household but her own. Those, she seems to think, drop from the clouds.[2]

The mother of my maternal grandfather was thirteen years old when my grandfather was born. Notwithstanding the fact that he was born more than a decade after slavery, kindly masters had

[1] Frances Anne Kimbel, *Journal of a Residence on a Georgian Plantation.*
[2] Mary Boykin Chesnut, *Diary from Dixie.*

not given up their devilish ways or their slavery-time prerogatives. Young Master, old Master's favorite son, raped my great-grandmother when she was twelve and he was at the gay-blade age of twenty-one. Needless to say, the young cut-up did not make an honest woman out of my great-grandmother. That is not the way things were done in those days. Neither is that the way things are done in these days by the Southern gentlemen of quality.

Evolving out of this mongrelization of a proud and pure race, there grew a people who came to be designated as Negroes, mulattoes, quadroons, or octoroons. The dictionary is very helpful and enlightening on this subject. Accordingly, an octoroon is "a person having one-eighth Negro blood, the offspring of a quadroon and a white."

Do I hear you ask, "But what in the devil is a quadroon?" A quadroon is "a person who is one-fourth Negro; the offspring of a mulatto and a white." And a mulatto is "the offspring of parents of whom one is white and the other a Negro." Now let us find out what a Negro is. A Negro is "a person having more or less Negro blood." So you see, after all the rigmarole, an octoroon is a Negro, a quadroon is a Negro, a mulatto is a Negro, a Negro is a Negro is a Negro is a Negro. Any questions?

In many Southern states, one drop of black blood in your white veins makes you an American Negro. We black folk are indeed a powerful race of people. I mean we really leave our imprint on a nation.

Explanation of the Black Psyche

This article first appeared in the New York Times Magazine *in 1964.*

When I was a boy in Macon, Ga. one of the greatest compliments a benevolent white man could give a Negro was usually found in the obituary column of the local newspaper: "He was a black man, but he had a white heart." And the burden of every black man was supposedly just a little easier to bear that day. It was a time when many of us black folk laughed at the antics of Amos 'n' Andy and wept copious tears at a ridiculous movie, very aptly titled "Imitation of Life." Most of us looked at life through the eyes of white America.

The great fictional and filmic masterpieces on the American racial theme usually fell into two categories. One theme dealt with the utter heartbreak of the mulatto, who rejected his black blood and was in turn rejected by his white blood. A variation of this theme was the shattering experience of "passing." The other theme was the "Uncle Tom," or what I like to call the "Gunga Din," theme. This one also had many variations, but over all there was the image created by that great apologist for colonialism, Rudyard Kipling, of a man who—

> *. . . For all 'is dirty 'ide*
> *'E was white, clear white, inside*
> *When 'e went to tend the wounded*
> *under fire!*

With some "additional dialogue" by Hollywood, dear old "white inside" Gunga was a marvelous figment of Western man's wistful imagination, the personification of his wish fulfillment. Gunga was a water boy for the British regiment and, in the movie, finally blew the bugle against his own people. And how "whiter" inside could a "noble savage" be?

I am waging a quiet little campaign at the moment to substitute the term "Gunga Din" for that much maligned character "Uncle Tom," in designating the contemporary water boys who still blow the bugles for ol' Massa, better known these days as "Mister Charlie." For, although Mrs. Stowe's beloved "Uncle Tom" was indeed an Uncle Tom, as we understand the term today, he, nevertheless, in the final confrontation, chose death rather than blow the bugle against his people.

Variations of the Gunga Din theme were seen in a rash of movie epics like "Gone with the Wind" and "Virginia" and "Kentucky," etc., ad infinitum, ad nauseam, always played magnificently with tongue in cheek by such stalwarts as Hattie Mc-

Daniel and Louise Beavers. In the great emotional scene the black mammy was usually in the big house, weeping and moaning over little pure-white-as-the-driven-snow Missy Anne, who had just sneezed, while mammy's own young'un was dying of double pneumonia, unattended down in the cabins. All in all, the slaves were presented as carefree and contented in their idyllic degradation. If the black man *really* believed in this romantic version of American slavery, he would have long since wasted away, pining for those good old happy-go-lucky days of bondage.

Last year I did considerable research on that bygone utopian era, and I got a very different picture, slightly less romantic. I found that the slaves were so happy that most of the plantation owners could not afford the astronomical rates of fire insurance. Those rapturous slaves were setting fire to the cotton patches, burning down the plantations, every day the good Lord sent them. They organized countless insurrections, killed their masters, poisoned their mistresses, put spiders in the big-house soup. They demonstrated their contentment in most peculiar ways.

I shall never forget an evening I spent in a movie house in Hollywood, watching a closed-circuit television broadcast of the first Patterson-Johansson fight, and the great shame I felt for my white countrymen that night, as they began to smell a possible victory for the white foreigner over the black American. Forgotten entirely was the fact that soft-hearted Floyd Patterson was a fellow-countryman. Color superseded patriotism. As I sat there hearing shouted exhortations like, "Kill the nigger!", I felt that Patterson and I were aliens in a strange and hostile country, and Ingemar was home amongst his people.

In fairness to my countrymen in the closed circuits of America that night, their reactions were not intellectual, not even willful. They were spontaneous, not unlike a conditioned reflex. This ecstasy at the sudden emergence of a new white hope came from the metaphoric guts of them; from their hearts, their souls, their bellies. This was their white insides reacting.

It has been rationalized to me that this incident had no racial implications at all, that these rabid Johansson fans were merely in the Old American tradition of rooting for the underdog. Well,

I was also rooting for the underdog, and I knew that, win or lose, the underdog in America was Floyd Patterson, Harry Belafonte, Emmett Till, Rosa Parks, Meredith, Poitier, the black American *me*. The words, "Kill the nigger!" could not possibly have come screaming from my throat, subconsciously, unconsciously or otherwise.

Just as surely as East is East and West is West, there is a "black" psyche in America and there is a "white" one, and the sooner we face up to this social and cultural reality, the sooner the twain shall meet. Our emotional chemistry is different from yours in many instances. Your joy is very often our anger and your despair our fervent hope. Most of us came here in chains and most of you came here to escape your chains. Your freedom was our slavery, and therein lies the bitter difference in the way we look at life.

You created the myth of the faithful slave, but we know that the "loyal slave" is a contradiction in terms. We understand, though, that the master must always make himself believe in the undying love of his slave. That is why white America put words in the black man's mouth and bade him sing—improbable lyrics like

All de darkeys am a-weepin'
Massa's in de cold, cold ground.

But my great-grandmother told me differently. "We wept all right, honey! Great God Almighty! We cried for joy and shouted hallelujah," when old master got the cold, cold ground that was coming to him.

In order to justify slavery in a courageous new world which was spouting slogans of freedom and equality and brotherhood, the enslavers, through their propagandists, had to create the fiction that the enslaved people were subhuman and undeserving of human rights and sympathies. The first job was to convince the outside world of the inherent inferiority of the enslaved. The second job was to convince the American people. And the third job, which was the cruelest hoax of all, was to convince the slaves themselves that they deserved to be slaves.

The propagandists for American slavery (the creative writers of the time) tackled these tasks with alacrity and a great measure of success, the effect of which still remain with us today, a hundred years after the Emancipation Proclamation, almost 200 years after the Declaration of Independence. Thus, the Negro was invented and the American Revolution thwarted. Knock on any door in Harlem. Ask any black man or woman in Alabama or Mississippi: Was 1776 for real?

Ironically enough, the fathers of our magnificent Revolution, Washington and Jefferson, themselves owned hundreds of human chattels and even though the great Thomas Jefferson made many speeches against the peculiar institution, he was never able to convince himself to the extent of manumitting his own slaves during his own lifetime.

Surely the great irony of the situation did not escape my ancestors back in the days of the Revolution. And now, today, it does not escape their great-great-grandchildren. When we black folk hear one of our white leaders use the phrase, "the free world," even though the same white leader may very well be the Governor of the state of Mississippi or Alabama, or any other state, for that matter, we—as the slaves of Washington and Jefferson must have done—stare at him incredulously and cannot believe our ears. And we wonder how this word "freedom" can have such vastly different meanings, such conflicting connotations.

But the time has come for you (white America) and me (black America) to work this thing out once and for all, to examine and evaluate the differences between us and the differences inside of us. Time is swiftly running out, and a new dialogue is indispensable. It is so long overdue it is almost half past midnight.

My fight is not to be a white man in a black skin, but to inject some black blood, some black intelligence into the pallid main stream of American life, culturally, socially, psychologically, philosophically. This is the truer deeper meaning of the Negro revolt, which is not yet a revolution—to get America ready for the middle of the 20th century, which is already magnificently here.

This new epoch has caught our country (yours and mine) napping in a sweet nostalgia of the good old days. Our country slumbers in a world of yesteryears, before Africa and Asia got up off their knees and threw off the black man's burden; the good old days when you threw pennies to the "natives" and there were gunboats in the China Sea and Big Stick Policies and Monroe Doctrines and "Old Coasters" from the U.K. sipped their gin-and-tonics in Accra and Lagos and talked about the "natives," as they basked in their roles of Great White Fathers in that best of all possible worlds.

That world is gone forever, and black and brown men everywhere are glad, deep in their hearts, but most Western men are chagrined, which is the understatement of the century. This is why the world is becoming much too much for Western men, even for most of you liberal Western men, even you radical Western men, whoever you are, and wherever.

But the world is becoming more and more to my liking, to my taste and in my image. It gladdens my heart to see black and brown men and women come with dignity to the United Nations in affirmation of the manhood and the selfhood of the entire human race.

The American Negro, then, is an Anglo-Saxon invention, a role the Anglo-Saxon gentlemen invented for the black man to play in this drama known euphemistically as the American Way of Life. It began as an economic expedient, frankly, because you wanted somebody to work for nothing. It is still that, but now it is much more than that. It has become a way of life within a way of life, socially, economically, psychologically, philosophically.

But now, in the middle of the 20th century, I, the Negro, am refusing to be your "nigrah" any longer. Even some of us "favored," "talented," "unusual" ones are refusing to be your educated, sophisticated, split-leveled "nigrahs" any longer. We refuse to look at ourselves through the eyes of white America.

We are not fighting for the right to be like you. We respect ourselves too much for that. When we fight for freedom, we mean freedom for us to be black, or brown, and you to be white and yet live together in a free and equal society. This is the only way that integration can mean dignity for both of us.

I, for one, am growing weary of those well-meaning white liberals who are forever telling me they don't know what color I am. The very fact that they single me out at the cocktail party and gratuitously make me the beneficiary of their blessed assurance gives the lie to their pronouncements.

My fight is not *for* racial sameness but for racial equality and *against* racial prejudice and discrimination. I work for the day when my people will be free of the racist pressures to be *white like you;* a day when "good hair" and "high yaller" and bleaching cream and hair-straighteners will be obsolete. What a tiresome place America would be if freedom meant we all had to think alike and be the same color and wear the same gray flannel suit!

If relationships are to improve between us Americans, black and white and otherwise, if the country is to be saved, we will have to face up to the fact that differences do exist between us. All men react to life through man-made symbols. Even our symbolic reactions are different from yours. To give a few examples:

In the center of a little Southern town near the border of Mississippi, there is a water tower atop which is a large white cross, illumined at night with a lovely (awesome to Negroes) neoned brightness. It can be seen for many miles away. To most white Americans who see it for the first time it is a beacon light that symbolizes the Cross upon which Jesus died, and it gives them a warm feeling in the face and shoulders. But the same view puts an angry knot in the black man's belly. To him it symbolizes the very, very "Christian" K.K.K.

To the average white man, a courthouse, even in Mississippi, is a place where justice is dispensed. To me, the black man, it is a place where justice is dispensed—with.

Even our white hero symbols are different from yours. You give us moody Abraham Lincoln, but many of us prefer John Brown, whom most of you hold in contempt and regard as a fanatic; meaning, of course, that the firm dedication of any white man to the freedom of the black man is *prima facie* evidence of perversion and insanity.

You look upon these times as the Atomic Age, the Space Age, the Cold War era. But I believe that when the history of these times is written, it will not be so important who reached the moon first or who made the largest bomb. I believe the great significance will be that this was the century when most of man-

John Oliver Killens

kind achieved freedom and human dignity. For me, this is the
Freedom Century.

So now it is time for you to understand us, because it is becoming increasingly hazardous for you not to. Dangerous for both
of us. As Richard Wright said in his "Twelve Million Black
Voices," voices you chose not to heed: "Each day when you see
us black folk upon the dusty land of your farms or upon the hard
pavement of your city streets, you usually take us for granted and
think you know us, but our history is far stranger than you suspect, and we are not what we seem."

The Rev. Ralph Abernathy of Montgomery placed the question
humorously when he said that the new Negro of Montgomery had
stopped laughing when he wasn't tickled and scratching when he
didn't itch.

In a word we are bringing down the curtain on this role you
cast us in, and we will no longer be a party to our own degradation. We have become unbelievers, no longer believing in the
absolute superiority of the white man's juju. You have never
practiced what you preached. Why would we want to be like you?
We have caught you in too many lies. You proud defenders of the
chastity of womanhood, you champions of racial purity, you are,
if I may coin a phrase, "the last of the great miscegenators."

Yes, we are different from you and we are not invisible men,
Ralph Ellison notwithstanding. We are the most visible of Americans. We are both Americans and Negroes. Other Americans, for
the most part, excepting Puerto Ricans and Mexicans, are just
Americans. But we are more than just Americans, not because of
our color but because of how America exploited our color. We
are different, not because we willed it, but because America set us
apart from the rest of the community for special exploitation.
And so we are special, with extraspecial insights.

In the summer and fall of 1961 I traveled in a Land Rover
12,000 miles through Africa. I talked to people in the cities, on
the farms, in the villages. I talked with workers, farmers, artists,
market women, ministers of state, politicians, teachers, and the
same question was asked me everywhere I went with variations:
"How can we believe your country's professions of goodwill to us,
with whom they have not lived, when they deny human dignity

144

to you who come from us and have lived with them for centuries and helped to build their great civilization?"

It is a question America has to answer to the entire New World of Africa and Asia. The only way we Americans, black and white, can answer this question affirmatively is to make freedom and democracy work *here* and *now*. Just as most Negroes still believe that the ultimate solution for us is in America, I am firmly convinced that the ultimate salvation of America is in the Negro.

The Negro loves America enough to criticize her fundamentally. Most of white America simply can't be bothered. Ironically enough, in the middle of the 20th century, the Negro is the new white hope. To live castrated in a great white harem and yet somehow maintain his black manhood and his humanity—this is the essence of the new man created out of the Negro Invention. History may render the verdict that this was the greatest legacy handed to the New World by the West.

Western man wrote *his* history as if it were the history of the entire human race. I hope that colored men all over the world have watched Western man too long to commit the fatal folly of writing history with a colored pencil. For there is great wisdom in the old Ghana proverb, which says "No one rules forever on the throne of time."

We black folk have learned many lessons during our sojourn in this place. One of them is the truth of another Ghana proverb that says: "Only a fool points to his heritage with his left hand." We are becoming prouder and prouder of our heritage in America and Africa. And we know the profound difference between pride and arrogance; the difference, if you will, between James Meredith and Ross Barnett, both of Mississippi. . . . Yes, we black people stand ready, eager, willing and able to make our contribution to the culture of the world. Our dialogue will not be protest but *affirmation* of the human dignity of all people everywhere.

I know there are white folk who want America to be the land of the free and the home of the brave, but there are far too few of them, and most of them are seldom brave. And I, too, cherish old John Brown and Garrison and William Moore. Let the winter patriots increase their ranks. Let those who truly love America join the valiant Negro Revolt and save the beloved country.

145

JOHN A. WILLIAMS

From *This Is My Country, Too*

At the request of Holiday *magazine, John A. Williams made a trip across the United States to gauge the attitudes of American whites toward Negroes. His account of that trip first appeared in* Holiday, *and in 1965 it was published in book form under the title* This Is My Country, Too.

"JOHN F. KENNEDY WAS MURDERED . . ."

John F. Kennedy was murdered in Dallas the next morning while I was shopping with my niece on Olivera Street. She tuned in her transistor, an instrument she is never without. Sobbing and broken voices rushed out of it: facts were helter-skelter and being altered every ten seconds.

"Close your mouth," I said to her. It was hanging open as if to trap flies.

Customers gathered near the small battered radio, stood shoulder to shoulder. One woman burst into tears on the spot. A Negro man was reported to have fled the scene. A Negro boy was reported to have seen two people struggling on an overpass along the route of the Kennedy car. "Negro" kept running through the reports like some lesser theme in a wild symphony, a theme that would at the finale become dominant.

146

My niece and I rushed back to the car, drove home, and turned on the television set. There, calmly holding his earphone was baggy-eyed Walter Cronkite, a man who often irritates me with his "personalized" reporting, but who that morning was a superb newsman. On the other channel, Frank McGee held forth as calm but more solemn. Both were a relief from the sobbing hysterical radio reporters.

I had an appointment at Lightcraft of California, where Joe works, and I was to meet his boss again, Arthur Addis. In the parking lot of the plant, a man sweeping up the grounds asked me, "Is he dead?"

"No, but critical." That had been the last report.

The sweeper was a beefy man with a red face. He heaved a sigh of relief. "A salesman just came in and said he was dead."

At that moment the salesman came out. The sweeper said, "You were wrong, he's still alive."

"Like hell he is," the salesman said, getting into his car. "They just announced it officially. He's dead, like I told you." The sweeper turned away and passed his broom over the road.

Inside, Arthur Addis said, "John, a hell of a day this is." He was a tall, graying man who looked more like a fashion model than the president of a light-fixture manufacturing company.

Then Joe came out and took me to his departments. "It's all over, huh?"

"Yes."

"These damned people have lost their minds," he said.

I met his men in a kind of a daze and listened while Joe told them of the murder. Addis was walking around the plant in shock. "Joe, get the boys together. I want to talk to them."

Solemnly the men gathered in a cleared space. The machinery had been turned off. The men crept through corridors and from behind doors, their faces open and expectant.

"You've heard by now," Addis said, "that the President has been assassinated. I don't know what to tell you about this kind of hatred. I don't know how it's going to affect any of us. The best thing we can do is to be stable. Don't do anything in panic. Don't rush and take your money out of the bank. I'm not. There are Constitutional safeguards that will keep us stable. Don't panic. The New York Stock Exchange closed early to avoid panic. It's going to be a long weekend. For God's sake don't do anything foolish."

Addis turned and wandered off again. Joe took me by the arm and walked me to the car. "He's scared shitless," he said. "He's Jewish, you know, and maybe he can smell the pogrom coming. I'm scared too, man. It's the end of something. What? Tell me, you're the writer. What's it the end of—liberalism?"

"Man, I don't know. You sense so many ugly things, so big, so cumbersome, but effective as hell."

At home my niece wandered around the house saying, "Uh, uh, uh." We watched a man-on-the-street show and heard an interviewee say, "Some nigger did it." And later in the afternoon my sister called to say that they had announced in her school over the public address system that a Negro had murdered Kennedy. "Johnny, *we* would never do a thing like *that!* We're not crazy like *they* are."

The reports of a Negro murderer seemed to prove how fearful the white public is, at least in Los Angeles, of an outbreak of racial violence. They expect it. When Lee Harvey Oswald was taken in, a sense of relief seemed to descend over the city, which had probably come closer to a race riot than it dared dream. (I later learned that only two or three other cities had been bombarded with such racially slanted news.)

My mother kept rising from her deep well of disgust ("They just haven't got any sense") and grief ("That poor boy riding with his wife on such a pretty day"), only to sink into it again.

The family dinner that Sunday was a quiet affair, with nearly everyone watching television. Lincoln had gone to his burial by train, I thought, and Kennedy by jet; only the way they travel varies. In this land of the free, this land given to the bold slogan, since the Revolution Americans have averaged one murdered President every forty-four and a quarter years.

I watched my family reach across generations of poverty and persecution and extend to the Kennedys deep and sincere sympathy. But a heavy air of irony remained, as if they had known all along that disaster, sickness, hate, and anarchy had to extend beyond them to encompass even the mightiest. They have known all their lives—and perhaps it was bred into them—that the power of government was an illusion and that the people who made them aware of that fact had to know it first. My family was fat and lean, tall and short, and ranged from uncontaminated black to high yellow. They knew that to be any degree of black was to scream down the ages that the American dream of the beginning was not yet fulfilled, and that when the opportunity to fulfill it has been presented like the seats on a Ferris wheel, it has only been ignored.

The flag Ola had ordered flown at half-mast on the lawn was limp. My car was idling in the driveway, and it was loaded. There had been hints in our final words of time, what it gives and what it takes away. Ola and Albert are not young and have worked hard; knowing that they must go is not an easy thing to digest, with so much distance between us.

Two blocks down the empty street I saw a young woman walking up, her head covered with a veil as if she were just coming from Mass. She was Negro and I wondered if Kennedy's grief for the plight of my people had been as sincere as hers was for him.

"THE FACE OF THE ENEMY IS VARIED"

It was growing cold the morning I left Denver. There was talk of snowstorms in the East. I bought chains for the tires. There was little snow in the streets. It was 7:15 in the morning when I had breakfast; 7:15 and a group of businessmen were discussing the fate of their employees over breakfast at a nearby table. Should they let this one go? What recommended him for further employment with the company? Should they bring in the guy— the guy—Mike, what the hell's his name? Jewish name? Yeah, that's it. Okay. What kind of Christmas bonus? Two hundred? Two-fifty? All the while there was the clatter of cups and saucers, the rattle of silverware on thick Iroquois china. I snatched a look at the circle of sleep-filled faces. Agreed, two-seventy-five bonus. I felt sorry for the men under discussion. I would not like to have

149

my fate decided that early in the morning; it is too close to the time people are executed by firing squads or hanged by the neck until dead. Sleep still clings; the stomach growls for food; the body has not become used to the rhythm of the day; the mind is sluggish, and perhaps the liver too; and the day seems infinitely and impossibly long.

For a Negro the face of the enemy is varied—all sizes and shapes and colors, even black. Often there is no face at all, but an attitude, one that I began to encounter after I had gone north through Cheyenne, where stack upon stack of rusted cars piled high on either side of the road seemed like the gates of ancient cities, and where I saw a youth crossing the street garbed in a ten-gallon hat, cowboy boots, and a continental suit. East of the Warren, Wyoming, missile site, the land becomes a long silent plain with tall, dull-green grasses bending in the wind as waves of the sea. The towns along the way are small and filled with a chill. It was in this region that whenever I presented my credit card at motels and gas stations, I began to encounter suspicion and deep distrust. After I handed them the card, their expressions changed; I no longer was a faceless black. Their eye came up and saw me for the first time. Often they fingered the precious bit of plastic and gave themselves time to trigger all the ugly hidden machinery that told them that, by everything they knew, I should not have it in my possession. But it *was* in my possession; that was a fact as hard as the card itself, an indisputable fact.

One attendant, his face falling as I handed him the card, rushed into his office. I followed him and watched while he peered at the lost, stolen, or canceled list.

"You won't find my name on there," I assured him.

"I'm supposed to look anyway," he said, and while this was perhaps true, I knew—and he knew—that he didn't make it a practice unless he thought he had a sure thing.

This attitude persists in many places: a Negro isn't supposed to have anything; if he has, he is a thief. Still, the very clerks and attendants who hold this attitude, expect a Negro to have a bundle of cash to pay the bills for cross-country travel. Paradox.

The middle of America is a lonely place; oases of life are few and far between, and usually small and cautious of strangers. The only response I got was coldness. Once in a while, standing outside the car while it was being gassed, I would see the attendants peeping at me, sizing me up. Their eyes would run the length of the car, linger on the guns, slide back to my face and then back to the gas nozzle.

I stumbled on a newly opened stretch of highway in Nebraska. There were only two or three other cars on it. I opened up the car and it galloped. The sun was behind me and it threw ahead the shadow of the car; humped and foreshortened, the gray image sped over the ground, always eight feet before me. The engine gave off a low, steady hum. The landscape, almost bare with winter, flashed by, and where there was green, browned by winter, the sun shone bronze. The land was level, unexciting, and I raced on, calculating the distance and feeling as one with the car. And when at dusk I reached the end of the new highway and joined another, a fleeting confusion and anger assailed me. That could not have been the end of it; there had to be more, more! But there was no more and I had to get in step with the mortals and tread the everyday highways once more.

Strangely, while tearing along that road at great speeds, I thought of New York and missed the trumpet and saxophone players on the subways, the jackleg preachers, the psychotics, the popcorn-caramel stink of the 14th Street subway stop.

IN MEMORY OF J.F.K.

UNITE

FORGET TO HATE

The sign was posted near a restaurant in Savannah, Missouri. Do they mean it, I wondered, flashing past in the grip of swiftly moving traffic en route to Kansas City, Missouri.

As usual, I entered the network of city speedways and chose an exit at random. And, as usual, I found myself very near my hotel. Sometimes I have a great deal of luck, and at others, none.

While waiting to register, an old-maid clerk nudged another, and looking straight at me, said, "Something stinks." The other turned and grimly shook her head. I ignored them both. By now I was a little weary of being the catalyst for white people to make fools of themselves.

MALCOLM X

From *The Autobiography of Malcolm X*

The Autobiography of Malcolm X *was written with the assistance of Alex Haley.*

ICARUS

The Deep South white press generally blacked me out. But they front-paged what I felt about Northern white and black Freedom Riders going *South* to "demonstrate." I called it "ridiculous"; their own Northern ghettoes, right at home, had enough rats and roaches to kill to keep all of the Freedom Riders busy. I said that ultra-liberal New York had more integration problems than Mississippi. If the Northern Freedom Riders wanted more to do, they could work on the roots of such ghetto evils as the little children out in the streets at midnight, with apartment keys on strings around their necks to let themselves in, and their mothers and fathers drunk, drug addicts, thieves, prostitutes. Or the Northern Freedom Riders could light some fires under Northern city halls, unions, and major industries to give more jobs to Negroes to remove so many of them from the relief and welfare rolls, which created laziness, and which deteriorated the ghettoes into steadily worse places for humans to live. It was all—it *is* all —the absolute truth; but what did I want to *say* it for? Snakes couldn't have turned on me faster than the liberal.

Yes, I will pull off that liberal's halo that he spends such efforts cultivating! The North's liberals have been for so long pointing accusing fingers at the South and getting away with it that they have fits when they are exposed as the world's worst hypocrites.

I believe my own life *mirrors* this hypocrisy. I know nothing about the South. I am a creation of the Northern white man and of his hypocritical attitude toward the Negro.

The white Southerner was always given his due by Mr. Muhammad. The white Southerner, you can say one thing—he is honest. He bares his teeth to the black man; he tells the black man, to his face, that Southern whites never will accept phony "integration." The Southern white goes further, to tell the black man that he means to fight him every inch of the way—against even the so-called "tokenism." The advantage of this is the Southern black man never has been under any illusions about the opposition he is dealing with.

You can say for many Southern white people that, individually, they have been paternalistically helpful to many individual Negroes. But the Northern white man, he grins with his teeth, and his mouth has always been full of tricks and lies of "equality" and "integration." When one day all over America, a black hand touched the white man's shoulder, and the white man turned, and there stood the Negro saying "Me, too . . ." why, that Northern liberal shrank from that black man with as much guilt and dread as any Southern white man.

Actually, America's most dangerous and threatening black man is the one who has been kept sealed up by the Northerner in the black ghettoes—the Northern white power structure's system to keep talking democracy while keeping the black man out of sight somewhere, around the corner.

The word "integration" was invented by a Northern liberal. The word has no real meaning. I ask you: in the racial sense in which it's used so much today, whatever "integration" is supposed to mean, can it precisely be defined? The truth is that "integration" is an *image,* it's a foxy Northern liberal's smoke-screen that confuses the true wants of the American black man. Here in these fifty racist and neo-racist states of North America, this word "integration" has millions of white people confused, and angry, believing wrongly that the black masses want to live mixed up with the white man. That is the case only with the relative handful of these "integration"-mad Negroes.

I'm talking about these "token-integrated" Negroes who flee from their poor, downtrodden black brothers—from their own self-hate, which is what they're really trying to escape. I'm talking about these Negroes you will see who can't get enough of nuzzling up to the white man. These "chosen few" Negroes are more white-minded, more anti-black, than even the white man is.

Human rights! Respect as *human beings!* That's what America's black masses want. That's the true problem. The black masses want not to be shrunk from as though they are plague-ridden. They want not to be walled up in slums, in the ghettoes, like animals. The want to live in an open, free society where they can walk with their heads up, like men, and women!

Few white people realize that many black people today dislike and avoid spending any more time than they must around white people. This "integration" image, as it is popularly interpreted, has millions of vain, self-exalted white people convinced that black people want to sleep in bed with them—and that's a lie! Or you can't *tell* the average white man that the Negro man's prime desire isn't to have a white woman—another lie! Like a black brother recently observed to me, "Look, you ever smell one of them *wet?*"

The black masses prefer the company of their own kind. Why, even these fancy, bourgeois Negroes—when they get back home from the fancy "integrated" cocktail parties, what do they do but kick off their shoes and talk about those white liberals they just left as if the liberals were dogs. And the white liberals probably do the very same thing. I can't be sure about the whites, I am never around them in private—but the bourgeois Negroes know I'm not lying.

I'm telling you like it *is!* You *never* have to worry about me biting my tongue if something I know as truth is on my mind. Raw, naked truth exchanged between the black man and the white man is what a whole lot more of is needed in this country—

to clear the air of the racial mirages, clichés, and lies that this country's atmosphere has been filled with for four hundred years.

In many communities, especially small communities, white people have created a benevolent image of themselves as having had so much "good-will toward our Negroes," every time any "local Negro" begins suddenly letting the local whites know the truth— that the black people are sick of being hind-tit, second-class, disfranchised, that's when you hear, uttered so sadly, "Unfortunately now because of this, our whites of good-will are starting to turn against the Negroes. . . . It's so regrettable . . . progress *was* being made . . . but now our communications between the races have broken down!"

What are they talking about? There never was any *communication*. Until after World War II, there wasn't a single community in the entire United States where the white man heard from any local Negro "leaders" the truth of what Negroes felt about the conditions that the white community imposed upon Negroes.

You need some proof? Well, then, why was it that when Negroes did start revolting across America, virtually all of white America was caught up in surprise and even shock? I would hate to be general of an army as badly informed as the American white man has been about the Negro in this country.

This is the situation which permitted Negro combustion to slowly build up to the revolution-point, without the white man realizing it. All over America, the local Negro "leader," in order to survive as a "leader," kept reassuring the local white man, in effect, "Everything's all right, everything's right in hand, boss!" When the "leader" wanted a little something for his people: "Er, boss, some of the people talking about we sure need a better school, boss." And if the local Negroes hadn't been causing any "trouble," the "benevolent" white man might nod and give them a school, or some jobs.

The white men belonging to the power structures in thousands of communities across America know that I'm right! They know that I am describing what has been the true pattern of "communications" between the "local whites of good-will" and the local Negroes. It has been a pattern created by domineering, ego-ridden whites. Its characteristic design permitted the white man to feel "noble" about throwing crumbs to the black man, instead of feeling guilty about the local community's system of cruelly exploiting Negroes.

But I want to tell you something. This pattern, this "system" that the white man created, of teaching Negroes to hide the truth from him behind a façade of grinning, "yessir-bossing," foot-shuffling and head-scratching—that system has done the American white man more harm than an invading army would do to him.

Why do I say this? Because all this has steadily helped this American white man to build up, deep in his psyche, absolute conviction that he *is* "superior." In how many, many communities have, thus, white men who didn't finish high school regarded condescendingly university-educated local Negro "leaders," principals of schools, teachers, doctors, other professionals?

The white man's system has been imposed upon non-white peoples all over the world. This is exactly the reason why wherever people who are anything but white live in this world today, the white man's governments are finding themselves in deeper and deeper trouble and peril.

Let's just face truth. Facts! Whether or not the white man of the world is able to face truth, and facts, about the true reasons for his trouble—that's what essentially will determine whether or not *he* will now survive.

Today we are seeing this revolution of the non-white peoples, who just a few years ago would have frozen in horror if the mighty white nations so much as lifted an eyebrow. What it is, simply, is that black and brown and red and yellow peoples have, after hundreds of years of exploitation and imposed "inferiority" and general misuse, become, finally, do-or-die sick and tired of the white man's heel on their necks.

How can the white American government figure on selling "democracy" and "brotherhood" to non-white peoples—if they read and hear every day what's going on right here in America, and see the better-than-a-thousand-words photographs of the American white man denying "democracy" and "brotherhood" even to America's native-born non-whites? The world's non-whites know how this Negro here has loved the American white man, and slaved for him, tended to him, nursed him. This Negro has jumped into uniform and gone off and died when this America was attacked by enemies both white and non-white. Such a faithful, loyal non-white as *this*—and *still* America bombs him, and sets dogs on him, and turns fire hoses on him, and jails him by the thousands, and beats him bloody, and inflicts upon him all manner of other crimes.

Of course these things, known and refreshed every day for the rest of the world's non-whites, are a vital factor in these burnings of ambassadors' limousines, these stonings, defilings, and wreckings of embassies and legations, these shouts of "White man, go home!" these attacks on white Christian missionaries, and these bombings and tearing down of flags.

Is it clear why I have said that the American white man's malignant superiority complex has done him more harm than an invading army?

The American black man should be focusing his every effort toward building his *own* businesses, and decent homes for himself. As other ethnic groups have done, let the black people, wherever possible, however possible, patronize their own kind, hire their own kind, and start in those ways to build up the black race's ability to do for itself. That's the only way the American black man is ever going to get respect. One thing the white man never can give the black man is self-respect! The black man never can become independent and recognized as a human being who is truly equal with other human beings until he has what they have, and until he is doing for himself what others are doing for themselves.

The black man in the ghettoes, for instance, has to start self-correcting his own material, moral, and spiritual defects and evils. The black man needs to start his own program to get rid of drunkenness, drug addiction, prostitution. The black man in America has to lift up his own sense of values.

Only a few thousands of Negroes, relatively a very tiny number, are taking any part in "integration." Here, again, it is those few bourgeois Negroes, rushing to throw away their little money in the white man's luxury hotels, his swanky nightclubs, and big, fine, exclusive restaurants. The white people patronizing those places can afford it. But these Negroes you see in those places can't afford it, certainly most of them can't. Why, what does some Negro one installment payment away from disaster look like somewhere downtown out to dine, grinning at some headwaiter who has more money than the Negro? Those bourgeois Negroes out draping big tablecloth-sized napkins over their knees and ordering quail under glass and stewed snails—why, Negroes don't even *like* snails! What they're doing is proving they're integrated.

If you want to get down to the real outcome of this so-called "integration," what you've got to arrive at is intermarriage.

I'm right *with* the Southern white man who believes that you can't have so-called "integration," at least not for long, without intermarriage increasing. And what good is this for anyone? Let's again face reality. In a world as color-hostile as this, man or woman, black or white, what do they want with a mate of the other race?

Certainly white people have served enough notice of their hostility to any blacks in their families and neighborhoods. And the way most Negroes feel today, a mixed couple probably finds that black families, black communities, are even more hostile than the white ones. So what's bound to face "integrated" marriages, except being unwelcomed, unwanted, "misfits" in whichever world they try to live in? What we arrive at is that "integration," socially, is no good for either side. "Integration," ultimately, would destroy the white race . . . and destroy the black race.

The white man's "integrating" with black women has already changed the complexion and characteristics of the black race in America. What's been proved by the "blacks" whose complexions are "whiter" than many "white" people? I'm told that there are in America today between two and five million "white Negroes," who are "passing" in white society. Imagine their torture! Living in constant fear that some black person they've known might meet and expose them. Imagine every day living a lie. *Imagine* hearing their own white husbands, their own white wives, even their own white children, talking about "those Negroes."

I would doubt if anyone in America has heard Negroes more bitter against the white man than some of those I have heard. But I will tell you that, without any question, the *most* bitter anti-white diatribes that I have ever heard have come from "passing" Negroes, living as whites, among whites, exposed every day to what white people say among themselves regarding Negroes—things that a recognized Negro never would hear. Why, if there was a racial showdown, these Negroes "passing" within white circles would become the black side's most valuable "spy" and ally.

OUT

I've strayed off onto some of the incidents and situations which have taught me to respect the danger in the ghettoes. I had been trying to explain how I honestly evaluated my own qualifications to be worthy of presenting myself as an independent "leader" among black men.

In the end, I reasoned that the decision already had been made for me. The ghetto masses already had entrusted me with an image of leadership among them. I knew the ghetto instinctively extends that trust only to one who had demonstrated that he would never sell them out to the white man. I not only had no such intention—to sell out was not even in my nature.

I felt a challenge to plan, and build, an organization that could help to cure the black man in North America of the sickness which has kept him under the white man's heel.

The black man in North America was mentally sick in his cooperative, sheeplike acceptance of the white man's culture.

The black man in North America was spiritually sick because for centuries he had accepted the white man's Christianity—which asked the black so-called Christian to expect no true Brotherhood of Man, but to endure the cruelties of the white so-called Christians. Christianity had made black men fuzzy, nebulous, confused in their thinking. It had taught the black man to think if he had no shoes, and was hungry, "we gonna get shoes and milk and honey and fish fries in Heaven."

The black man in North America was economically sick and that was evident in one simple fact: as a consumer, he got less than his share, and as a producer gave *least*. The black American today shows us the perfect parasite image—the black tick under the delusion that he is progressing because he rides on the udder of the fat, three-stomached cow that is white America. For instance, annually, the black man spends over $3 billion for automobiles, but America contains hardly any franchised black automobile dealers. For instance, forty per cent of the expensive imported Scotch whisky consumed in America goes down the throats of the status-sick black man; but the only black-owned distilleries are in bathtubs, or in the woods somewhere. Or for instance—a scandalous shame—in New York City, with over a million Negroes, there aren't twenty black-owned businesses employing over ten people. It's because black men don't own and control their own community's retail establishments that they can't stabilize their own community.

The black man in North America was sickest of all politically. He let the white man divide him into such foolishness as considering himself a black "Democrat," a black "Republican," a black "Conservative," or a black "Liberal" . . . when a ten-million black vote bloc could be the deciding balance of power in American politics, because the white man's vote is almost always evenly divided. The polls are one place where every black man could fight the black man's cause with dignity, and with the power and the tools that the white man understands, and respects, and fears, and cooperates with. Listen, let me tell you something! If a black bloc committee told Washington's worst "nigger-hater," "We represent ten million votes," why, that "nigger-hater" would leap up: "Well, how *are* you? Come on *in* here!" Why, if the Mississippi black man voted in a bloc, Eastland would pretend to be more liberal than Jacob Javits—or Eastland would not survive in his office. Why else is it that racist politicians fight to keep black men from the polls?

Malcolm X

Whenever any group can vote in a bloc, and decide the outcome of elections, and it *fails* to do this, then that group is politically sick. Immigrants once made Tammany Hall the most powerful single force in American politics. In 1880, New York City's first Irish Catholic Mayor was elected and by 1960 America had its first Irish Catholic President. America's black man, voting as a bloc, could wield an even more powerful force.

U.S. politics is ruled by special-interest blocs and lobbies. What group has a more urgent special interest, what group needs a bloc, a lobby, more than the black man? Labor owns one of Washington's largest non-government buildings—situated where they can literally watch the White House—and no political move is made that doesn't involve how Labor feels about it. A lobby got Big Oil its depletion allowance. The farmer, through his lobby, is the most government-subsidized special-interest group in America today, because a million farmers vote, not as Democrats, or Republicans, liberals, conservatives, but as farmers.

Doctors have the best lobby in Washington. Their special-interest influence successfully fights the Medicare program that's wanted, and needed, by millions of other people. Why, there's a Beet Growers' Lobby! A Wheat Lobby! A Cattle Lobby! A China Lobby! Little countries no one ever heard of have their Washington lobbies, representing their special interests.

The government has departments to deal with the special-interest groups that make themselves heard and felt. A Department of Agriculture cares for the farmers' needs. There is a Department of Health, Education and Welfare. There is a Department of the Interior—in which the Indians are included. Is the farmer, the doctor, the Indian, the greatest problem in America today? No—it is the black man! There ought to be a Pentagon-sized Washington department dealing with every segment of the black man's problems.

Twenty-two million black men! They have given America four hundred years of toil; they have bled and died in every battle since the Revolution; they were in America before the Pilgrims, and long before the mass immigrations—and they are still today at the bottom of everything!

Why, twenty-two million black people should tomorrow give a dollar apiece to build a skyscraper lobby building in Washington, D.C. Every morning, every legislator should receive a communication about what the black man in America expects and wants and needs. The demanding voice of the black lobby should be in the ears of every legislator who votes on any issue.

The cornerstones of this country's operation are economic and political strength and power. The black man doesn't have the economic strength—and it will take time for him to build it. But right now the American black man has the political strength and power to change his destiny overnight.

It was a big order—the organization I was creating in my mind, one which would help to challenge the American black man to gain his human rights, and to cure his mental, spiritual, economic, and political sicknesses. But if you ever intend to do anything worthwhile, you have to start with a worthwhile plan.

Substantially, as I saw it, the organization I hoped to build would differ from the Nation of Islam in that it would embrace all faiths of black men, and it would carry into practice what the Nation of Islam had only preached.

Rumors were swirling, particularly in East Coast cities—what was I going to do? Well, the first thing I was going to have to do was to attract far more willing heads and hands than my own. Each day, more militant, action brothers who had been with me in Mosque Seven announced their break from the Nation of Islam to come with me. And each day, I learned, in one or another way, of more support from non-Muslim Negroes, including a surprising lot of the "middle" and "upper class" black bourgeoisie, who were sick of the status-symbol charade. There was a growing clamor: "When are you going to call a meeting, to get organized?"

To hold a first meeting, I arranged to rent the Carver Ballroom of the Hotel Theresa, which is at the corner of 125th Street and Seventh Avenue, which might be called one of Harlem's fusebox locations.

The *Amsterdam News* reported the planned meeting and many

readers inferred that we were establishing our beginning mosque in the Theresa. Telegrams and letters and telephone calls came to the hotel for me, from across the country. Their general tone was that this was a move that people had waited for. People I'd never heard of expressed confidence in me in moving ways. Numerous people said that the Nation of Islam's stringent moral restrictions had repelled them—and they wanted to join me.

A doctor who owned a small hospital telephoned long-distance to join. Many others sent contributions—even before our policies had been publicly stated. Muslims wrote from other cities that they would join me, their remarks being generally along the lines that "Islam is too inactive" . . . "The Nation is moving too slow."

Astonishing numbers of white people called, and wrote, offering contributions, or asking could *they* join? The answer was, no, they couldn't join; our membership was all black—but if their consciences dictated, they could financially help our constructive approach to America's race problems.

Speaking-engagement requests came in—twenty-two of them in one particular Monday morning's mail. It was startling to me that an unusual number of the requests came from groups of white Christian ministers.

I called a press conference. The microphones stuck up before me. The flashbulbs popped. The reporters, men and women, white and black, representing media that reached around the world, sat looking at me with their pencils and open notebooks.

I made the announcement: "I am going to organize and head a new mosque in New York City known as the Muslim Mosque, Inc. This will give us a religious base, and the spiritual force necessary to rid our people of the vices that destroy the moral fiber of our community.

"Muslim Mosque, Inc. will have its temporary headquarters in the Hotel Theresa in Harlem. It will be the working base for an action program designed to eliminate the political oppression, the economic exploitation, and the social degradation suffered daily by twenty-two million Afro-Americans."

1965

Anything I do today, I regard as urgent. No man is given but so much time to accomplish whatever is his life's work. My life in particular never has stayed fixed in one position for very long. You have seen how throughout my life, I have often known unexpected drastic changes.

I am only facing the facts when I know that any moment of any day, or any night, could bring me death. This is particularly true since the last trip that I made abroad. I have seen the nature of things that are happening, and I have heard things from sources which are reliable.

To speculate about dying doesn't disturb me as it might some people. I never have felt that I would live to become an old man. Even before I was a Muslim—when I was a hustler in the ghetto jungle, and then a criminal in prison, it always stayed on my mind that I would die a violent death. In fact, it runs in my family. My father and most of his brothers died by violence —my father because of what he believed in. To come right down to it, if I take the kind of things in which I believe, then add to that the kind of temperament that I have, plus the one hundred per cent dedication I have to whatever I believe in—these are ingredients which make it just about impossible for me to die of old age.

I have given to this book so much of whatever time I have because I feel, and I hope, that if I honestly and fully tell my life's account, read objectively it might prove to be a testimony of some social value.

I think that an objective reader may see how in the society to which I was exposed as a black youth here in America, for me to wind up in a prison was really just about inevitable. It happens to so many thousands of black youth.

I think that an objective reader may see how when I heard "The white man is the devil," when I played back what had been my own experiences, it was inevitable that I would respond positively; then the next twelve years of my life were devoted and dedicated to propagating that phrase among the black people.

I think, I hope, that the objective reader, in following my life—the life of only one ghetto-created Negro—may gain a better picture and understanding than he has previously had of the black ghettoes which are shaping the lives and the thinking of almost all of the 22 million Negroes who live in America.

Thicker each year in these ghettoes is the kind of teen-ager that I was—with the wrong kinds of heroes, and the wrong kinds of influences. I am not saying that all of them become the kind of parasite that I was. Fortunately, by far most do not. But still, the small fraction who do add up to an annual total of more and more costly, dangerous youthful criminals. The F.B.I. not long ago released a report of a shocking rise in crime each successive year since the end of World War II—ten to twelve per cent each year. The report did not say so in so many words, but I am saying that the majority of that crime increase is annually spawned in the black ghettoes which the American racist society permits to exist. In the 1964 "long, hot summer" riots in major cities across the United States, the socially disinherited black ghetto youth were always at the forefront.

In this year, 1965, I am certain that more—and worse—riots are going to erupt, in yet more cities, in spite of the conscience-salving Civil Rights Bill. The reason is that the *cause* of these riots, the racist malignancy in America, has been too long unattended.

I believe that it would be almost impossible to find anywhere in America a black man who has lived further down in the mud of human society than I have; or a black man who has been any more ignorant than I have been; or a black man who has suffered more anguish during his life than I have. But it is only after the deepest darkness that the greatest joy can come; it is only after slavery and prison that the sweetest appreciation of freedom can come.

For the freedom of my 22 million black brothers and sisters here in America, I do believe that I have fought the best that I knew how, and the best that I could, with the shortcomings that I have had. I know that my shortcomings are many.

My greatest lack has been, I believe, that I don't have the kind of academic education I wish I had been able to get—to have been a lawyer, perhaps. I do believe that I might have made a good lawyer. I have always loved verbal battle, and challenge. You can believe me that if I had the time right now, I would not be one bit ashamed to go back into any New York City public school and start where I left off at the ninth grade, and go on through a degree. Because I don't begin to be academically equipped for so many of the interests that I have. For instance, I love languages. I wish I were an accomplished linguist. I don't know anything more frustrating than to be around people talking something you can't understand. Especially when they are people who look just like you. In Africa, I heard original mother tongues, such as Hausa, and Swahili, being spoken, and there I was standing like some little boy, waiting for someone to tell me what had been said; I never will forget how ignorant I felt.

Aside from the basic African dialects, I would try to learn Chinese, because it looks as if Chinese will be the most powerful political language of the future. And already I have begun studying Arabic, which I think is going to be the most powerful spiritual language of the future.

I would just like to *study*. I mean ranging study, because I have a wide-open mind. I'm interested in almost any subject you can mention. I know this is the reason I have come to really like, as individuals, some of the hosts of radio or television panel programs I have been on, and to respect their minds—because even if they have been almost steadily in disagreement with me on the race issue, they still have kept their minds open and objective about the truths of things happening in this world. Irv Kupcinet in Chicago, and Barry Farber, Barry Gray and Mike Wallace in New York—people like them. They also let me see that they respected my mind—in a way I know they never realized. The way I knew was that often they would invite my opinion on subjects off the race issue. Sometimes, after the programs, we would sit around and talk about all kinds of things, current events and other things, for an hour or more. You see, most whites, even when they credit a Negro with some intelligence, will still feel that all he can talk about is the race issue; most whites never feel that Negroes can contribute anything to other areas of thought, and ideas. You just notice how rarely you will ever hear whites asking any Negroes what they think about the problem of world health, or the space race to land men on the moon.

Every morning when I wake up, now, I regard it as having another borrowed day. In any city, wherever I go, making speeches, holding meetings of my organization, or attending to other business, black men are watching every move I make, awaiting their chance to kill me. I have said publicly many times that I know that they have their orders. Anyone who chooses not to believe what I am saying doesn't know the Muslims in the Nation of Islam.

But I am also blessed with faithful followers who are, I believe, as dedicated to me as I once was to Mr. Elijah Muhammad. Those who would hunt a man need to remember that a jungle also contains those who hunt the hunters.

I know, too, that I could suddenly die at the hands of some white racists. Or I could die at the hands of some Negro hired by the white man. Or it could be some brainwashed Negro acting on his own idea that by eliminating me he would be helping out the white man, because I talk about the white man the way I do.

Anyway, now, each day I live as if I am already dead, and I tell you what I would like for you to do. When I *am* dead—I say it that way because from the things I *know,* I do not expect to live long enough to read this book in its finished form—I want you to just watch and see if I'm not right in what I say: that the white man, in his press, is going to identify me with "hate."

He will make use of me dead, as he has made use of me alive, as a convenient symbol of "hatred"—and that will help him to escape facing the truth that all I have been doing is holding up a mirror to reflect, to show, the history of unspeakable crimes that his race has committed against my race.

You watch. I will be labelled as, at best, an "irresponsible" black man. I have always felt about this accusation that the black "leader" whom white men consider to be "responsible" is invariably the black "leader" who never gets any results. You only get action as a black man if you are regarded by the white man as "irresponsible." In fact, this much I had learned when I was just a little boy. And since I have been some kind of a "leader" of black people here in the racist society of America, I have been more reassured each time the white man resisted me, or attacked me harder—because each time made me more certain that I was on the right track in the American black man's best interests. The racist white man's opposition automatically made me know that I did offer the black man something worthwhile.

Yes, I have cherished my "demagogue" role. I know that societies often have killed the people who have helped to change those societies. And if I can die having brought any light, having exposed any meaningful truth that will help to destroy the racist cancer that is malignant in the body of America—then, all of the credit is due to Allah. Only the mistakes have been mine.

OSSIE DAVIS

Why I Eulogized Malcolm X

Ossie Davis, the actor-playwright, was one of the first people publicly to express shock over the assassination of Malcolm X. In his eulogy at Malcolm X's funeral, Mr. Davis referred to him as "Our Black Shining Prince." The selection that follows is Mr. Davis's reply to a magazine editor's question, "Why did you eulogize Malcolm X?"

You are not the only person curious to know why I would eulogize a man like Malcolm X. Many who know and respect me have written letters. Of these letters I am proudest of those from a sixth-grade class of young white boys and girls who asked me to explain. I appreciate your giving me this chance to do so.

You may anticipate my defense somewhat by considering the following fact: no Negro has yet asked me that question. (My pastor in Grace Baptist Church where I teach Sunday school preached a sermon about Malcolm in which he called him a "giant in a sick world.") Every one of the many letters I got from my own people lauded Malcolm as a man, and commended me for having spoken at his funeral.

At the same time—and this is important—most all of them took special pains to disagree with much or all of what Malcolm said and what he stood for. That is, with one singing exception,

170

they all, every last, black, glory-hugging one of them, knew that Malcolm—whatever else he was or was not—*Malcolm was a man!*

White folks do not need anybody to remind them that they are men. We do! This was his one incontrovertible benefit to his people.

Protocol and common sense require that Negroes stand back and let the white man speak up for us, defend us, and lead us from behind the scene in our fight. This is the essence of Negro politics. But Malcolm said to hell with that! Get up off your knees and fight your own battles. That's the way to win back your self-respect. That's the way to make the white man respect you. And if he won't let you live like a man, he certainly can't keep you from dying like one!

Malcolm, as you can see, was refreshing excitement; he scared hell out of the rest of us, bred as we are to caution, to hypocrisy in the presence of white folks, to the smile that never fades. Malcolm knew that every white man in America profits directly or indirectly from his position vis-á-vis Negroes, profits from racism even though he does not practice it or believe it.

He also knew that every Negro who did not challenge on the spot every instance of racism, overt or covert, committed against him and his people, who chose instead to swallow his spit and go on smiling, was an Uncle Tom and a traitor, without balls or guts, or any other commonly accepted aspects of manhood!

Now, we knew all these things as well as Malcolm did, but we also knew what happened to people who stick their necks out and say them. And if all the lies we tell ourselves by way of extenuation were put into print, it would constitute one of the great chapters in the history of man's justifiable cowardice in the face of other men.

But Malcolm kept snatching our lies away. He kept shouting the painful truth we whites and blacks did not want to hear from all the housetops. And he wouldn't stop for love nor money.

You can imagine what a howling, shocking nuisance this man was to both Negroes and whites. Once Malcolm fastened on you, you could not escape. He was one of the most fascinating and charming men I have ever met, and never hesitated to take his attractiveness and beat you to death with it. Yet his irritation, though painful to us, was most salutary. He would make you angry as hell, but he would also make you proud. It was impossible to remain defensive and apologetic about being a Negro in his presence. He wouldn't let you. And you always left his presence with the sneaky suspicion that maybe, after all, you were a man!

But in explaining Malcolm, let me take care not to explain him away. He had been a criminal, an addict, a pimp, and a prisoner; a racist, and a hater, he had really believed the white man was a devil. But all this had changed. Two days before his death, in commenting to Gordon Parks about his past life he said: "That was a mad scene. The sickness and madness of those days! I'm glad to be free of them."

And Malcolm was free. No one who knew him before and after his trip to Mecca could doubt that he had completely abandoned racism, separatism, and hatred. But he had not abandoned his shock-effect statements, his bristling agitation for immediate freedom in this country not only for blacks, but for everybody.

And most of all, in the area of race relations, he still delighted in twisting the white man's tail, and in making Uncle Toms, compromisers and accommodationists—I deliberately include myself—thoroughly ashamed of the urbane and smiling hypocrisy we practice merely to exist in a world whose values we both envy and despise.

But even had Malcolm not changed, he would still have been a relevant figure on the American scene, standing in relation as he does, to the "responsible" civil rights leaders, just about where John Brown stood in relation to the "responsible" abolitionist in the fight against slavery. Almost all disagreed with Brown's mad and fanatical tactics which led him foolishly to attack a Federal arsenal at Harpers Ferry, to lose two sons there, and later to be hanged for treason.

Yet, today the world, and especially the Negro people, proclaim Brown not a traitor, but a hero and a martyr in a noble cause. So in future, I will not be surprised if men come to see that

Malcolm X was, within his own limitations, and in his own inimitable style, also a martyr in that cause.

But there is much controversy still about this most controversial American, and I am content to wait for history to make the final decision.

But in personal judgment, there is no appeal from instinct. I knew the man personally, and however much I disagreed with him, I never doubted that Malcolm X, even when he was wrong, was always that rarest thing in the world among us Negroes: a true man.

And if, to protect my relations with the many good white folks who make it possible for me to earn a fairly good living in the entertainment industry, I was too chicken, too cautious, to admit that fact when he was alive, I thought at least that now, when all the white folks are safe from him at last, I could be honest with myself enough to lift my hat for one final salute to that brave, black, ironic gallantry, which was his style and hallmark, that shocking zing of fire-and-be-damned-to-you, so absolutely absent in every other Negro man I know, which brought him, too soon, to his death.

MARTIN LUTHER KING, Jr.

From *Why We Can't Wait*

*After his arrest in a civil rights demonstration in 1963,
Dr. Martin Luther King, Jr., wrote this letter, which
appears in its entirety.*

LETTER FROM BIRMINGHAM JAIL

April 16, 1963

MY DEAR FELLOW CLERGYMEN:

While confined here in the Birmingham city jail, I came
across your recent statement calling my present activities "un-
wise and untimely." Seldom do I pause to answer criticism of
my work and ideas. If I sought to answer all the criticisms that
cross my desk, my secretaries would have little time for anything

AUTHOR'S NOTE: This response to a published statement by eight fellow
clergymen from Alabama (Bishop C. C. J. Carpenter, Bishop Joseph A.
Durick, Rabbi Hilton L. Grafman, Bishop Paul Hardin, Bishop Holan B.
Harmon, the Reverend George M. Murray, the Reverend Edward V.
Ramage and the Reverend Earl Stallings) was composed under somewhat
constricting circumstances. Begun on the margins of the newspaper in
which the statement appeared while I was in jail, the letter was continued
on scraps of writing paper supplied by a friendly Negro trusty, and concluded on a pad my attorneys were eventually permitted to leave me.
Although the text remains in substance unaltered, I have indulged in the
author's prerogative of polishing it for publication.

other than such correspondence in the course of the day, and I would have no time for constructive work. But since I feel that you are men of genuine good will and that your criticisms are sincerely set forth, I want to try to answer your statement in what I hope will be patient and reasonable terms.

I think I should indicate why I am here in Birmingham, since you have been influenced by the view which argues against "outsiders coming in." I have the honor of serving as president of the Southern Christian Leadership Conference, an organization operating in every southern state, with headquarters in Atlanta, Georgia. We have some eighty-five affiliated organizations across the South, and one of them is the Alabama Christian Movement for Human Rights. Frequently we share staff, educational and financial resources with our affiliates. Several months ago the affiliate here in Birmingham asked us to be on call to engage in a nonviolent direct-action program if such were deemed necessary. We readily consented, and when the hour came we lived up to our promise. So I, along with several members of my staff, am here because I was invited here. I am here because I have organizational ties here.

But more basically, I am in Birmingham because injustice is here. Just as the prophets of the eighth century B.C. left their villages and carried their "thus saith the Lord" far beyond the boundaries of their tome towns, and just as the Apostle Paul left his village of Tarsus and carried the gospel of Jesus Christ to the far corners of the Greco-Roman world, so am I compelled to carry the gospel of freedom beyond my own home town. Like Paul, I must constantly respond to the Macedonian call for aid.

Moreover, I am cognizant of the interrelatedness of all communities and states. I cannot sit idly by in Atlanta and not be concerned about what happens in Birmingham. Injustice anywhere is a threat to justice everywhere. We are caught in an inescapable network of mutuality, tied in a single garment of destiny. Whatever affects one directly, affects all indirectly. Never again can we afford to live with the narrow, provincial "outside agitator" idea. Anyone who lives inside the United States can never be considered an outsider anywhere within its bounds.

You deplore the demonstrations taking place in Birmingham.

But your statement, I am sorry to say, fails to express a similar concern for the conditions that brought about the demonstrations. I am sure that none of you would want to rest content with the superficial kind of social analysis that deals merely with effects and does not grapple with underlying causes. It is unfortunate that demonstrations are taking place in Birmingham, but it is even more unfortunate that the city's white power structure left the Negro community with no alternative.

In any nonviolent campaign there are four basic steps: collection of the facts to determine whether injustices exist; negotiation; self-purification; and direct action. We have gone through all these steps in Birmingham. There can be no gainsaying the fact that racial injustice engulfs this community. Birmingham is probably the most thoroughly segregated city in the United States. Its ugly record of brutality is widely known. Negroes have experienced grossly unjust treatment in the courts. There have been more unsolved bombings of Negro homes and churches in Birmingham than in any other city in the nation. These are the hard, brutal facts of the case. On the basis of these conditions, Negro leaders sought to negotiate with the city fathers. But the latter consistently refused to engage in good-faith negotiation.

Then, last September, came the opportunity to talk with leaders of Birmingham's economic community. In the course of the negotiations, certain promises were made by the merchants —for example, to remove the stores' humiliating racial signs. On the basis of these promises, the Reverend Fred Shuttlesworth and the leaders of the Alabama Christian Movement for Human Rights agreed to a moratorium on all demonstrations. As the weeks and months went by, we realized that we were the victims of a broken promise. A few signs, briefly removed, returned; the others remained.

As in so many past experiences, our hopes had been blasted, and the shadow of deep disappointment settled upon us. We had no alternative except to prepare for direct action, whereby we would present our very bodies as a means of laying our case before the conscience of the local and the national community. Mindful of the difficulties involved, we decided to undertake a process of self-purification. We began a series of workshops on nonviolence, and we repeatedly asked ourselves: "Are you able to accept blows without retaliating?" "Are you able to endure the ordeal of jail?" We decided to schedule our direct-action program for the Easter season, realizing that except for Christmas, this is the main shopping period of the year. Knowing that a strong economic-withdrawal program would be the by-product of direct action, we felt that this would be the best time to bring pressure to bear on the merchants for the needed change.

Then it occurred to us that Birmingham's mayoral election was coming up in March, and we speedily decided to postpone action until after election day. When we discovered that the Commissioner of Public Safety, Eugene "Bull" Connor, had piled up enough votes to be in the runoff, we decided again to postpone action until the day after the run-off so that the demonstrations could not be used to cloud the issues. Like many others, we waited to see Mr. Connor defeated, and to this end we endured postponement after postponement. Having aided in this community need, we felt that our direct-action program could be delayed no longer.

You may well ask: "Why direct action? Why sit-ins, marches and so forth? Isn't negotiation a better path?" You are quite right in calling for negotiation. Indeed, this is the very purpose of direct action. Nonviolent direct action seeks to create such a crisis and foster such a tension that a community which has constantly refused to negotiate is forced to confront the issue. It seeks so to dramatize the issue that it can no longer be ignored. My citing the creation of tension as part of the work of the nonviolent-resister may sound rather shocking. But I must confess that I am not afraid of the word "tension." I have earnestly opposed violent tension, but there is a type of constructive, non-violent tension which is necessary for growth. Just as Socrates felt that it was necessary to create a tension in the mind so that individuals could rise from the bondage of myths and half-truths to the unfettered realm of creative analysis and objective appraisal, so must we see the need for nonviolent gadflies to create the kind of tension in society that will help men rise from the dark depths of prejudice and racism to the majestic heights of understanding and brotherhood.

The purpose of our direct-action program is to create a situation so crisis-packed that it will inevitably open the door to negotiation. I therefore concur with you in your call for negotiation. Too long has our beloved Southland been bogged down in a tragic effort to live in monologue rather than dialogue.

One of the basic points in your statement is that the action that I and my associates have taken in Birmingham is untimely. Some have asked: "Why didn't you give the new city administration time to act?" The only answer that I can give to this query is that the new Birmingham administration must be prodded about as much as the outgoing one, before it will act. We are sadly mistaken if we feel that the election of Albert Boutwell as mayor will bring the millennium to Birmingham. While Mr. Boutwell is a much more gentle person than Mr. Connor, they are both segregationists, dedicated to maintenance of the status quo. I have hope that Mr. Boutwell will be reasonable enough to see the futility of massive resistance to desegregation. But he will not see this without pressure from devotees of civil rights. My friends, I must say to you that we have not made a single gain in civil rights without determined legal and nonviolent pressure. Lamentably, it is an historical fact that privileged groups seldom give up their privileges voluntarily. Individuals may see the moral light and voluntarily give up their unjust posture; but, as Reinhold Niebuhr has reminded us, groups tend to be more immoral than individuals.

We know through painful experience that freedom is never voluntarily given by the oppressor; it must be demanded by the oppressed. Frankly, I have yet to engage in a direct-action campaign that was "well timed" in the view of those who have not suffered unduly from the disease of segregation. For years now I have heard the word "Wait!" It rings in the ear of every Negro with piercing familiarity. This "Wait" has almost always meant "Never." We must come to see, with one of our distinguished jurists, that "justice too long delayed is justice denied."

We have waited for more than 340 years for our constitutional and God-given rights. The nations of Asia and Africa are moving with jetlike speed toward gaining political independence, but we still creep at horse-and-buggy pace toward gaining a cup of coffee at a lunch counter. Perhaps it is easy for those who have never felt the stinging darts of segregation to say, "Wait." But when you have seen vicious mobs lynch your mothers and fathers at will and drown your sisters and brothers at whim; when you have seen hate-filled policemen curse, kick and even kill your black brothers and sisters; when you see the vast majority of your twenty million Negro brothers smothering in an airtight cage of poverty in the midst of an affluent society; when you suddenly find your tongue twisted and your speech stammering as you seek to explain to your six-year-old daughter why she can't go to the public amusement park that has just been advertised on television, and see tears welling up in her eyes when she is told that Funtown is closed to colored children, and see ominous clouds of inferiority beginning to form in her little mental sky, and see her beginning to distort her personality by developing an unconscious bitterness toward white people; when you have to concoct an answer for a five-year-old son who is asking: "Daddy, why do white people treat colored people so mean?"; when you take a cross-country drive and find it necessary to sleep night after night in the uncomfortable corners of your automobile because no motel will accept you; when you are humiliated day in and day out by nagging signs reading "white" and "colored"; when your first name becomes "nigger," your middle name becomes "boy" (however old you are) and your last name becomes "John," and your wife and mother are never given the respected title "Mrs."; when you are harried by day and haunted by night by the fact that you are a Negro, living constantly at tiptoe stance, never quite knowing what to expect next, and are plagued with inner fears and outer resentments; when you are forever fighting a degenerating sense of "nobodiness"—then you will understand why we find it difficult to wait. There comes a time when the cup of endurance runs over, and men are no longer willing to be plunged into the abyss of despair. I hope, sirs, you can understand our legitimate and unavoidable impatience.

You express a great deal of anxiety over our willingness to

break laws. This is certainly a legitimate concern. Since we so diligently urge people to obey the Supreme Court's decision of 1954 outlawing segregation in the public schools, at first glance it may seem rather paradoxical for us consciously to break laws. One may well ask: "How can you advocate breaking some laws and obeying others?" The answer lies in the fact that there are two types of laws: just and unjust. I would be the first to advocate obeying just laws. One has not only a legal but a moral responsibility to obey just laws. Conversely, one has a moral responsibility to disobey unjust laws. I would agree with St. Augustine that "an unjust law is no law at all."

Now, what is the difference between the two? How does one determine whether a law is just or unjust? A just law is a man-made code that squares with the moral law or the law of God. An unjust law is a code that is out of harmony with the moral law. To put it in the terms of St. Thomas Aquinas: An unjust law is a human law that is not rooted in eternal law and natural law. Any law that uplifts human personality is just. Any law that degrades human personality is unjust. All segregation statutes are unjust because segregation distorts the soul and damages the personality. It gives the segregator a false sense of superiority and the segregated a false sense of inferiority. Segregation, to use the terminology of the Jewish philosopher Martin Buber, substitutes an "I–it" relationship for an "I–thou" relationship and ends up relegating persons to the status of things. Hence segregation is not only politically, economically and sociologically unsound, it is morally wrong and sinful. Paul Tillich has said that sin is separation. Is not segregation an existential expression of man's tragic separation, his awful estrangement, his terrible sinfulness? Thus it is that I can urge men to obey the 1954 decision of the Supreme Court, for it is morally right; and I can urge them to disobey segregation ordinances, for they are morally wrong.

Let us consider a more concrete example of just and unjust laws. An unjust law is a code that a numerical or power majority group compels a minority group to obey but does not make binding on itself. This is *difference* made legal. By the same token, a just law is a code that a majority compels a minority to follow and that it is willing to follow itself. This is *sameness* made legal.

Let me give another explanation. A law is unjust if it is inflicted on a minority that, as a result of being denied the right to vote, had no part in enacting or devising the law. Who can say that the legislature of Alabama which set up the state's segregation laws was democratically elected? Throughout Alabama all sorts of devious methods are used to prevent Negroes from becoming registered voters, and there are some counties in which, even though Negroes constitute a majority of the population, not a single Negro is registered. Can any law enacted under such circumstances be considered democratically structured?

Sometimes a law is just on its face and unjust in its application. For instance, I have been arrested on a charge of parading without a permit. Now, there is nothing wrong in having an ordinance which requires a permit for a parade. But such an ordinance becomes unjust when it is used to maintain segregation and to deny citizens the First-Amendment privilege of peaceful assembly and protest.

I hope you are able to see the distinction I am trying to point out. In no sense do I advocate evading or defying the law, as would the rabid segregationist. That would lead to anarchy. One who breaks an unjust law must do so openly, lovingly, and with a willingness to accept the penalty. I submit that an individual who breaks a law that conscience tells him is unjust, and who willingly accepts the penalty of imprisonment in order to arouse the conscience of the community over its injustice, is in reality expressing the highest respect for law.

Of course, there is nothing new about this kind of civil disobedience. It was evidenced sublimely in the refusal of Shadrach, Meshach and Abednego to obey the laws of Nebuchadnezzar, on the ground that a higher moral law was at stake. It was practiced superbly by the early Christians, who were willing to face hungry lions and the excruciating pain of chopping blocks rather than submit to certain unjust laws of the Roman Empire. To a degree, academic freedom is a reality today because Socrates practiced civil disobedience. In our own nation, the Boston Tea Party represented a massive act of civil disobedience.

We should never forget that everything Adolf Hitler did in Germany was "legal" and everything the Hungarian freedom fighters did in Hungary was "illegal." It was "illegal" to aid and comfort a Jew in Hitler's Germany. Even so, I am sure that, had I lived in Germany at the time, I would have aided and comforted my Jewish brothers. If today I lived in a Communist country where certain principles dear to the Christian faith are suppressed, I would openly advocate disobeying that country's antireligious laws.

I must make two honest confessions to you, my Christian and Jewish brothers. First, I must confess that over the past few years I have been gravely disappointed with the white moderate. I have almost reached the regrettable conclusion that the Negro's great stumbling block in his stride toward freedom is not the White Citizen's Counciler or the Ku Klux Klanner, but the white moderate, who is more devoted to "order" than to justice; who prefers a negative peace which is the absence of tension to a positive peace which is the presence of justice; who constantly says: "I agree with you in the goal you seek, but I cannot agree with your methods of direct action"; who paternalistically believes he can set the timetable for another man's freedom; who lives by a mythical concept of time and who constantly advises the Negro to wait for a "more convenient season." Shallow understanding from people of good will is more frustrating than absolute misunderstanding from people of ill will. Lukewarm acceptance is much more bewildering than outright rejection.

I had hoped that the white moderate would understand that law and order exist for the purpose of establishing justice and that when they fail in this purpose they become the dangerously structured dams that block the flow of social progress. I had hoped that the white moderate would understand that the present tension in the South is a necessary phase of the transition from an obnoxious negative peace, in which the Negro passively accepted his unjust plight, to a substantive and positive peace, in which all men will respect the dignity and worth of human personality. Actually, we who engage in nonviolent direct action are not the creators of tension. We merely bring to the surface the hidden tension that is already alive. We bring it out in the open, where it can be seen and dealt with. Like a boil that can never be cured so long as it is covered up but must be opened with all its ugliness to the natural medicines of air and light, injustice must be exposed, with all the tension its exposure creates, to the light of human conscience and the air of national opinion before it can be cured.

In your statement you assert that our actions, even though peaceful, must be condemned because they precipitate violence. But is this a logical assertion? Isn't this like condemning a robbed man because his possession of money precipitated the evil act of robbery? Isn't this like condemning Socrates because his unswerving commitment to truth and his philosophical inquiries precipitated the act by the misguided populace in which they made him drink hemlock? Isn't this like condemning Jesus because his unique God-consciousness and never-ceasing devotion to God's will precipitated the evil act of crucifixion? We must come to see that, as the federal courts have consistently affirmed, it is wrong to urge an individual to cease his efforts to gain his basic constitutional rights because the quest may precipitate violence. Society must protect the robbed and punish the robber.

I had also hoped that the white moderate would reject the myth concerning time in relation to the struggle for freedom. I have received a letter from a white brother in Texas. He writes: "All Christians know that the colored people will receive equal rights eventually, but it is possible that you are in too great a religious hurry. It has taken Christianity almost two thousand years to accomplish what it has. The teachings of Christ take time to come to earth." Such an attitude stems from a tragic misconception of time, from the strangely irrational notion that there is something in the very flow of time that will inevitably cure all ills. Actually, time itself is neutral; it can be used either destructively or constructively. More and more I feel that the people of ill will have used time much more effectively than have the people of good will. We will have to repent in this generation not merely for the hateful words and actions of the bad people but for the appalling silence of the good people. Human progress never rolls in on wheels of inevitability; it comes through the tireless efforts of men willing to be co-workers with God, and without this hard work, time itself becomes an ally of the forces of social stagnation. We must use time creatively, in the knowledge that the time is always ripe to do right. Now is the time to make real the promise of democracy and transform our pending national elegy into a creative psalm of brotherhood. Now is the time to lift our national policy from the quicksand of racial injustice to the solid rock of human dignity.

You speak of our activity in Birmingham as extreme. At first I was rather disappointed that fellow clergymen would see my nonviolent efforts as those of an extremist. I began thinking about the fact that I stand in the middle of two opposing forces in the Negro community. One is a force of complacency, made up in part of Negroes who, as a result of long years of oppression, are so drained of self-respect and a sense of "somebodiness" that they have adjusted to segregation; and in part of a few middle-class Negroes who, because of a degree of academic and economic security and because in some ways they profit by segregation, have become insensitive to the problems of the masses. The other force is one of bitterness and hatred, and it comes perilously close to advocating violence. It is expressed in the various black nationalist groups that are springing up across the nation, the largest and best-known being Elijah Muhammad's Muslim movement. Nourished by the Negro's frustration over the continued existence of racial discrimination, this movement is made up of people who have lost faith in America, who have absolutely repudiated Christianity, and who have concluded that the white man is an incorrigible "devil."

I have tried to stand between these two forces, saying that we need emulate neither the "do-nothingism" of the complacent nor the hatred and despair of the black nationalist. For there is the more excellent way of love and non-violent protest. I am grateful to God that, through the influence of the Negro church, the way of nonviolence became an integral part of our struggle.

184

If this philosophy had not emerged, by now many streets of the South would, I am convinced, be flowing with blood. And I am further convinced that if our white brothers dismiss as "rabble-rousers" and "outside agitators" those of us who employ non-violent direct action, and if they refuse to support our nonviolent efforts, millions of Negroes will, out of frustration and despair, seek solace and security in black-nationalist ideologies—a development that would inevitably lead to a frightening racial nightmare.

Oppressed people cannot remain oppressed forever. The yearning for freedom eventually manifests itself, and that is what has happened to the American Negro. Something within has reminded him of his birthright of freedom, and something without has reminded him that it can be gained. Consciously or unconsciously, he has been caught up by the *Zeitgeist,* and with his black brothers of Africa and his brown and yellow brothers of Asia, South America and the Caribbean, the United States Negro is moving with a sense of great urgency toward the promised land of racial justice. If one recognizes this vital urge that has engulfed the Negro community, one should readily understand why public demonstrations are taking place. The Negro has many pent-up resentments and latent frustrations, and he must release them. So let him march; let him make prayer pilgrimages to the city hall; let him go on freedom rides—and try to understand why he must do so. If his repressed emotions are not released in nonviolent ways, they will seek expression through violence; this is not a threat but a fact of history. So I have not said to my people: "Get rid of your discontent." Rather, I have tried to say that this normal and healthy discontent can be channeled into the creative outlet of nonviolent direct action. And now this approach is being termed extremist.

But though I was initially disappointed at being categorized as an extremist, as I continued to think about the matter I gradually gained a measure of satisfaction from the label. Was not Jesus an extremist for love: "Love your enemies, bless them that curse you, do good to them that hate you, and pray for them which despitefully use you, and persecute you." Was not

Amos an extremist for justice: "Let justice roll down like waters and righteousness like an ever-flowing stream." Was not Paul an extremist for the Christian gospel: "I bear in my body the marks of the Lord Jesus." Was not Martin Luther an extremist: "Here I stand; I cannot do otherwise, so help me God." And John Bunyan: "I will stay in jail to the end of my days before I make a butchery of my conscience." And Abraham Lincoln: "This nation cannot survive half slave and half free." And Thomas Jefferson: "We hold these truths to be self-evident, that all men are created equal . . ." So the question is not whether we will be extremists, but what kind of extremists we will be. Will we be extremists for hate or for love? Will we be extremists for the preservation of injustice or for the extension of justice? In that dramatic scene on Calvary's hill three men were crucified. We must never forget that all three were crucified for the same crime—the crime of extremism. Two were extremists for immorality, and thus fell below their environment. The other, Jesus Christ, was an extremist for love, truth and goodness, and thereby rose above his environment. Perhaps the South, the nation and the world are in dire need of creative extremists.

I had hoped that the white moderate would see this need. Perhaps I was too optimistic; perhaps I expected too much. I suppose I should have realized that few members of the oppressor race can understand the deep groans and passionate yearnings of the oppressed race, and still fewer have the vision to see that injustice must be rooted out by strong, persistent and determined action. I am thankful, however, that some of our white brothers in the South have grasped the meaning of this social revolution and committed themselves to it. They are still all too few in quantity, but they are big in quality. Some—such as Ralph McGill, Lillian Smith, Harry Golden, James McBride Dabbs, Ann Braden and Sarah Patton Boyle—have written about our struggle in eloquent and prophetic terms. Others have marched with us down nameless streets of the South. They have languished in filthy, roach-infested jails, suffering the abuse and brutality of policemen who view them as "dirty nigger-lovers." Unlike so many of their moderate brothers and sisters, they have recognized the urgency of the moment and sensed the need for powerful "action" antidotes to combat the disease of segregation.

Let me take note of my other major disappointment. I have been so greatly disappointed with the white church and its leadership. Of course, there are some notable exceptions. I am not unmindful of the fact that each of you has taken some significant stands on this issue. I commend you, Reverend Stallings, for your Christian stand on this past Sunday, in welcoming Negroes to your worship service on a nonsegregated basis. I commend the Catholic leaders of this state for integrating Spring Hill College several years ago.

But despite these notable exceptions, I must honestly reiterate that I have been disappointed with the church. I do not say this as one of those negative critics who can always find something wrong with the church. I say this as a minister of the gospel, who loves the church; who was nurtured in its bosom; who has been sustained by its spiritual blessings and who will remain true to it as long as the cord of life shall lengthen.

When I was suddenly catapulted into the leadership of the bus protest in Montgomery, Alabama, a few years ago, I felt we would be supported by the white church. I felt that the white ministers, priests and rabbis of the South would be among our strongest allies. Instead, some have been outright opponents, refusing to understand the freedom movement and misrepresenting its leaders; all too many others have been more cautious than courageous and have remained silent behind the anesthetizing security of stained-glass windows.

In spite of my shattered dreams, I came to Birmingham with the hope that the white religious leadership of this community would see the justice of our cause and, with deep moral concern, would serve as the channel through which our just grievances could reach the power structure. I had hoped that each of you would understand. But again I have been disappointed.

I have heard numerous southern religious leaders admonish their worshipers to comply with a desegregation decision because it is the law, but I have longed to hear white ministers declare: "Follow this decree because integration is morally right and because the Negro is your brother." In the midst of blatant injustices inflicted upon the Negro, I have watched white churchmen stand on the sideline and mouth pious irrelevancies and sanctimonious trivialities. In the midst of a mighty struggle to rid our nation of racial and economic injustice, I have heard many ministers say: "Those are social issues, with which the gospel has no real concern." And I have watched many churches commit themselves to a completely otherworldly religion which makes a strange, un-Biblical distinction between body and soul, between the sacred and the secular.

I have traveled the length and breadth of Alabama, Mississippi and all the other southern states. On sweltering summer days and crisp autumn mornings I have looked at the South's beautiful churches with their lofty spires pointing heavenward. I have beheld the impressive outlines of her massive religious-education buildings. Over and over I have found myself asking: "What kind of people worship here? Who is their God? Where were their voices when the lips of Governor Barnett dripped with words of interposition and nullification? Where were they when Governor Wallace gave a clarion call for defiance and hatred? Where were their voices of support when bruised and weary Negro men and women decided to rise from the dark dungeons of complacency to the bright hills of creative protest?"

Yes, these questions are still in my mind. In deep disappointment I have wept over the laxity of the church. But be assured that my tears have been tears of love. There can be no deep disappointment where there is not deep love. Yes, I love the church. How could I do otherwise? I am in the rather unique position of being the son, the grandson and the great-grandson of preachers. Yes, I see the church as the body of Christ. But, oh! How we have blemished and scarred that body through social neglect and through fear of being nonconformists.

There was a time when the church was very powerful—in the time when the early Christians rejoiced at being deemed worthy to suffer for what they believed. In those days the church was not merely a thermometer that recorded the ideas and principles of popular opinion; it was a thermostat that transformed the mores of society. Whenever the early Christians entered a town, the people in power became disturbed and immediately sought to convict the Christians for being "disturbers of the peace" and "outside agitators." But the Christians pressed on, in the conviction that they were "a colony of heaven," called to obey God rather than man. Small in number, they were big in commitment. They were too God-intoxicated to be "astronomically intimidated." By their effort and example they brought an end to such ancient evils as infanticide and gladiatorial contests.

Things are different now. So often the contemporary church is a weak, ineffectual voice with an uncertain sound. So often it is an arch defender of the status quo. Far from being disturbed by the presence of the church, the power structure of the average community is consoled by the church's silent—and often even vocal—sanction of things as they are.

But the judgment of God is upon the church as never before. If today's church does not recapture the sacrificial spirit of the early church, it will lose its authenticity, forfeit the loyalty of millions, and be dismissed as an irrelevant social club with no meaning for the twentieth century. Every day I meet young people whose disappointment with the church has turned into outright disgust.

Perhaps I have once again been too optimistic. Is organized religion too inextricably bound to the status quo to save our nation and the world? Perhaps I must turn my faith to the inner spiritual church, the church within the church, as the true *ekklesia* and the hope of the world. But again I am thankful to God that some noble souls from the ranks of organized religion have broken loose from the paralyzing chains of conformity and joined us as active partners in the struggle for freedom. They have left their secure congregations and walked the streets of Albany, Georgia, with us. They have gone down the highways of the South on tortuous rides for freedom. Yes, they have gone to jail with us. Some have been dismissed from their churches, have lost the support of their bishops and fellow ministers. But they have acted in the faith that right defeated is stronger than evil triumphant. Their witness has been the spiritual salt that has preserved the true meaning of the gospel in these troubled times. They have carved a tunnel of hope through the dark mountain of disappointment.

I hope the church as a whole will meet the challenge of this decisive hour. But even if the church does not come to the aid of justice, I have no despair about the future. I have no fear about the outcome of our struggle in Birmingham, even if our motives are at present misunderstood. We will reach the goal of freedom in Birmingham and all over the nation, because the goal of America is freedom. Abused and scorned though we may be, our destiny is tied up with America's destiny. Before the pilgrims landed at Plymouth, we were here. Before the pen of Jefferson etched the majestic words of the Declaration of Independence across the pages of history, we were here. For more than two centuries our forebears labored in this country without wages; they made cotton king; they built the homes of their masters while suffering gross injustice and shameful humiliation —and yet out of a bottomless vitality they continued to thrive and develop. If the inexpressible cruelties of slavery could not stop us, the opposition we now face will surely fail. We will win our freedom because the sacred heritage of our nation and the eternal will of God are embodied in our echoing demands.

Before closing I feel impelled to mention one other point in your statement that has troubled me profoundly. You warmly commended the Birmingham police force for keeping "order" and "preventing violence." I doubt that you would have so warmly commended the police force if you had seen its dogs sinking their teeth into unarmed, nonviolent Negroes. I doubt that you would so quickly commend the policemen if you were to observe their ugly and inhumane treatment of Negroes here in the city jail; if you were to watch them push and curse old Negro women and young Negro girls; if you were to see them slap and kick old Negro men and young boys; if you were to observe them, as they did on two occasions, refuse to give us food because we wanted to sing our grace together. I cannot join you in your praise of the Birmingham police department.

It is true that the police have exercised a degree of discipline in handling the demonstrators. In this sense they have conducted themselves rather "nonviolently" in public. But for what purpose? To preserve the evil system of segregation. Over the past few years I have consistently preached that nonviolence demands that the means we use must be as pure as the ends we seek. I have tried to make clear that it is wrong to use immoral means to attain moral ends. But now I must affirm that it is just as wrong, or perhaps even more so, to use moral means to preserve immoral ends. Perhaps Mr. Connor and his policemen have been rather nonviolent in public, as was Chief Pritchett in Albany, Georgia, but they have used the moral means of nonviolence to maintain the immoral end of racial injustice. As T. S. Eliot has said: "The last temptation is the greatest treason: To do the right deed for the wrong reason."

I wish you had commended the Negro sit-inners and demonstrators of Birmingham for their sublime courage, their willingness to suffer and their amazing discipline in the midst of great provocation. One day the South will recognize its real heroes. They will be the James Merediths, with the noble sense of purpose that enables them to face jeering and hostile mobs, and with the agonizing loneliness that characterizes the life of the pioneer. They will be old, oppressed, battered Negro women, symbolized in a seventy-two-year-old woman in Montgomery, Alabama, who rose up with a sense of dignity and with her people decided not to ride segregated buses, and who responded with ungrammatical profundity to one who inquired about her weariness: "My feets is tired, but my soul is at rest." They will be the young high school and college students, the young ministers of the gospel and a host of their elders, courageously and nonviolently sitting in at lunch counters and willingly going to jail for conscience' sake. One day the South will know that when these disinherited children of God sat down at lunch counters, they were in reality standing up for what is best in the American dream and for the most sacred values in our Judaeo-Christian heritage, thereby bringing our nation back to those great wells

191

of democracy which were dug deep by the founding fathers in their formulation of the Constitution and the Declaration of Independence.

Never before have I written so long a letter. I'm afraid it is much too long to take your precious time. I can assure you that it would have been much shorter if I had been writing from a comfortable desk, but what else can one do when he is alone in a narrow jail cell, other than write long letters, think long thoughts and pray long prayers?

If I have said anything in this letter that overstates the truth and indicates an unreasonable impatience, I beg you to forgive me. If I have said anything that understates the truth and indicates my having a patience that allows me to settle for anything less than brotherhood, I beg God to forgive me.

I hope this letter finds you strong in the faith. I also hope that circumstances will soon make it possible for me to meet each of you, not as an integrationist or a civil-rights leader but as a fellow clergyman and a Christian brother. Let us all hope that the dark clouds of racial prejudice will soon pass away and the deep fog of misunderstanding will be lifted from our fear-drenched communities, and in some not too distant tomorrow the radiant stars of love and brotherhood will shine over our great nation with all their scintillating beauty.

Yours for the cause of Peace and Brotherhood,

MARTIN LUTHER KING, JR.

ROBERT F. WILLIAMS

From *Negroes with Guns*

FROM EXILE

Why do I speak to you from exile?

Because a Negro community in the South took up guns in self-defense against racist violence—and used them. I am held responsible for this action, that for the first time in history American Negroes have armed themselves as a group, to defend their homes, their wives, their children, in a situation where law and order had broken down, where the authorities could not, or rather would not, enforce their duty to protect Americans from a lawless mob. I accept this responsibility and am proud of it. I have asserted the right of Negroes to meet the violence of the Ku Klux Klan by armed self-defense—and have acted on it. It has always been an accepted right of Americans, as the history of our Western states proves, that where the law is unable, or unwilling, to enforce order, the citizens can, and must, act in self-defense against lawless violence. I believe this right holds for black Americans as well as whites.

Many people will remember that in the summer of 1957 the Ku Klux Klan made an armed raid on an Indian community in the South and were met with determined rifle fire from the Indians acting in self-defense. The nation approved of the action and there were widespread expressions of pleasure at the defeat of the Kluxers, who showed their courage by running away despite their armed superiority. What the nation doesn't know, because it has never been told, is that the Negro community in Monroe, North Carolina, had set the example two weeks before when we shot up an armed motorcade of the Ku Klux Klan, including two police cars, which had come to attack the home of Dr. Albert E. Perry, vice-president of the Monroe chapter of the National Association for the Advancement of Colored People. The stand taken by our chapter resulted in the official re-affirmation by the NAACP of the right of self-defense. The Preamble to the resolution of the 50th Convention of the NAACP, New York City, July 1959, states: ". . . we do not deny, but reaffirm, the right of an individual and collective self-defense against unlawful assaults."

Because there has been much distortion of my position, I wish to make it clear that I do not advocate violence for its own sake, or for the sake of reprisals against whites. Nor am I against the passive resistance advocated by the Reverend Martin Luther King and others. My only difference with Dr. King is that I believe in flexibility in the freedom struggle. This means that I believe in non-violent tactics where feasible and the mere fact that I have a Sit-In case pending before the U.S. Supreme Court bears this out. Massive civil disobedience is a powerful weapon under civilized conditions, where the law safeguards the citizens' right of peaceful demonstrations. In civilized society the law serves as a deterrent against lawless forces that would destroy the democratic process. But where there is a breakdown of the law, the individual citizen has a right to protect his person, his family, his home and his property. To me this is so simple and proper that it is self-evident.

When an oppressed people show a willingness to defend themselves, the enemy, who is a moral weakling and coward is more willing to grant concessions and work for a respectable compromise. Psychologically, moreover, racists consider themselves superior beings and they are not willing to exchange their superior

194

lives for our inferior ones. They are most vicious and violent when they can practice violence with impunity. This we have shown in Monroe. Moreover, when because of our self-defense there is a danger that the blood of whites may be spilled, the local authorities in the South suddenly enforce law and order when previously they had been complaisant toward lawless, racist violence. This too we have proven in Monroe. It is remarkable how easily and quickly state and local police control and disperse lawless mobs when the Negro is ready to defend himself with arms.

Furthermore, because of the international situation, the Federal Government does not want racial incidents which draw the attention of the world to the situation in the South. Negro self-defense draws such attention, and the Federal Government will be more willing to enforce law and order if the local authorities don't. When our people become fighters, our leaders will be able to sit at the conference table as equals, not dependent on the whim and the generosity of the oppressors. It will be to the best interests of both sides to negotiate just, honorable and lasting settlements.

The majority of white people in the United States have literally no idea of the violence with which Negroes in the South are treated daily—nay, hourly. This violence is deliberate, conscious, condoned by the authorities. It has gone on for centuries and is going on today, every day, unceasing and unremitting. It is our way of life. Negro existence in the South has been one long travail, steeped in terror and blood—our blood. The incidents which took place in Monroe, which I witnessed and which I suffered, will give some idea of the conditions in the South, such conditions that can no longer be borne. That is why, one hundred years after the Civil War began, we Negroes in Monroe armed ourselves in self-defense and used our weapons. We showed that our policy worked. The lawful authorities of Monroe and North Carolina acted to enforce order only after, and as a direct result of, our being armed. Previously they had connived with the Ku Klux Klan in the racist violence against our people. Self-

Robert F. Williams

defense prevented bloodshed and forced the law to establish order. This is the meaning of Monroe and I believe it marks a historic change in the life of my people.

From *U.S.A.: The Potential of a Minority Revolution*

This selection was included in the May–June 1964 issue of Crusader Monthly Newsletter, *edited and published by Mr. Williams in Cuba.*

It is a universally known fact that the power structure of the racist USA is rabidly opposed to self-defense on the part of our oppressed people. They have a morbid fear of violent self-preservation on the part of U.S. freedom fighters. Is this because they love the dehumanized Negro? Is this because they are concerned with the welfare and well-being of our brutalized people? Is this because the American society is a pacifist society with an aversion for violence? No! A thousand times No! If the power structure had ever manifested any true concern for the welfare of our people (for whom it now professes great fear that we may commit suicide by fighting for the right to live as human beings) there would be no question of a violent liberation struggle. The question of peaceful persuasion, as a moral issue, is belied by its imperialist military actions against Cuba, South Vietnam, Cambodia, Laos and other liberated areas. Why is such a belligerently imperialist government not concerned about black Americans, and whites as well, being exterminated in a nuclear war? Was it not Kennedy, as the very head of the U.S. Government and white so-called liberal society, who said, ". . . We will live up to our commitments even if victory turns to ashes in our mouths?" Where were the panic preachers then, who express such great concern and alarm for the possibility of black Americans being exterminated in violently resisting racial oppression? Is not a black American just as dead when killed in an international war of conquest as in a national struggle for liberation?

Why are the liberals, Uncle Toms and the power structure so hysterical about the possibility of massive violence erupting on the national human rights scene?

The fact is that the racist oppressors of the Afroamerican realize the insecurity and vulnerability of the most powerful military complex in the world to a violent internal struggle, wherein its horrible and sophisticated weapons of war will be ineffective. The internal defense of the U.S. is a possibility that money cannot buy. Only a change in the moral and social structure of the system offers security against an enraged oppressed citizenry. The USA is either unwilling or morally incapable of bearing the cost of this type of internal security. The race question is her Achilles heel, her Maginot line.

The power structure, the liberals and Uncle Toms are in essence asking Afroamericans to cooperate with the very forces that are opposing them. How can oppressed people who seek liberation, afford to allow the enemy to dictate the method of struggle? How can a people, who are dead serious about their freedom, allow themselves to be duped into limiting themselves to the most ineffective method of struggle? It is not logical to accommodate the will of the oppressor, who has a vested interest in maintaining the status quo, and to wage a successful liberation struggle simultaneously.

The fact is that racist white America is not worried about the possibility of Negroes being exterminated. It is more worried about the loss of its privileged position in its racist caste society; its system of white supremacy and world domination. . . .

Is it possible for a minority revolution to succeed in powerful America? The cynics, prophets of doom, and agents of the oppressive establishment maintain that to even raise such a question is insane. They energetically, with a clairvoyant air, assure us that violent self-defense or violent resistance to brutal racial oppression can lead only to suicide. How do they know? What is the basis of their logic? Are they any wiser than those cynics who brazenly stated that "man will never fly," that "it is impossible to cross the oceans," that "man can never reach the speed of a mile a minute and survive," and that "the American Revolution can never succeed against the military might of the Crown?" How do they know that violent resistance on the part of our people will lead to suicide? Yes, they have been conditioned to accept America's racist tyranny as a condition bound to prevail until the tyrant himself elects to abandon the throne of tyranny. They are more than resigned to the premise that white supremacy might is the God of the fate and destiny of oppressed black humanity.

Yes, a minority revolution has as much, or more, chance of succeeding in the racist USA as any place else in the world. At the very outset, all revolutions are minority revolutions. In the early stages cynics think that all revolutions have a very remote chance of succeeding. Revolutionaries display a propensity to accomplish the impossible. Is the Afroamerican revolution to be an exception? Do we subscribe to the premise of white supremacy? Is it because the oppressor is white and the oppressed is black that most of the world accepts the premise that our struggle must be white-led and supported by the majority race or that it is insignificant and doomed to failure?

The fact of the matter is that the Afroamerican wants and has been seeking brotherhood with the white masses since his enslavement in the New World. A people as brutally oppressed as American Negroes cannot wait forever for the support of mythological and theoretical allies. Most white workers in the USA today have a vested interest in the status quo. The present system grants them special privileges in a jungle society. The cow of production may be lean and diseased but the Negro is the only herdsman limited to the cutlets of feet and tail. The vast majority of the whites have also been mentally poisoned with racism. It is asinine to expect them to recover from their race psychosis without a severe shock treatment.

The American society is a highly industrialized complex. A highly industrialized and mechanized system is also a very sensitive one. The more machinery required to serve a community, the greater the incidence of mechanical breakdown. The more dependent a community is on mechanization, the more important it is for the wheels of industry to perpetually turn smoothly.

Social systems, like biological systems, tend to adjust to environmental conditions and requirements. The American society, over a long period of time, has adjusted itself to a high rate of productivity directly bearing on the relativity of consumption.

The physical conditioning of a society also manifests certain relative psychological traits. The American mind has been conditioned to think of great calamities, wars and revolutionary upheavals as taking place on distant soil. Because of the vast upper and middle classes in the USA, that have grown accustomed to comfortable living, the nation is not psychologically prepared for massive violence and a sudden disruption of the essential agencies of the affluent society. The soft society is highly susceptible to panic.

Afroamericans have long sought a peaceful solution to the race question. It is more than obvious that a people, who have manifested an unshakable faith in the vain hope that the government would eventually grant citizenship and justice, prefers a peaceful solution. Our people have dreamed and prayed for a peaceful transition from slavery to first class citizenship and human dignity. Peaceful evolution, through the mediums of legislation, law and negotiation are the methods that have been pursued for almost 200 years under the present government. The results are bitter and frustrating indeed. The orderly social process has been stymied by savage violence and brute force.

Instead of the majority race extending brotherhood and justice, it has resorted to a campaign of a massive drive aimed at extermination. The fascist elements are arming, not to liberate our brutally oppressed people but to liquidate us. It is becoming next to impossible for Negroes to conduct a "peaceful" demonstration in America. A Civil Rights Bill will have no more effect than the U.S. Constitution. What is integration when the law says yes, but the police and howling mobs say no? Our only logical and successful answer is to meet organized and massive violence with massive and organized violence. Our people must prepare to wage an urban guerrilla war of self-defense. Self-defense develops to the stage wherein the source of evil and terror must be eliminated. . . .

Robert F. Williams

Afroamericans must remember that such a campaign of massive self-defense should not be based upon a lust for sadistical gratification. It cannot be a campaign for vengeance, however sweet and deserving vengeance may be. Such a campaign of self-defense and survival must be based on the righteous cause of justice. It must not be anti-white but anti-oppression and injustice. Uncle Toms should be as much a target as racist whites.

Like it or not, we cannot escape the trend of history. The hour is fast approaching when our people must make a decision to meekly submit to fascist forces of terror and extermination or surge forth to the battle to liberate ourselves, save America and liquidate its domestic enemies. If we truly seek freedom and human dignity we must be willing to pay for it in the fashion of the Algerians. Great multitudes of our people must be willing to fight and die in America's true cause and commitment to her Constitution, democratic principles and the rights of man, and for a victory that will not ". . . turn to ashes in our mouths," but to eternal freedom and happiness in our hearts. Such a victory would truly make the world safe for democracy. It would secure the world from extermination by hydrogen war. Not only is America's peace and security involved but also the peace and security of the whole world.

The horrible nightmare of massive violence need not fall upon the American scene. It can be staved off by the birth of a sincere spirit of humanity, dedicated to the proposition of brotherhood, peace and security.

When a brutally oppressed and dehumanized people are denied the peaceful channels through which to activate redress, and when their peaceful petitions are answered with ruthless violence, the only recourse left to them is to meet violence with violence.

We do not advocate the violent overthrow of the U.S. Government. We merely advocate self-defense for brutalized Afroamericans. If in the process of executing our Constitutional and God-given right of self-defense, the racist U.S. Government, which refuses to protect our people, is destroyed, the end result stems from certain historical factors of social relativity.

". . . This country, with its institutions, belongs to the people

200

who inhabit it. Whenever they shall grow weary of the existing government they can exercise their Constitutional right of amending it, or their revolutionary right to dismember or overthrow it. . . . If by the mere force of numbers a majority should deprive a minority of any clearly written Constitutional right, it might, in any moral point of view, justify revolution . . . ," Abraham Lincoln, 1861.

The oppressor's heart is hard. The experience of history teaches that he only relents under violent pressure and force. There is very little hope that he will see the handwriting on the wall before it is too late. This year, 1964 is going to be a violent one, the storm will reach hurricane proportions by 1965 and the eye of the hurricane will hover over America by 1966. America is a house on fire—FREEDOM NOW!—or let it burn, let it burn. Praise the Lord and pass the ammunition!!!

LEROI JONES

From *Home*

COLD, HURT, AND SORROW
(Streets of Despair)

These streets stretch from one end of America to the other and connect like a maze from which very few can fully escape. Despair sits on this country in most places like a charm, but there is a special gray death that loiters in the streets of an urban Negro slum. And the men who walk those streets, tracing and retracing their steps to some hopeless job or a pitiful rooming house or apartment or furnished room, sometimes stagger under the weight of that gray, humiliated because it is not even "real."

Sometimes walking along among the ruined shacks and lives of the worst Harlem slum, there is a feeling that just around the next corner you'll find yourself in South Chicago or South Philadelphia, maybe even Newark's Third Ward. In these places life, and its possibility, has been distorted almost identically. And the distortion is as old as its sources: the fear, frustration, and hatred that Negroes have always been heir to in America. It is just that in the cities, which were once the black man's twentieth century "Jordan," *promise* is a dying bitch with rotting eyes. And the stink of her dying is a deadly killing fume.

The blues singers know all this. They knew before they got

to the cities. "I'd rather drink muddy water, sleep in a hollow log, than be in New York City treated like a dirty dog." And when they arrived, in those various cities, it was much worse than even they had imagined. The city blues singers are still running all that down. Specifically, it's what a man once named for me unnatural adversity. It is social, it is economic, it is cultural and historical. Some of its products are emotional and psychological; some are even artistic, as if Negroes suffered better than anyone else. But it's hard enough to be a human being under any circumstances, but when there is an entire civilization determined to stop you from being one, things get a little more desperately complicated. What do you do then?

You can stand in doorways late nights and hit people in the head. You can go to church Saturday nights and Sundays and three or four times during the week. You can stick a needle in your arm four or five times a day, and bolster the economy. You can buy charms and herbs and roots, or wear your hat backwards to keep things from getting worse. You can drink till screaming is not loud enough, and the coldest night is all right to sleep outside in. You can buy a big car . . . if the deal goes down. There's so much, then, you can do, to yourself, or to somebody else. Another man sings, "I'm drinkin' t.n.t., I'm smokin' dynamite, I hope some screwball starts a fight."

One can never talk about Harlem in purely social terms, though there are ghetto facts that make any honest man shudder. It is the tone, the quality of suffering each man knows as his own that finally must be important, but this is the most difficult thing to get to. (There are about twenty young people from one small Southern town, all friends, all living within the same few blocks of the black city, all of whom are junkies, communally hooked. What kind of statistic is *that?* And what can you say when you read it?)

The old folks kept singing, there will be a better day . . . or, the sun's gonna shine in my back door some day . . . or, I've had my fun if I don't get well no more. What did they want? What would that sun turn out to be?

203

LeRoi Jones

Hope is a delicate suffering. Its waste products vary, but most of them are meaningful. And as a cat named Mean William once said, can you be glad, if you've never been sad?

STREET PROTEST

There have been black men trying to get other black men to protest and rise against the weight of America's oppression since those first clipper ships bringing them in in chains. There have been black men willing even to die, and not for an abstract freedom they teach you in grammar school which belongs largely to dead patriots masquerading as Indians, but for the simple need to say exactly what they think, and explain exactly what they think America is. But any black American who ever tried to say something factual about the black man's life in America, even in the uncomplicated circumstance of slavery, was either killed or, as the slave ship grew more sophisticated and gave a few Negroes radios or air conditioning in the hold, driven crazy or driven away for daring to protest.

But to a large extent America convinced itself that the black man didn't mind being a slave. (You remember those grinning woogies strumming on the cotton bales? The happy-go-lucky image of Harlem is an extension of this.) Although the records of slave revolts are too numerous to support such a faked conclusion, and men like Caesar, Gabriel, Denmark Vesey, Nat Turner, and so many others were not killed for strumming banjos.

Before the Negro came North at the beginning of the century there was not much room for any protest except one that would have to begin at violence. But the North offered at least a little more room to swing, buoyed up as it was, and is, by a kindly Liberal/Missionary syndrome that will let you say almost anything you want, as long as you don't threaten to *do* anything. (The missionary types would tell the more repressive Americans, "Such protest is good for business.")

But ever since the early years of this century there have been a great many formal Negro protest groups thriving in the North:

not only the large, more respectable groups like the NAACP, but the quickly organized and usually quickly disbanded protest groups, who have no clearly outlined "program" and of course no wealthy supporters and therefore very little influence—except that they represent all the people with no influence.

Some men take it upon themselves, even alone, to make some noise about the filth they see. In Harlem such men are easy to hear; their persistence makes them available. They don't even need a soapbox and an American flag, or a place on the stand in front of Michaux's House Of Proper Propaganda on Seventh Avenue just above 125th Street. They just stand out somewhere and talk loud, and a few people stand and listen.

At an NAACP-Church rally recently, in front of the Hotel Theresa, where the large, money-financed, more organized "protests" take place, a single speaker took up a stand directly across the street from the main rally and tried to shout the electronic equipment down with a rolled-up magazine. There were about one hundred cops watching the main rally and about two watching the loner.

There are some protest speakers who wear African robes and sandals, and study African history. And now, as Africa rises, there are some who speak of "teaching the children about their heritage," though they ought to know also that that heritage is one that is cruelly local.

Since the twenties there have been all kinds of local betterment leaders and social prophets in Harlem. Marcus Garvey was both, and even before he began his Back To Africa movement and the Universal Negro Improvement Association, he was shouting at people on Lenox Avenue to get themselves together and get the white man off their backs. The sentiment is still strong in Harlem, and leaflets and speakers urging Negroes to "Buy Black" are still ubiquitous. And now, young clean-headed, clean-suited boys wave their copies of *Muhammad Speaks,* spreading the word of Elijah Muhammad and Malcolm X.

Any weekend will find some speakers out, singly or encouraged —especially if the weather's good. There is always a picket line getting ready to form or a neophyte protest group, and there are always reasons why they should form. There are even some speakers with personal uniforms to specify their utopias. But an open and very public understanding of what all these protests are about has come to Harlem, just as it has come to Negroes throughout the rest of the country, whose local Harlems are equally impossible, equally repressive. In many cases, the men on the platforms are just repeating what they hear. From people's mouths, and people's horns.

STOKELY CARMICHAEL
and CHARLES V. HAMILTON

From *Black Power*

"FIRST CLOSE RANKS"

The adoption of the concept of Black Power is one of the most legitimate and healthy developments in American politics and race relations in our time. The concept of Black Power speaks to all the needs mentioned in this chapter. It is a call for black people in this country to unite, to recognize their heritage, to build a sense of community. It is a call for black people to begin to define their own goals, to lead their own organizations and to support those organizations. It is a call to reject the racist institutions and values of this society.

The concept of Black Power rests on a fundamental premise: *Before a group can enter the open society, it must first close ranks.* By this we mean that group solidarity is necessary before a group can operate effectively from a bargaining position of strength in a pluralistic society. Traditionally, each new ethnic group in this society has found the route to social and political viability through the organization of its own institutions with which to represent its needs within the larger society. Studies in voting behavior specifically, and political behavior generally, have made it clear that politically the American pot has not melted. Italians vote for Rubino over O'Brien; Irish for Murphy over Goldberg, etc. This phenomenon may seem distasteful to

207

some, but it has been and remains today a central fact of the American political system.

"BLACK PEOPLE MUST LEAD"

The point is obvious: black people must lead and run their own organizations. Only black people can convey the revolutionary idea—and it is a revolutionary idea—that black people are able to do things themselves. Only they can help create in the community an aroused and continuing black consciousness that will provide the basis for political strength. In the past, white allies have often furthered white supremacy without the whites involved realizing it, or even wanting to do so. Black people must come together and do things for themselves. They must achieve self-identity and self-determination in order to have their daily needs met.

Black Power means, for example, that in Lowndes County, Alabama, a black sheriff can end police brutality. A black tax assessor and tax collector and county board of revenue can lay, collect, and channel tax monies for the building of better roads and schools serving black people. In such areas as Lowndes, where black people have a majority, they will attempt to use power to exercise control. This is what they seek: control. When black people lack a majority, Black Power means proper representation and sharing of control. It means the creation of power bases, of strength, from which black people can press to change local or nation-wide patterns of oppression—instead of from weakness.

It does not mean *merely* putting black faces into office. Black visibility is not Black Power. Most of the black politicians around the country today are not examples of Black Power. The power must be that of a community, and emanate from there. The black politicians must start from there. The black politicians must stop being representatives of "downtown" machines, whatever the cost might be in terms of lost patronage and holiday handouts.

Black Power recognizes—it must recognize—the ethnic basis of American politics as well as the power-oriented nature of American politics. Black Power therefore calls for black people to consolidate behind their own, so that they can bargain from a position of strength. But while we endorse the *procedure* of group solidarity and identity for the purpose of attaining certain goals in the body politic, this does not mean that black people should strive for the same kind of rewards (i.e., end results) obtained by the white society. The ultimate values and goals are not domination or exploitation of other groups, but rather an effective share in the total power of the society.

Nevertheless, some observers have labeled those who advocate Black Power as racists; they have said that the call for self-identification and self-determination is "racism in reverse" or "black supremacy." This is a deliberate and absurd lie. There is no analogy—by any stretch of definition of imagination—between the advocates of Black Power and white racists. Racism is not merely exclusion on the basis of race but exclusion for the purpose of subjugating or maintaining subjugation. The goal of the racists is to keep black people on the bottom, arbitrarily and dictatorially, as they have done in this country for over three hundred years. The goal of black self-determination and black self-identity—Black Power—is full participation in the decision-making processes affecting the lives of black people, and recognition of the virtues in themselves as black people. The black people of this country have not lynched whites, bombed their churches, murdered their children and manipulated laws and institutions to maintain oppression. White racists have. Congressional laws, one after the other, have not been necessary to stop black people from oppressing others and denying others the full enjoyment of their rights. White racists have made such laws necessary. The goal of Black Power is positive and functional to a free and viable society. No white racist can make this claim.

THE MYTHS OF COALITION

At the beginning of our discussion of Black Power, we said that black people must redefine themselves, state new values and goals. The same holds true for white people of good will; they too need to redefine themselves and their role.

209

Stokely Carmichael and Charles V. Hamilton

Some people see the advocates of Black Power as concerned with ridding the civil rights struggle of white people. This has been untrue from the beginning. There is a definite, much-needed role whites can play. This role can best be examined on three different, yet interrelated, levels: educative, organizational, supportive. Given the pervasive nature of racism in the society and the extent to which attitudes of white superiority and black inferiority have become embedded, it is very necessary that white people begin to disabuse themselves of such notions. Black people, as we stated earlier, will lead the challenge to old values and norms, but whites who recognize the need must also work in this sphere. Whites have access to groups in the society never reached by black people. They must get within those groups and help perform this essential educative function.

One of the most disturbing things about almost all white supporters has been that they are reluctant to go into their own communities—which is where the racism exists—and work to get rid of it. We are not now speaking of whites who have worked to get black people "accepted," on an individual basis, by the white society. Of these there have been many; their efforts are undoubtedly well-intended and individually helpful. But too often those efforts are geared to the same false premises as integration; too often the society in which they seek acceptance of a few black people can afford to make the gesture. We are speaking, rather, of those whites who see the need for basic change and have hooked up with the black liberation movement because it seemed the most promising agent of such change. Yet they often admonish black people to be non-violent. They should preach non-violence in the white community. Where possible, they might also educate other white people to the need for Black Power. The range is great, with much depending on the white person's own class background and environment.

On a broader scale, there is the very important function of working to reorient this society's attitudes and policies toward African and Asian countries. Across the country, smug white communities show a poverty of awareness, a poverty of humanity, indeed, a poverty of ability to act in a civilized manner toward non-

Anglo human beings. The white middle-class suburbs need "free-dom schools" as badly as the black communities. Anglo-conformity is a dead weight on their necks too. All this is an educative role crying to be performed by those whites so inclined.

The organizational role is next. It is hoped that eventually there will be a coalition of poor blacks and poor whites. This is the only coalition which seems acceptable to us, and we see such a coalition as the major internal instrument of change in the American society. It is purely academic today to talk about bringing poor blacks and poor whites together, but the task of creating a poor-white power block dedicated to the goals of a free, open society—not one based on racism and subordination—must be attempted. The main responsibility for this task falls upon whites. Black and white *can* work together in the white community where possible; it is not possible, however, to go into a poor Southern town and talk about "integration," or even desegregation. Poor white people are becoming more hostile—not less—toward black people, partly because they see the nation's attention focused on black poverty and few, if any, people coming to them.

Only whites can mobilize and organize those communities along the lines necessary and possible for effective alliances with the black communities. This job cannot be left to the existing institutions and agencies, because those structures, for the most part, are reflections of institutional racism. If the job is to be done, there must be new forms created. Thus, the political modernization process must involve the white community as well as the black.

It is our position that black organizations should be black-led and essentially black-staffed, with policy being made by black people. White people can and do play very important supportive roles in those organizations. Where they come with specific skills and techniques, they will be evaluated in those terms. All too frequently, however, many young, middle-class, white Americans, like some sort of Pepsi generation, have wanted to "come alive" through the black community and black groups. They have wanted to be where the action is—and the action has been in those places. They have sought refuge among blacks from a sterile, meaningless, irrelevant life in middle-class America. They have been unable to deal with the stifling, racist, parochial, split-level mentality of their parents, teachers, preachers and friends. Many have come seeing "no difference in color," they have come "color blind." But at this time and in this land, color *is* a factor and we should not overlook or deny this. The black organizations do not need this kind of idealism, which borders on paternalism. White people working in SNCC have understood this. There are white lawyers who defend black civil rights workers in court, and white activists who support indigenous black movements across the country. Their function is not to lead or to set policy or to attempt to define black people to black people. Their role is supportive.

Ultimately, the gains of our struggle will be meaningful only when consolidated by viable coalitions between blacks and whites who accept each other as co-equal partners and who identify their goals as politically and economically similar. At this stage, given the nature of the society, distinct roles must be played. The charge that this approach is "anti-white" remains as inaccurate as almost all the other public commentary on Black Power. There is nothing new about this; whenever black people have moved toward genuinely independent action, the society has distorted their intention or damned their performance.

DYNAMITE IN THE GHETTO

The core problem within the ghetto is the vicious circle created by the lack of decent housing, decent jobs and adequate education. The failure of these three fundamental institutions to work has led to alienation of the ghetto from the rest of the urban area as well as to deep political rifts between the two communities.

In America we judge by American standards, and by this yardstick we find that the black man lives in incredibly inadequate housing, shabby shelters that are dangerous to mental and physical health and to life itself. It has been estimated that twenty million black people put fifteen billion dollars into rents, mortgage payments and housing expenses every year. But because his choice is largely limited to the ghettos, and because the black population is increasing at a rate which is 150 percent over that of the increase in the white population, the shelter shortage for the black person is not only acute and perennial, but getting increasingly tighter. Black people are automatically forced to pay top dollar for whatever they get, even a 6 x 6 cold-water flat.

Urban renewal and highway clearance programs have forced black people more and more into congested pockets of the inner city. Since suburban zoning laws have kept out low-income housing, and the Federal Government has failed to pass open-occupancy laws, black people are forced to stay in the deteriorating ghettos. Thus crowding increases, and slum conditions worsen.

In the Mill Creek (East St. Louis), Illinois, urban renewal undertaking, for instance, a black slum was cleared and in its place rose a middle-income housing development. What happened to those evicted to make way for this great advance? The majority were forced into what remained of the black ghetto; in other words, the crowding was intensified.

Here we begin to understand the pervasive, cyclic implications of institutional racism. Barred from most housing, black people are forced to live in segregated neighborhoods and with this comes de facto segregated schooling, which means poor education, which leads in turn to ill-paying jobs.

It is impossible to talk about the problems of education in the black community without at some point dealing with the issue of desegregation and integration, especially since the Supreme Court decision of May 17, 1954: " . . . In the field of public education the doctrine of separate but equal has no place. Separate education facilities are inherently unequal." However, all the discussion of integration or bussing today seems highly irrelevant; it allows a lot of highly paid school administrators to talk around and never deal with the problem. For example, in Washington, D.C., the schools were supposedly integrated immediately after the 1954 decision, but as a result of the population movements of whites into suburbs and blacks into the inner (ghetto) city, black children attend what are in fact segregated schools. Today, roughly 85 percent of the children in the Washington, D.C. public schools are black. Nor is integration very relevant or meaningful in any of the other major urban areas. In Chicago, 87 percent of the black students in elementary school attend virtually all-black public schools. In Detroit, 45 percent of the black students are in public schools that are overwhelmingly black. In Philadelphia, thirty-eight elementary schools have a black enrollment of 99 percent. In April, 1967, the Rev. Henry Nichols, vice president of the Philadelphia School Board, stated on television that the city had two separate school systems: one for the ghetto, the other for the rest of the city. There was no public denial from any other knowledgeable sources in the city. In Los Angeles, forty-three elementary schools have at least 85 percent black attendance. In the Borough of Manhattan in New York City, 77 percent of the elementary school students and 72 percent of the junior high school students are black.[1]

Clearly, "integration"—even if it would solve the educational problem—has not proved feasible. The alternative presented is usually the large-scale transfer of black children to schools in white neighborhoods. This too raises several problems . . . Implicit is the idea that the closer you get to whiteness, the better you are. Another problem is that it makes the majority of black youth expendable. Probably the maximum number of blacks who could transfer from ghetto schools to white schools, given the over-crowded conditions of city schools anyway, is about 20 percent. The 80 percent left behind are therefore expendable.

The real need at present is not integration but quality education.

In Central Harlem, for example, there are twenty elementary schools, four junior high schools and no high schools. A total of 31,469 students—virtually all black—attend these schools. In New York as a whole, only 50.3 percent of the teachers in the black and Puerto Rican elementary schools were fully licensed as compared with 78.2 percent in white schools.[2]

In 1960, in Central Harlem, 21.6 percent of third-grade stu-

[1] Tom Kahn, *The Economics of Equality*. League for Industrial Democracy, 1964, pp. 31–32.
[2] *Ibid.*, p. 32.

dents were reading above grade level and 30 percent were reading below. By the sixth grade, 11.7 per cent are reading above and 80 per cent are reading below grade level. The median equivalent grades reading comprehension for Central Harlem, third grade, was a full year behind the city median and the national norm, and by the sixth grade it was two years behind. The same is true of word knowledge. In arithmetic, the students of Central Harlem are one and a half years behind the rest of the city by the sixth grade, and by the time they are in the eighth grade, they are two years behind. The I. Q. scores are 90.6 in the third grade, and by the sixth grade they have gone down to 86.3.[3]

The basic story of education in Central Harlem emerges as one of inefficiency, inferiority and mass deterioration. It is a system which typifies colonialism and the colonist's attitude. Nor is Harlem unique. Rev. Henry Nichols, vice president of the Philadelphia Board of Education, stated in 1967 that 75 percent of the black children who would be graduated that year were "functional illiterates. . . . The reason for this," he added, "is the attitude of school administrators toward black people."[4]

There can be no doubt that in today's world a thorough and comprehensive education is an absolute necessity. Yet it is obvious from the data that a not even minimum education is being received in most ghetto schools. White decision-makers have been running those schools with injustice, indifference and inadequacy for too long; the result has been an educationally crippled black child turned out onto the labor market equipped to do little more than stand in welfare lines to receive his miserable dole.

It should not be hard to understand why approximately 41 percent of the pupils entering high school from Central Harlem drop out before receiving a diploma, 52 percent of these being boys. When one couples school conditions with the overcrowded and deteriorating housing in which black pupils must live and study, additional factors become clear. Males, in particular, must leave school because of financial pressure. The young drop-out or even

[3] *Youth in the Ghetto,* New York: Harlem Youth Opportunities Unlimited (HARYOU), 1964, pp. 166–80.
[4] *The New York Times* (May 4, 1967), p. 23.

high school graduate with an inadequate education, burdened also by the emotional deprivations which are the consequences of poverty, is now on the street looking for a job.

TAKE CARE OF BUSINESS

We are calling at this time for new political forms which will be the link between broadened participation (now occurring) and legitimate government. These forms will provide a means whereby a newly politicized people can get what they need from the government. It is not enough to add more and more people to the voter rolls and then send them into the old "do-nothing," compromise-oriented political parties. Those new voters will only become frustrated and alienated. It is no good to enact an anti-poverty program calling for "maximum feasible participation of the poor" and then saddle that program with old City Hall and bureaucratic restrictions. The people will see this only as a perpetuation of the same old colonial situation. This country can continue to appropriate money for programs to be run by the same kinds of insensitive people with paternalistic, Anglo-conformity attitudes and the programs will continue to fail. They should fail, because they do not have the confidence and trust of the masses. In order to gain that confidence and trust, the people must be much more involved in the formulation and implementation of policy. Black people are indeed saying: "Mr. Charlie, we'd rather do it ourselves." And in doing it themselves, they will be developing the *habit* of participation, the *consciousness* of ability to achieve, and the experience and wisdom to govern. Only this can ultimately create a viable body politic. It is not enough that shiny new school buildings be built in the ghettos, if the black people whose children attend them basically feel no attachment to those schools. Learning will not take place. . . .

It is difficult, if not impossible, for white America, or for those blacks who want to be like white America, to understand this basically revolutionary mentality. But in the final analysis, white America would save itself a lot of trouble if it did try to understand and to come to terms with this new black-oriented mentality. Because one thing stands clear: whatever the consequences, there is a growing—a rapidly growing—body of black people determined to "T.C.B."—take care of business. They will not be stopped in their drive to achieve dignity, to achieve their share of power, indeed, to become their own men and women—in this time and in this land—by whatever means necessary.

KENNETH B. CLARK

From *Dark Ghetto*

Statements in "The Cry of the Ghetto," a chapter in Dr. Clark's book, Dark Ghetto, *were obtained from residents of Harlem by Willie Jones, a staff interviewer for Harlem Youth Opportunities Unlimited (HARYOU).*

THE CRY OF THE GHETTO

A lot of times, when I'm working, I become as despondent as hell and I feel like crying. I'm not a man, none of us are men! I don't own anything. I'm not a man enough to own a store; none of us are.

—MAN, AGE ABOUT 30

You know the average young person out here don't have a job, man, they don't have anything to do. They don't have any alternative, you know, but to go out there and try to make a living for themselves. Like when you come down to the Tombs down there, they're down there for robbing and breaking in. They want to know why you did it and where you live, but you have to live. You go down to the employment agency and you can't get a job. They have you waiting all day, but you can't get a job. They don't have a job for you. Yet you have to live. I'm ready to do anything anyone else is ready to do—because I want to live— I want to live. No one wants to die. I want to live.

—DRUG ADDICT, MALE, AGE 30

If a man qualifies, it should be first come, first serve. You understand what I mean? Regardless of whether we're black or white, we all have families! It should be first come, first serve. But that's not how they do you! If you're black, you're automatically turned down on a lot of jobs. They'll take your application, but no sooner than you walk out of the office, or wherever it is, they take the application and put it in the wastebasket, and tell you they'll let you know in a couple of weeks.

—MAN, AGE ABOUT 24

No one with a mop can expect respect from a banker, or an attorney, or men who create jobs, and all you have is a mop. Are you crazy? Whoever heard of integration between a mop and a banker?

—MAN, AGE ABOUT 38

The way the Man has us, he has us wanting to kill one another. Dog eat dog, amongst us! He has us, like we're so hungry up here, he has us up so tight! Like his rent is due, my rent is due. It's Friday. The Man wants sixty-five dollars. If you are three days over, or don't have the money; like that, he wants to give you a dispossess! Take you to court! The courts won't go along with you, they say get the money or get out! Yet they don't tell you how to get the money, you understand? They say get the money and pay the Man, but they don't say how to get it. Now, if you use illegal means to obey his ruling to try to get it—which he's not going to let you do—if you use illegal means to pay your bills according to his ruling—he will put you in jail.

—MAN, AGE 31

They are raising the rents so high, like that, with a job, the menial jobs that we have or get, the money we will receive—we won't be able to pay the rent! So where we going to go? They are pushing us further, and further, and further—out of Harlem.

—MAN, AGE 31

If you could get onto the ninth floor of the Tombs, you would see for yourself. They are lying there like dogs, vomiting and what not, over one another. It is awful. It smells like a pigpen up there. If you look, you'll see nothing but Spanish. And the black

219

man. You'll seldom see a white man. When you do, he is from a
very poor group. They are 20 years old, looking like they were 40.

DRUG ADDICT, MALE, AGE ABOUT 37

Discrimination is even in the school I attend right now. I know
my teacher is very prejudiced because I have certain questions
that have to be answered for my knowledge, but he will never
answer. He would always call on a little white boy to give the
answer. I told him one night, to his face, that if he didn't want
to answer my questions just tell me and I would leave. There are
always other teachers. He didn't say anything. He just looked at
me and figured I was going to—so he said, "Well, maybe next
time." There is no next time—this is the time and I'm not taking
second best from any white man.

—BOY, AGE 17

The conditions here are the way they are because of white domination of this community, and when that changes, as is being
attempted here, by these [Black] Nationalists, or by any other
nationalist groups, or by the Muslims; when they can unite and
change these conditions, change the white domination for Black
domination, the conditions will change.

—MAN, AGE 28

Why in the hell—now this is more or less a colored neighborhood—why do we have so many white cops? As if we got to have
somebody white standing over us. Not that I am prejudiced or
anything, but I can't understand why we have to have so many
white cops! Now if I go to a white neighborhood, I'm not going
to see a lot of colored cops in no white neighborhood, standing
guard over the white people. I'm not going to see that; and I
know it, and I get sick and tired of seeing so many white cops,
standing around.

—WOMAN, AGE 38

My wife was even robbed coming back from the store. They
tried to snatch her pocketbook, and she came upstairs crying to

me. What could I do? Where was the police? Where is the protection?

—MAN, AGE ABOUT 50

The white cops, they have a damn sadistic nature. They are
really a sadistic type of people and we, I mean me, myself, we
don't need them here in Harlem. We don't need them! They
don't do the neighborhood any good. They deteriorate the neighborhood. They start more violence than any other people start.
They start violence, that's right. A bunch of us could be playing
some music, or dancing, which we have as an outlet for ourselves.
We can't dance in the house, we don't have clubs or things like
that. So we're out on the sidewalk, right on the sidewalk; we
might feel like dancing, or one might want to play something on
his horn. Right away here comes a cop. "You're disturbing the
peace!" No one has said anything, you understand; no one has
made a complaint. Everyone is enjoying themselves. But here
comes one cop, and he'll want to chase everyone. And gets mad.
I mean, he gets mad! We aren't mad. He comes into the neighborhood, aggravated and mad.

—MAN, AGE ABOUT 33

Last night, for instance, the officer stopped some fellows on
125th Street, Car No. ——, that was the number of the car, and
because this fellow spoke so nicely for his protection and his
rights, the officer said, "All right, everybody get off the street or
inside!" Now, it's very hot. We don't have air-conditioned apart-
ments in most of these houses up here, so where are we going if
we get off the streets? We can't go back in the house because we
almost suffocate. So we sit down on the curb, or stand on the sidewalk, or on the steps, things like that, till the wee hours of the
morning, especially in the summer when it's too hot to go up.
Now where were we going? But he came out with his nightstick
and wants to beat people on the head, and wanted to—he arrested
one fellow. The other fellow said, "Well, I'll move, but you don't
have to talk to me like a dog." I think we should all get together
—everybody—all get together and every time one draws back his
stick to do something to us, or hits one of us on the head, take the

stick and hit *him* on *his* head, so he'll know how it feels to be hit on the head, or kill him, if necessary. Yes, kill him, if necessary. That's how I feel. There is no other way to deal with this man. The only way you can deal with him is the way he has been dealing with us.

—MAN, ABOUT 35

Everything is a big laugh in this dump unless you kill a cop. Then they don't laugh. I had a cop walk up to me a couple of days ago. You know what he said? "Move over." They have the street blocked up and he's going to tell me you can go around them. I said, "Hell if I do." He said, "What did you say?" I said, "Hell if I do." He said, "I'll slap your black ass." I told him, "That's one day you'll know if you're living or dying." He just looked at me. I said, "Why don't you say it? You want to say nigger so bad."

—MAN, AGE 21

The flag here in America is for the white man. The blue is for justice; the fifty white stars you see in the blue are for the fifty white states; and the white you see in it is the White House. It represents white folks. The red in it is the white man's blood— he doesn't even respect your blood, that's why he will lynch you, hang you, barbecue you, and fry you.

—MAN, AGE ABOUT 35

A stereotyped Negro you see him in the movies or on TV, walking down the levee with a watermelon in his hand, his shiny teeth, and his straw hat on his head. That's the one you see on television, yassuh, yassuh, and the showboys come in Stepin Fetchit, because that's what every Negro is associated with. To me, the middle-class Negro and the upper-class Negro is one that's trying to get away from that stereotype. They're the ones trying to get away.

—MAN, AGE 18

I don't see why we've got to always look up to the white man's life. That's what we've been exposed to, you know. Be like the white man. I think we have to have criteria of our own. They had

"Amos and Andy" on radio, they were done by white men. You hear the fellows saying, "Oh, I'm going to get me a white broad." We should form our own criteria. We should try and have some more people like Martin Luther King, like James Baldwin. We can send some draftsmen to school, some engineers; people can come back and build a city for Negroes to live in, or you know, not just for Negroes but for Negroes and anyone else who wants to live there. Why do we always have to get up—come up to the white man's level? We struggle like the devil to get up there, and we hardly ever do it. Why can't we form our own level?

—GIRL, AGE 15

I have been uncomfortable being a Negro. I came from the South—Kentucky, on the Ohio River line—and I have had white people spit on me in my Sunday suit.

—WOMAN

The main thing is to know just where he comes from, knowing about his race. The main thing. He will then disregard every time he turns on the television that he sees a white face. That won't mean anything to him; it will be just another program because he will know that the conditions of the way of this world are based on only the white man's psychology, that makes these things. It won't be because this man is better fitted than he is on the television; it is because he dominates, he capitalizes, he corrupts.

—MAN, AGE 35

First stop wearing the white man's clothes. Dress in your ancestral clothes. Learn your history and your heritage. This is part of my culture and I'm proud. Wear your clothes! Put on your *abdaba,* your *dashiki* and your *fella.* You can do it.

—WOMAN, AGE ABOUT 45

The Honorable Elijah Mohammed teaches, but the only thing is, some of our people still don't take that old blue-eyed, hook-nosed picture of Christ off their wall—take it down and step on it. These people have been exploiting us for years.

—MAN, AGE ABOUT 35

223

Hear me now, hear me. Thy kingdom come, thy will be done, on earth as it is in Heaven. The kingdom is ours, black man's kingdom. We want our own God, our own paradise, our own joys on this earth, and if we are not getting that, then something must be wrong somewhere, so with all of your Gospel and all your preaching, if you cannot benefit the children, it has no value.

—MAN, AGE ABOUT 50

Churches don't mean us no good. We've been having churches all our lives under the same conditions, and look at the condition we're still in. The church must not have meant anything. See, when you go to church you don't learn how to read and write, and count, at church. You learn that in school. See what I mean? So what good the churches doing us? They are not doing us any good! You could build some factories or something in Harlem and give our people some work near home. That would do us more good than a church.

—MAN, AGE ABOUT 45

We don't want any bloodshed if we can help it, but if there has to be a little bloodletting, well and good. But this is only the beginning—what happened here today. Our next big step is the Harlem Police Department—we want black captains and we're going to have them. I've been fighting for dozens of years here in Harlem, where the so-called leaders play—Uncle Tom—play politics and let the people starve. You have district leaders here that draw a big fat salary. You can't hardly walk the street for trash. You have captains here—district captains and what not— all kinds of leaders here in Harlem. You never see them until election.

—WOMAN, AGE ABOUT 30

I think there's a great lack of offensive direction and most of the adults have, more or less, succumbed to the situation and have decided, what the hell can I do? This is the attitude; that we can do nothing, so leave it alone. People think you're always going to be under pressure from the white man and he owns and runs everything, and we are so dependent on him that there's nothing

I can do. This is the general impression I've gotten from most of the adults in Harlem.

—GIRL, AGE 15

It's got to get better. It can't get worse—it's got to get better, and they'll open up. They have to open up because they will find themselves going down all over the world, not only here. It's not just us picketing that forced them to do this; all over the world people are talking about American imperialism, and it's forcing them to do all these things. Because whether I walk the line or not, whoever walks the line that has a black face is walking the line for me. Whether they are walking in Alabama, Arizona, Mississippi, or wherever they're walking. And there isn't anything for the Man to do but begin giving us an equal chance if he wants to save himself, because he's going down and we're the only ones that are holding him up.

—MAN, AGE ABOUT 45

All right, so you get into the school and you get your rights, but in the whole scope of the black man in America, how can you accomplish anything by doing this? Yes, all right, you are accepted into Woolworths; you fought and got your heads beat in. But what do your children think of you? Do you have any economic or political power? The people like you who're going into Greenwood, Mississippi, say, where the people are living—you are all dependent. It's unthinkable. The people have nothing. At this point they are living on things that are being sent to them from New York, Chicago, and other places in the United States. Do you know how much money we spend on foreign aid while here in the United States we people are starving?

—MAN, AGE 18, AND GIRL, AGE 15

When the time comes, it is going to be too late. Everything will explode because the people they live under tension now; they going to a point where they can't stand it no more. When they get to that point. . . . They want us to go to Africa, they say.

That would be the best thing they would want in the world

225

because then they could get all of us together. All they would have to do is drop one bomb and we're dead.

—MEN, AGES 30 TO 35

I would like to see the day when my people have dignity and pride in themselves as black people. And when this comes about, when they realize that we are capable of all things, and can do anything under the sun that a man can do, then all these things will come about—equality, great people, presidents—everything.

—MAN, AGE 19

I would like to be the first Negro president.

—BOY, AGE ABOUT 17

Biographical Notes

JAMES BALDWIN was born in New York City in 1924. At the age of twenty-one he received a Saxon Fellowship, followed by a period of residence in France, where his first novel, *Go Tell It on the Mountain,* was completed. Mr. Baldwin has also received Rosenwald, Guggenheim, and Ford Foundation fellowships. He is the author of several novels, including *Giovanni's Room* and *Another Country,* many short stories, articles, plays and essays. His essays have been widely acclaimed for their analyses of racial problems in the United States. They have been collected in *Notes of a Native Son, Nobody Knows My Name,* and *The Fire Next Time.*

LERONE BENNETT, JR., worked while he was still in high school for *The Mississippi Enterprise,* the weekly Negro newspaper in his home town, Clarksdale. Later, at Morehouse College in Atlanta, he was the editor of the school newspaper. After graduating from Morehouse, Mr. Bennett became city editor of the *Atlanta Daily World,* a Negro newspaper, and then joined the staff of Johnson Publications, the publisher of *Ebony, Jet,* and other Negro magazines. He worked as an assistant editor for *Jet* and *Ebony,* and eventually became *Ebony*'s senior editor. He has written numerous articles for *Ebony* and other magazines and is the author of *Before the Mayflower,* an important historical study of the Negro in America, as well as other books.

STOKELY CARMICHAEL was born in Trinidad, and he grew up there and in New York City where he attended the Bronx High School of Science. In 1964 he graduated from Howard University, where he had been active in student government and local civil rights activities. He has worked with the Student Nonviolent Coordinating Committee (SNCC) since its inception in 1960, and he has been arrested more than fifteen times in civil rights demonstrations in both the North and the South. Mr. Carmichael was a founder of the Lowndes County Freedom Organization (the "Black Panther" Party) in Alabama, and he was a leader of the 1964 Mississippi Summer Project, a civil rights project sponsored by SNCC. After serving as national chairman of SNCC for the 1966–67 term, Mr. Carmichael went back into "field work" for SNCC, concentrating on organizing the black ghetto in Washington, D.C. He has lectured on "black power" in many cities throughout the United States, and, together with Charles V. Hamilton, is the author of *Black Power* (1967).

KENNETH B. CLARK, director of the Social Dynamics Research Institute at the City College of New York, is one of the nation's leading psychologists and social scientists. A graduate of Howard University, Dr. Clark received his Ph.D. from Columbia University. After teaching at Howard, he became professor of psychology at C.C.N.Y. in 1942 and established the Northside Center for Child Development in Harlem in 1946. His testimony on the effects of racial prejudice on children was cited in *Brown* v. *Board of Education,* the United States Supreme Court school desegregation decision of 1954. Dr. Clark was a founder of Harlem Youth Opportunities Unlimited (HARYOU), a government-supported social service agency, and he has been a member of the New York State Board of Regents. He is the author of *Dark Ghetto, Prejudice and Your Child* and the editor of *The Negro Protest.*

OSSIE DAVIS was born in Cogdell, Georgia, in 1917 and attended Howard University. He is a well-known actor and playwright, having starred on Broadway in *A Raisin in the Sun* (1959) and *Purlie Victorious* (1962), a three-act comedy which he wrote. He is the author of many articles and speaks frequently on life for the Negro in the United States, including the problems faced by Negroes in the American theater. Mr. Davis has also participated in many civil rights demonstrations. He appears in movies and television plays and has performed frequently with his wife, Ruby Dee, the noted actress.

FREDERICK DOUGLASS was born a slave in 1817. He escaped to freedom from Maryland in 1838 and began a career as a speaker for the Massachusetts Anti-Slavery Society. His powerful physical appearance and eloquent descriptions of the evils of slavery soon made him famous throughout the North. Still a fugitive, in 1845 Mr.

Douglass traveled to England to avoid reenslavement, where he continued his lectures and raised money to buy his freedom. Upon his return to the United States, he started his own abolitionist newspaper, *The North Star.* He continued to agitate against slavery and was an adviser to John Brown. After Brown's unsuccessful raid on Harper's Ferry in 1859, Douglass had to leave the United States again, going first to Canada, and eventually to England. During the Civil War he was active in recruiting troops for Negro regiments. Mr. Douglass's autobiography, *Life and Times of Frederick Douglass,* is a well-written and moving account of the life of a Southern slave. In 1889 he was appointed U.S. Consul General to Haiti.

Frederick Douglass fought for equality in suffrage and education for the Negro American until his death in 1895. His writings have provided a philosophical basis for programs aimed at social and economic equality, both in his own time and today.

W. E. B. DuBois (William Edward Burghardt DuBois) was born in Great Barrington, Massachusetts, in 1868. He studied at Fisk University, and Harvard, where he received his Ph.D. in 1895. Dr. DuBois was a professor of sociology, economics, and history, and an expert on Negro American history. He wrote many books, the first of which was *Suppression of the Black African Trade* (1896). *The Souls of Black Folk* (1903) has had enormous influence on black writers and continues to be praised for the beauty of its poetic prose as well as its penetrating insights into Negro American life. Dr. DuBois' study of the post-Civil War period, *Black Reconstruction* (1935), is regarded as one of the outstanding works on that era. His autobiography, *Dusk of Dawn,* was published in 1940.

A founder of the NAACP in 1909, Dr. DuBois became editor of its magazine, *Crisis,* and continued in that position until 1934. He also initiated Pan-African Congresses of African and American Negroes to focus attention on the social and economic problems of black people. For over fifty years, through his speeches, articles, books, and poetry, Dr. DuBois was the leading spokesman for a militant and radical attack on all forms of economic exploitation and racial discrimination. Because his approach was in conflict with that of those Negro leaders who advocated accommodation with the white majority, Dr. DuBois was a controversial figure during most of his life.

He left the United States in 1961 to take up permanent residence in Ghana, where he died on August 28, 1963.

RALPH ELLISON was born in Oklahoma City in 1914, and he studied at Tuskegee Institute in Alabama. He has distinguished himself as a writer and lecturer during the past twenty years and has been both a jazz musician and free-lance photographer. Mr. Ellison has been Writer in Residence at Rutgers University, Visiting Fellow at Yale, and he has also taught at the University of Chicago. He has lectured at many other universities in this country. His widely acclaimed novel *Invisible Man* won the National Book Award in 1952, and it was voted "the most distinguished single work" published in the last twenty years by the *Chicago Tribune Book Week* poll in 1965. Mr. Ellison's short stories, essays, and reviews have appeared in many major American magazines, and a collection of his essays, *Shadow and Act,* was published in 1966.

DICK GREGORY was born in St. Louis, Missouri, in 1932. He attended school there and became a track star, which won for him a scholarship to Southern Illinois University. Mr. Gregory left school to enter the army, and as a member of Special Services entertainment troupes, he began to develop and perform the comedy routines for which he eventually became famous. After completing his army service, he returned to college, but left again, working at a series of jobs in Chicago. After breaking into the entertainment world by performances in small nightclubs, he achieved national recognition and his recordings became bestsellers. Since the early 1960's Mr. Gregory has appeared at many rallies and demonstrations in behalf of civil rights organizations throughout the North and the South, and in this connection he has been arrested several times. He has fasted in protest of American involvement in the war in South Vietnam and has often spoken out on crises concerning Negro American life.

CHARLES V. HAMILTON is a graduate of Roosevelt University in Chicago, where he has served as chairman of the Department of Political Science. He also holds a law degree from Loyola University, as well as an M.A. and a Ph.D. from the University of Chicago. He has taught at Rutgers University, Tuskegee Institute in Alabama, and Lincoln University. Mr. Hamilton's articles on civil rights and constitutional law have appeared in the

Journal of Negro Education, The Wisconsin Law Review, Negro Digest, and *Phylon,* the scholarly quarterly of Atlanta University. He is an active participant in civil rights organizations and often serves as a legal adviser to these groups and to colleges and government agencies. Mr. Hamilton wrote *Minority Politics in Black Belt Alabama,* and he is the co-author with Stokely Carmichael of *Black Power* (1967).

LANGSTON HUGHES is known best for his poems, which have been collected in *The Weary Blues, Selected Poems,* and *Panther and the Lash.* He was a prolific writer for over forty years and crossed the country on numerous occasions to give public readings of his work. In addition to poetry Mr. Hughes wrote short stories, plays, newspaper columns, historical works, books for children, and two autobiographical works, *I Wonder As I Wander* and *The Big Sea.*

Born in Joplin, Missouri, in 1902, Mr. Hughes went to school in Kansas and Ohio and then traveled in Africa and Europe. He completed his formal education at Columbia University and Lincoln University in Pennsylvania. He lived most of his life in New York City, where he was very helpful to young writers who sought his advice and encouragement. He died there in 1967.

LEROI JONES, poet, playwright, and social essayist, was born in Newark, New Jersey, in 1934. He attended Howard and Columbia universities and the New School for Social Research. Mr. Jones's work has been published in many magazines, including the *Saturday Review, Evergreen Review,* and *The Nation,* and he has been the editor of several small literary magazines. His books of poems include *Preface to a Twenty Volume Suicide Note* (1961) and *The Dead Lecturer* (1964). He is the author of *Dutchman, The Slave* and other plays which have been produced in New York and many major cities abroad. His prose works include *Blues People, The System of Dante's Hell,* and *Home.* Mr. Jones was a founder of the Black Arts Repertory Theater in Harlem, and when he returned to live in Newark, he began producing and directing plays in a theater he established there. He also assisted neighborhood teenagers in publishing a community newspaper. In the fall of 1967, Mr. Jones was convicted on a charge of illegal possession of weapons during the "rebellions" in Newark that summer. His conviction and heavy sentence aroused much controversy, and the case was appealed. In the days following the assassination of Dr. Martin Luther King, Mr. Jones worked with a community organization and the Newark city administration to maintain calm and prevent violence.

JOHN OLIVER KILLENS was born in Macon, Georgia, in 1916. He attended Howard, Columbia, and New York universities, among others.

Mr. Killens is an outstanding novelist, and his published works include *Youngblood, And Then We Heard the Thunder, 'Sippi,* and *Black Man's Burden.* He established the Harlem Writers Guild Workshop for young writers, and he has written for television and motion pictures. Mr. Killens has also taught and lectured at universities and has been Writer in Residence at Fisk College in Nashville, Tennessee.

MARTIN LUTHER KING, JR., was born in Atlanta, Georgia, in 1929, and attended Morehouse College in Atlanta, Crozer Theological Seminary in Pennsylvania, and Boston University. After being ordained as a minister, he became the pastor of a church in Montgomery, Alabama, where he led the famous 1955–56 bus boycott. As a result of this protest, the Southern Christian Leadership Conference, a nonviolent organization, was formed to continue the struggle for improved conditions for Negroes in the United States. Dr. King was one of the founders of this group, and he soon became the dominant force in the nonviolent movement in this country. He had organized and participated in numerous civil rights demonstrations, including the Birmingham, Alabama, demonstrations in the spring of 1963, and the massive "March on Washington" that same year, at which he delivered his stirring speech "I Have a Dream." In 1964 Dr. King received the Nobel Peace Prize. He had openly opposed United States involvement in the war in South Vietnam and had also attacked the American draft system, which he had felt was racially unjust. Concentrating on a "poor people's" campaign in Washington, D.C., Dr. King was continuing his opposition to all forms of discrimination against Negro Americans. On April 4, 1968, while in Memphis, Tennessee, to lead a demonstration for striking garbage collectors of that city, Dr. King was shot and killed by a white assassin. His murder shocked a nation already in the midst of examining its legacy of violence and denial.

MALCOLM X was born "Malcolm Little" on May 19, 1925, in Omaha, Nebraska. His family moved from Omaha to East Lansing, Michigan, and after the eighth grade Malcolm X went to Roxbury, Massachusetts, to live with his sister, Ella. He later came to New York, and in his autobiography he tells of his experiences in the Negro ghettoes of these Eastern cities. In 1946 Malcolm X was sentenced to imprisonment, and it was there that he became a member of the Nation of Islam, the Black Muslim group headed by Elijah Muhammed. Upon his parole, Malcolm X established many temples for Elijah Muhammed, and he lectured often in person, and on radio and television. He won nationwide attention, but after much conflict with the leaders of the Nation of Islam, and after two trips to Africa, he formed his own group, the Organization of Afro-American Unity. On Sunday, February 21, 1965, Malcolm X was assassinated while making a speech in the Audubon Ballroom in New York. His autobiography, published in 1965, has been widely read by both Negroes and Whites, and, together with his speeches, has had an important effect on the struggle of black Americans for dignity and full equality.

LOFTEN MITCHELL was born in Harlem, where he began writing theatrical sketches and acted with the Rose McClendon Players, a local theater group. He studied at the City College of New York, Talladega College in Alabama, and Columbia University. In his book *Black Drama* (1967) he tells how he gave up acting and decided to devote himself to writing plays. Among the plays he has written are *Blood in the Night, A Land Beyond the River,* and *Star of the Morning.* In 1958 Mr. Mitchell was awarded a Guggenheim grant to support his work as a playwright. His articles on drama have often appeared in *Theatre Arts Monthly,* and he has written and lectured on the Negro in the American theater.

GORDON PARKS was born in 1912 on a small farm in Fort Scott, Kansas. He moved to St. Paul, Minnesota, in his youth and held a succession of jobs until he went to Chicago to establish himself as a photographer. His photographs became known, and he received a Rosenwald Fellowship to help support his work.

233

Since 1949 Mr. Parks has been a member of the staff of *Life* magazine, and he has written and photographed stories on a wide variety of subjects. His work has won international recognition, and he has written a book on photography, a novel, *The Learning Tree* (1963), and an autobiography, *A Choice of Weapons* (1966).

TED POSTON, a native of Hopkinsville, Kentucky, was educated at Tennessee State College and New York University. At various times he was an editor of the *New York Contender,* the *Pittsburgh Courier,* and the New York *Amsterdam News,* all Negro newspapers. He has also been a staff member of the *New York Post.* Mr. Poston's short stories have appeared in anthologies and magazines, and for many years his articles have been published by many leading American magazines, including *The Nation* and the *New Republic.*

BILL RUSSELL was born in Monroe, Louisiana, during the Depression and grew up in the South and in Oakland, California. He received a basketball scholarship to San Francisco University, which achieved prominence in college basketball when its team, led by Mr. Russell, won two National Collegiate Athletic Association championships. Mr. Russell starred on the undefeated United States Olympic Team in 1956 and has had an outstanding career as a center for the Boston Celtics. The Celtics have won more than seven world championships, and Mr. Russell has been voted Most Valuable Player and a member of numerous All-Time National Basketball Association teams. He has also been named player-coach of the Boston Celtics, the first time a Negro American athlete has been hired to coach a professional team in the United States. His autobiography, *Go Up for Glory,* written with William McSweeney, was published in 1966.

WALTER WHITE was born in Atlanta, Georgia, in 1896 and moved to New York in 1918. He became an official of the NAACP and, because he was Caucasian in appearance, he was able to investigate lynchings by posing as a white man. He interviewed many white Southerners, usually without arousing suspicion; but this was not always the case, and on several occasions his life was threatened when it was discovered that he was a Negro. Mr. White wrote many articles and a number of books based on the information he gathered during these investigations, and they served to alert Americans to the brutal treatment of many Southern Negroes. He also wrote an autobiography, *A Man Called White*.

JOHN A. WILLIAMS was born in Jackson, Mississippi, in 1925 and grew up in Syracuse, New York. After graduating from Syracuse University, he held jobs as a social worker and journalist. Mr. Williams' novels include *The Angry Ones* (1960), *Night Song* (1961), *Sissie* (1963), and *The Man Who Cried I Am* (1967), which has received great critical acclaim. He has written many short stories and has also edited a collection of stories and articles, *The Angry Black*. *This Is My Country, Too*, a nonfiction work based on a trip across the United States, was published in 1965.

ROBERT F. WILLIAMS left his home in Monroe, North Carolina, where he was born in 1925, to live in the North. After working at various odd jobs, he joined the Marine Corps. When he returned to Monroe in 1953, he became a member of the local chapter of the NAACP and was soon elected president. Hostilities against Negroes in Monroe were extreme at that time, and Williams declared that Negroes should arm themselves as a deterrent against violence. Because of this stand, he was suspended from office by the national board of the NAACP and eventually was permanently expelled from that organization. Mr. Williams held to his position and organized a group of similar-thinking Negro militants in Monroe. In 1961 his group defended many nonviolent "freedom riders" who came into conflict with state and local police while demonstrating against segregation in North Carolina. As a result of a complex situation arising from that confrontation, and despite conflicting reports of what actually happened, Mr. Williams was accused of kidnaping a white couple who were in the Negro neighborhood at the time. He left the United States, going first to Cuba, and a warrant for his arrest was issued by the FBI. Mr. Williams later went to China, where he has proclaimed his innocence and has continued to voice his support for Negro self-defense. He has also advocated preparation by Negroes for widespread armed racial conflicts.

RICHARD WRIGHT was born in 1908 on a plantation near Natchez, Mississippi. He was self-educated, for the most part, and worked at many varied jobs, both in the South and later in Chicago. During the Depression he worked as a writer with the Federal Writers' Project, a government-sponsored program. His first book, *Uncle Tom's Children,* a collection of short stories, was published in 1938, and in 1939 he received a Guggenheim fellowship. *Native Son,* Mr. Wright's first novel, was published in 1949, and it soon brought him national fame and international recognition. Its success was equaled in 1945 with the publication of *Black Boy,* an autobiography.

In 1946 Richard Wright moved to Paris with his family, where he continued to write about life for Negroes in the United States. In 1953 he visited the African Gold Coast, now Ghana, and wrote *Black Power,* a description of his experiences in that country. He remained an expatriate until his death in Paris in 1960.